DIGGING THROUGH DARKNESS

Chronicles of an Archaeologist

DIGGING THROUGH DARKNESS

Chronicles of an Archaeologist

CARMEL SCHRIRE

UNIVERSITY PRESS OF VIRGINIA

Charlottesville and London

THE UNIVERSITY PRESS OF VIRGINIA

Copyright © 1995 by the Rector and Visitors of the University of Virginia

First published 1995

Library of Congress Cataloging-in-Publication Data

Schrire, Carmel.
   Digging through darkness : chronicles of an archaeologist / Carmel Schrire.
      p.   cm.
   Includes bibliographical references and index.
   ISBN 0–8139-1558-9
   1. Archaeology—Field work.   2. Archaeology and history.
3. Schrire, Carmel.   I. Title.
CC76.S37   1995
930.1—dc20   94–30778
                                                              CIP

Designed by Christine Leonard Raquepaw

PRINTED IN THE UNITED STATES OF AMERICA

To Reuben and Nina

Contents

Illustrations

Acknowledgments

The research on which this book is based received financial support from many sources, including the National Science Foundation (BNS 85-08990), the John Simon Guggenheim Foundation, the Rutgers University Research Council, the Mauerberger Foundation, the Human Sciences Research Council, and the Australian Institute of Aboriginal Studies. I owe a deep debt of gratitude to professional colleagues, in the Department of Prehistory, Research School of Pacific Studies, Australian National University, the Department of Archaeology, University of Cape Town, and the Department of Anthropology, Rutgers University.

I owe much to my teachers, including M. Wilson, R. Inskeep, G. Isaac, C. McBurney, E. Higgs, J. Golson and D. J. Mulvaney. The Oudepost excavations and research were immeasurably helped by friends, family, and colleagues, including, G. Abrahams, J. Adler, G. Avery, M. Avery, M. Cairns, J. Cavallo, M. Conkey, K. Cruz-Uribe, H. Deacon, J. Deacon, D. Duco, R. Elphick, G. Fagan, E. February, T. Figueira, G. Flesch, S. Godfrey, M. Hall, C. Henshilwood, M. Herbert, R. Hoosain, S. Jordan, K. Karklins, R. Klein, H. Klose, J. Klose, J. Lanham, J. A. Loos, L. Meltzer, D. Miller, A. Morris, J. Parkington, N. Penn, G. Pieczenik, C. Poggenpoel, Ch. Poggenpoel, F. Poggenpoel, G. Poggenpoel, R. Ross, K. Schoeman, M. Shaw, J. Sealy, R. C.-H. Shell, R. Siegel, A. Sillen, M. Simons, D. Sleigh, A. Smith, T. Smith, M. Sponheimer, N. J. van der Merwe, H. Vos, L. Webley, B. Werz, M. West, M. Winer, and R. Yates.

I thank the Oudepost Syndicate and the National Parks Board for facilitating access to the site.

The wide variety of sources used in this book led me into many different fields. I thank Jim Deetz for making historical archaeology seem fun, and Ivor Noël Hume for making fragments intelligible. Rhys Isaac taught me that we must learn to tell stories to make things come alive. The writings of three particular authors inspired me to strive for the liveliness and passion of true scholarship; for this, I thank C. R. Boxer, J. M. Coetzee, and Greg Dening.

I acknowledge special debts of gratitude to my parents, Toddy and Sylvia Schrire, for a lifetime of encouragement, and to Bill Steiger and our children Reuben and Nina, for help and affection at home and in the field.

DIGGING THROUGH DARKNESS

Chronicles of an Archaeologist

Introduction

This is a book about the history and consequences of colonialism and racism, seen through the eyes of a colonial-born archaeologist.

Digging through Darkness centers on my research in South Africa and Australia over the past thirty years. The work falls under the formal rubrics of archaeology, history, and anthropology, but its perspectives are every bit as personal as they are academic. Their mixture of formality and intimacy deliberately mirrors an interplay reflected in the wider colonial enterprise, for although European expansion swept through the globe with theatrical grandeur, on occasion it was also writ exceeding small in the lives of those people who endured it. Thus a single event may be viewed as part of the political history of a great chartered company, and at the same time it may be seen through the eyes of a hunter-forager girl, spurned for dalliance with drunken soldiers.

The written histories of South Africa and Australia are part of the broader canvas of European expansion, which began about a thousand years ago. Domination was slow and lumbering at first, but around the start of the sixteenth century, it quickened to engulf much of the world. Great nations moved to control primary commodities. People, food, feathers, gold, silver, cloth, and jewels were shipped worldwide. Fleets sailed down the English Channel, through the Bay of Biscay, or, if they needed to avoid the sandbanks and pirates in the Channel, north through the Shetland Islands, and then south, into the open sea. Regrouping at Madeira and the Cape Verdes for refreshments, they swooped across to the West Indies and America or else headed down to the roaring forties, to catch the winds for the Cape of Good Hope. Here, at the tip of Africa, half-way to the East Indies, ships took stock of their situation. They buried their dead, left a last message under an inscribed post-office stone, and set sail for the Orient. By the seventeenth century there was a choice of two routes: Either make a clear run up the African coast, past the slavers of Mozambique and Madagascar, and out across the Indian Ocean, or else head southwards from the Cape, back into the forties, and sail toward the Great Southland or New Holland, turning north for the Sunda Straits before hitting the west Australian coast.[1]

The impact of these voyages and the systems that propelled them reverberated through Europe and its new colonies. It still resounds today in the evidence of documents, genetics, languages, and broken artifacts. Diaries, ships' logs, songs, manifests, law suits, and even novels tell of the reconciliations. Historians analyze the documents of adventure and commerce. Biologists plot flares of new diseases carried intercontinental in rats, bedding, and breath, and linguists decode phrases and intonations to infer the intensity of these new and potent interactions. Archaeologists excavate discarded fragments lost and buried in the lee of crumbling forts and in the sodden bowels of sunken ships.

Exchanges of substances, including genes and viruses, spices, narcotics, food and drink, trinkets and jewels, profoundly altered the lives of all the people concerned. Native people breathed the warmth of a woolen blanket traded from a colonial sailor, only to fall ill and die of the same virus that had killed its previous owner and put the blanket on the market in the first place! The sight of a squat, green bottle was often sufficient to ensure the abrogation of their land by avid, if unsuspecting, hunter-foragers. Tobacco from Virginia and Brazil set African hunters' hearts racing for a narcotic hit to exceed the effect of local weeds or dance-induced trances. American maize became a staple food in Africa, where it possibly sustained huge armies, such as those mustered by the Zulu king Chaka to challenge the entire British Empire. West African slaves cut sugar cane and boiled molasses in Barbados and Surinam; their masters shipped it out to London, Paris, and Rotterdam to tease the appetites of the poor even as it rotted their teeth. Pepper, nutmeg and cloves from the Spice Islands of Banda, Molucca, and Java enlivened rotten meat in Holland and France, engorging the poor and enriching those who invested in these strange fruits. The good burghers of Delft grew plump from profits gained by imitating Oriental porcelains, while their relatives in Gouda waxed wealthy from pipes that they made to hold the tobacco picked by Gambian slaves in the sweltering fields of Virginia and Brazil.

These linkages epitomize colonialism. They emanate largely from the viewpoint of the aggressor, from his writings, his cargoes, and his garbage. Natives had plenty to say, but they were for the most part illiterate. Revisionist scholars have labored hard to find and understand the "Other." Names of indigenous people, or those that they were given by their new masters, appear in colonial accounts, and their crosses and fingerprints embellish an occasional treaty, but their opinions seldom, if ever, survive. For all the anger, argument, and confusion that must have attended every exchange, when all was said and done, colonial masters were hardly obliged to record whatever the other side said. Indeed, as they saw it, for the most part the other side was better left unsaid.

Some argue that archaeology fills the gap created by indigenous illiteracy. Along the encroaching frontiers of European penetration lies a series of mounds and ruins marking the position of native kraals and colonial outposts. Here, in stockaded villages and buttressed forts, the currency of the newcomer greased the palm of the native to ensure the transfer of land and power. The refuse of contact contains the material signatures of both sides. Broken bones, pots, stone spears, and burials announce the indigenous presence, while glass, porcelain, coins, beads, and pipes signal the colonial invaders. Archaeologists reconstruct bottles from broken glass and pipes from fractured stems and then go beyond their form and function to decode a deeper message. Spear points, chipped from the broken base of a wine bottle, reveal the hunter's demand for glass over stone, and bottles and pipes record the delivery of narcotic liquor and tobacco from Europe to the new worlds.

Inferences such as these lend voice to the otherwise silent villages, slave quarters, and hunting camps. Dick Gregory, the African-American political satirist, praised the reconstruction of a community of freed slaves at Parting Ways, Massachusetts, when he told archaeologist Jim Deetz: "You've given us a piece of the ink!" Some argue that his optimism was misplaced. For although residues denote interactions and, on occasion, even give them voice, the actual temper of these moments is lost forever. Archaeologists may infer diet, technology, exchanges, and economy, but the flavor of their findings can never match the punch of the written word. For illiteracy is incontrovertible, and one price illiterates pay to history is prejudice. Ignorance of the other person's view brings with it a disinterest, a contempt for the history, and for even for the sufferings, of those who could not write. Where invasion is concerned silence blunts the impact of the newcomers on the lives and spirit of colonized people.[2]

Population estimates are a case in point. Efforts have been made for many years to quantify the impact of colonial contact by estimating the toll it took in native lives. This is more than a mere academic game, because such findings often serve as grounds for the restitution of indigenous Land Rights. The procedure involves computing the precontact growth rate, which rests in turn, on the estimated time of first human settlement. This has proved very changeable in countries like Australia and North America, where the date of the earliest human presence is constantly being revised by findings from new sites and new dating techniques. Then, too, there is such a vast gulf between a modern census of living people and an archaeological estimate drawn from a small sample of village dwellings and burial mounds that if only one prehistoric variable alters just a fraction, all the bets on the size of a precontact population are off. At the other end of the time span, questions abound about the date and nature of the first external contact. It is not certain, for example, whether the Portuguese or the Phoenicians first rounded the Cape of Good Hope or the degree to which Southeast Asian influences affected Australian Aboriginal life long before European penetration occurred. These considerations are central to the question of exactly when foreign pathogens first appeared on an otherwise pristine front and whether a particular epidemic was actually transmitted by the invaders or indigenous to the native population. Lacking, as we do, the genetic signature of historic epidemics, we cannot be certain that what was called measles or even smallpox five hundred years ago, was, in fact, the same disease we know today. Finally, historical accounts of contact populations are also open to question. Travelers' accounts have, on occasion, turned out to be fictitious, as in the case of an Arctic factor who overstated the number of warlike Inuit living around his trading post in order to inflate his own bravery and importance.[3]

Technicalities notwithstanding, a sense of unfairness permeates all efforts to reconstruct the world of native people at contact because so much of what the conquerors wrote was of no great moment or even, on occasion, of any consequence at all! For instance, housed in the gleaming, white confines of the Royal Archives at The Hague are innumerable documents that have been nurtured and curated for centuries. One such find consists of a number of large, thick, parchments inscribed with an elegantly curlicued script and bound with ribbon and addressed to the Lords and Masters of the Grand Chamber in Amsterdam in humble gratitude and soaring praise. It is officially listed as an account of a committee's findings in the bays at the southernmost tip of

Africa, where the Dutch settled in the mid-seventeenth century along-side some of the most controversial and interesting indigenous folk in the world. The document's title leads one to hope for descriptions of many people and places, but in fact, it renders in great detail, only the winds that blew in the bays around the Cape of Good Hope over a short six-week period in the early eighteenth century. Prolix and repetitive, interlarded with obsequiousness, it enraged even the company to whom it was written, so much so, that they took off time to write back and say that this kind of reportage was a waste of everyone's time!

The condemnation may prove unjustified in the long run, because detailed weather reports such as this are useful to climatologists trying to reconstruct the fabric of past regimes. But whatever its potential contribution to meteorology, this particular document emanated from a visit to a remote region where strange and wondrous people wandered along the shore, camping on the river banks and watching the horizon for the ships carrying exotic wares. If asked, they might have told about their lives. If watched, they might have inspired a corpus of life drawings; if listened to, they might have yielded a new language. As far as this particular document is concerned, they did not exist. For all intents and purposes, they have vanished from the record, whereas the document itself has survived to carry its vapid message down the years. The fact that its preservation took care and cost serves to drive home the injustice that while the words of a petty clerk on board ship still echo after three hundred years, not a single thought of the native cattlemen watching from the beach remains for us today.[4]

These essays try to redress this silence in part by rooting themselves in historical and archaeological sources. Palpable though the documents and artifacts may be, in the end their deeper messages can only be read though acts of imagination. As a result, I turn, on occasion, to fiction to enhance and enlarge the experiences under discussion. I make no pretensions about writing historical fiction per se, though some of my writing clings as closely to the facts as do fictional renditions. A recent novel, *The Birthday Boys,* centers on the actual events that took place on five sequential birthdays of members of the Scott expedition to the South Pole. It adheres so strongly to a welter of documentary sources, official reports, diaries, logs, letters home that they reverberate in every sentence of the book. Yet the author, Beryl Bainbridge, never quotes a single source, as if, by virtue of this omission, she intends to maintain the illusion and, one might argue, the power of her fiction. J. M. Coetzee addresses a similar issue in a more complex way in a series of accounts of an expedition to the interior of South Africa. Some are entirely fictional, but others stem directly from archival accounts. Their interfacing is crafted to reveal how fine is the line that separates assumed reality from imagination. Coetzee seems to challenge the informed reader to spot the seams when he transforms the actual Van Riebeeck Society into the fictional Van Plettenberg Society, and the well-known Cape Archives, into the unknown South African National Archives. His teasing is light, but his message is profound. Attribution is moot because historic documents that seek to alter the truth are more fictional than inventions. "Truth," he declares, talking about modern South Africa, "overwhelms and swamps every act of the imagination."[5]

Unlike these writers, I have taken care to annotate my fictions, with references that anchor the text to the written or excavated record. A simple example of how I have tried to flesh out the details, might be useful here. In excavating a small colonial outpost at the tip of Africa, we unearthed three artifacts: a fragment of porcelain, a piece of copper with irregular perforations, and the mandible of a fish. They lay close together in a pile of charred wood and bone, heaped up outside the ruined wall of a stone house. Documentary sources reveal that the structure was part of an outpost of the Dutch East India Company that was built and occupied about 300 years ago, and a deeper reading reveals the trade, succor, and violence that colored its sixty-year occupancy.[6]

Archaeological wisdom, on the other hand, uses the artifacts to create a story. First, the fragment of porcelain: the curvature of the sherd identifies the vessel of which it was once part as a bowl. Numerous, crisscrossing scratches on its inner surface reveal that it was used for some time in conjunction with a metal spoon or fork. A wisp of cerulean blue, part of the tail of a prancing horse, denotes its point of origin as China, where this pattern was produced in middle of the seventeenth century. The bowl was probably traded into island Southeast Asia and then shipped by the Dutch East India Company to its African resting place. Next, the copper fragment: it was perforated by two different-sized square nails and patched with a broken scrap of iron. Its shape suggests that it was part of a large skimmer, and its odd perforations and rough repair show how unwilling its owners were to dump it, even after the holes clogged up and the neck broke. This reluctance is typical of people living on small outposts, far from the main supply depot. Finally, the fish bone: it came from a haarder, or mackerel, identical to those that are netted in the bay today, and its clean, uncharred appearance in a heap of charcoal suggests that the fish was boiled clean.

Let us now turn these identifications into the simplest actions. A Company soldier enters the lodge where a kettle of fish is bubbling on a hearth set against the low wall. He sniffs, and leans over to stir the cauldron with the large copper skimmer. Then reaching toward the rough table, he takes a small, chipped bowl, and fills it with fish. Pulling a bent pewter spoon from the belt that cinches his coarse, ill-fitting trousers, he walks outside, and squats in the sun while he spoons the stew greedily. He finishes his meal, wipes his mouth on his sleeve, and throws out the residue of bones and scales. His greasy fingers slip, and the bowl shatters against the wall. Overhead, gulls wheel and shriek, frantic for him to leave so that they can jostle in to squabble over the remains scattered in the sand.

The charcoal lying in and around these objects has not been radiometrically dated, but assuming for the moment that it were to yield a date in the vicinity of the late seventeenth century, then we might marry the artifacts to a well-documented episode of violence that occurred here in July 1673, when a party of natives led by a certain Kees descended on the post and slaughtered the corporal, a soldier, and two colonists who were visiting at the time.[7]

Corporal Dirk van der Heerengraaff watches from the dim recess of the Company lodge as two of the soldiers under his command pull the seine way up on the beach. A light winter rain mists the shore, whipped by occasional gusts off the sea. The bulging purse flashes as it disgorges its load of silver haarders. The men rinse the fish in the sea, throw them into a kettle, and carry the pot to the fire. One skims the bubbling scum with a long-handled copper skimmer. The corporal can stay his hunger no longer. He ladles a mess of stew into a small, chipped bowl. Leaning against the large rock at the corner of the fort, he watches the small fishing boat bobbing offshore, then bends his head to spoon the fragrant broth. He never gets a taste. From behind the rock where he has been hiding, a small, brown man whom the Dutch call Kees springs up, and with a blow of his club, sends the soldier reeling. The bowl smashes on the rock. Men run to the door of the lodge only to be met by daggers and clubs. One staggers away and splashes a frantic passage to the small boat anchored offshore. Kees runs inside, kicks the pot away, and holds a burning brand to the thatch. His accomplices pillage the supplies. They crack the neck off a bottle of brandy and drink deep. Their cries and laughter reach a survivor, who is vomiting with fear in the small boat. Above his head, smoke mingles with the gray drizzle.

These are simple renditions, based on straightforward accounts, objects, and inferences. Others I have written are earthier and feature strong language and coarse epithets that deserve some explanation here. My vision of the colonial exchange system is colored by violence, pain, and death. Where some view the moment that the first settlers landed as a noble moment of conquest, I imagine their dirty, wet clothes and squelching shoes. Where some see brave soldiers of the Company, I find illiterate youths struggling to survive their tour of duty. An architect who visited our excavations at Oudepost noticed that the residues lay in and around the living quarters at the Company outpost, rather than being dumped in garbage pits. Realizing that this implied a dirty, fly-ridden post, she insisted that our identification of the site was wrong. Whatever this camp might have been, it could not have housed Dutchmen, because they were immaculate and tidy people, epitomized as such in genre paintings. She spoke with some authority, having reconstructed a number of colonial Dutch houses at the Cape, all of which featured waxed, tiled floors, gleaming brass fixtures, and well-pressed drapes. Archaeology, with its evidence of squalid outpost life, and history, with its repetitive chronicle of rape, dismemberment, rats, typhus, flux, and puerpural fever, belie this orderly vision. I do not envisage the soldiers of the Dutch East India Company as oil-painted gentlemen but as seventeenth-century grunts, enlisted men drawn from the ranks of the poor and dispossessed, who were probably every bit as violent and unthinking as their twentieth-century equivalents, at play in the fields of Vietnam and Somalia. Consequently, if the reader is offended by the invective I have put in their mouths, I urge that it be judged not by today's standards of political correctness but by my reading of the past.

Here now is a series of chronicles of colonial contact. Each one begins with a different tale, told from a fresh point of view, but in the end they are all talking about the same thing. The first is an account of my childhood, which starts with the arrival of my own colonist ancestor in South Africa a hundred years ago. The interplay of being Jewish, white, and female in South Africa sets the stage for a chronicle of colonial contacts, when the natives of distant lands encountered the settlers, merchants, and soldiers of Europe, worldwide.

The next three accounts describe colonial contact through the lens of archaeology and history. They start with the excavations at Oudepost I, a colonial site in South Africa, that lies 100 km north of where my great-grandfather landed a century ago. Evidence of European invasion is marked in gun flints, lead shot, and bones; the traces of indigenous people, in stone tools, broken pots, and bone points. The lessons of archaeological interpretation are followed by an account of the events that culminated in the savage massacre at Oudepost in 1673. Old documents serve as a framework into which is woven the story of a Company deserter who made common cause with the pastoral foragers, only to become embroiled in the hatred and violence that were the hallmarks of race relations at the Cape of Good Hope. The tale reiterates similar interactions today, setting the stage for us to swing back into the history of the region, this time writ small, through the eyes of two old women living in the shadow of the site today.

Leaving archaeology, the geographical reach of the book now widens out to detail a craze that abounded a century ago, when colonial officials amassed body parts of the very same native people they purported to explore and administer. This grisly hobby, and its resultant Halloween-type practices, take us from South Africa to the Pacific, through dusty shelves and filing cabinets of modern museums, to reveal what each side thought of the other. Colonial explorers were every bit as exotic and mystifying to the watchers on the beaches of Australia, Hawaii, and the Cape of Good Hope, as were the so-called savages to the emissaries of Europe; and as assiduously as explorers bartered for native skulls, so eagerly did the Pacific islanders curate the bones of certain Englishmen.

The stage now shifts to Australia, to the life of a burned-out leper working on an archaeological site in north Australia. The focus oscillates between past and present, setting Aboriginal lives in the larger sweep of European expansion and anthropological wisdom. This in turn, carries us into the lives of certain anthropological icons by documenting the complex life of what was once regarded as a prototypically simple person. Bushmen have featured in many scientific discourses, and even today molecular biologists theorize that they encode the most ancient genes of all modern people. Our particular old man crossed paths with some of the most famous exponents of human evolution. His relatives adorn the pages of numerous scientific papers, and his myths form the basis for new visions of prehistoric rock art. Today, we find him transported to what his present-day promoters think was his ancestral home. In the cold mountains of the western Cape, the old man sees snow for the first time and wonders about his future.

Finally, the book comes full circle with a joke told over port and wine at a dinner party in Cape Town. The language is idiomatic, but the event it describes occurred 350 years ago, when the first Dutch colonists landed at the Cape, setting off the tales of contact with which this book began.

These chronicles are all in large part true, but at the same time all of them raise the question of what is true? An event recorded in a document need not have happened. The document may look old and authoritative, but the author may have had a more complicated motive than mere recording of actual events. And conversely, a conversation set in a hunters' camp three hundred years ago may bear no written testimony, yet it might well have taken place. The bibliography of these chronicles identifies which is which, but in some respects the distinction is of little consequence. For if the official diaries of the Cape of Good Hope describe three fires lighted in succession in the year 1673, was this actually so? Do they become any more or less real if I invent the arsonist? Is a murder at a remote outpost less reprehensible because we sense the motive of the killer, and is apartheid more poignant if we see it through the eyes of two old women who emasculate their cat as a gesture of control?

"Possessing the other," wrote Greg Dening in an analysis of the encounter between Europeans and Pacific islanders a good two centuries ago, "Possessing the other, like possessing the past, is always full of delusions." These chronicles must now speak for themselves. It is time to give them voice.[8]

2

Chronicle of a Childhood

Archaeologists deal in artifacts. They traffic in bones and chipped stone tools from stratified caves, in sherds from the ruins of ancient towns, and in shattered goblets and encrusted jars sucked out of shipwrecks. The rules of the discipline prescribe standard methods to find and decode the messages and meanings of these objects, which are then classified according to provenance, shape, usage, and age. But rules do not enliven the context of an empty cave, nor do they lend voice to the cobbled lane of a walled city or the heaving deck of an East Indiaman bound for Ceylon. Only imagination fleshes out the sound and taste of time past, anchoring the flavor of lost moments in the welter of objects left behind. Where better, then, to start this archaeological memoir than in the artifacts of the archaeologist's life?

My father's study is a large dim room in the house he built in Cape Town on the slopes of the mountain overlooking the bay. Light gleaming through a stained glass roundel paints colored strips on the Oriental rugs and the dark, polished floor. Four-square, in the middle of the room, stands his massive Victorian desk in its heavy glass shoes. A revolving bookcase stacked with dictionaries in French, Hebrew, German, Latin, and Dutch is placed in easy reach of the chair. Books dominate the room. One wall is packed with Judaica, with massive tomes dealing with ritual and magic, and a well-thumbed section on angelology. A Georgian glass-fronted bookcase houses African exploration and travel, with the earliest volumes bound in creamy vellum and later adventures in gaudy, gold-embossed, Victorian covers. Shelved below the window are the bound annals of medicine and surgery that begin around 1930 and end abruptly in the mid 1950s. Between the bookshelves are display cases where silver Hebrew amulets, spice boxes, and goblets gleam in velvet settings. Rows of pewter ceremonial plates and brass Sabbath candlesticks alternate with Chinese roof tiles of mythical beasts and warriors striding to the kill. Elsewhere is folk art, fragments of embroidery, fretwork renditions of the Holy City, and a memorial plaque whose neat gold Hebrew letters are framed with twining roses and horns of plenty that converge in a basket filled with five eggs and guarded by a plump, gilded dove. It commemorates one Sarah, and is the handiwork of my great-grandfather, Reb Yehuda Leb Schrire, who carved it in honor of his large family.

Reb Schrire was born in Oshmanya, Lithuania, in 1851, the son of rabbis who traced their name and its roots back a thousand years to Reb Sherira Ben Hanina Gaon, an author of the Babylonian Talmud. Yehuda Leb was small, chirpy, and lame. After a bout of childhood polio, he limped for the rest of his life. He was educated in Vilna, where his possibilities were so circumscribed by virtue of being a Jew that he could not become a doctor, lawyer, or secular scholar. Instead, he became a man of many parts, moving from place to place as a scholar, cantor, teacher, ritual slaughterer, circumciser, butcher, and baker.[1]

Around 1885 he was appointed to the synagogue at Neustadt-Sugind on the Prussian border of Lithuania, where he met and taught one Sammy Marks. Marks emigrated to South Africa, where instead of siding with the Englishmen, who had come to the new diamond and goldfields, he allied himself with the newly independent Boers of the South African Republic to become an industrial and orchard magnate under President Paul Kruger. Marks did not forget his roots, and he sponsored so much immigration from his home town that the region was almost depopulated of Jews.

One such immigrant was Reb Yehuda Leb Schrire.[2]

Marks brought his former teacher to the goldfields around 1892–93 to attend to the new congregation. Reb Yehuda Leb hated to leave his wife and children, but he was flattered by the invitation and eager to break the restrictions of his East European life. The long sea journey brought him to the Cape of Good Hope, and the railroad sped him northwards from Cape Town. Since its tracks had not yet reached Johannesburg, he crossed the final stretch by wagon, trundling across the dusty flats as though on the back of a lumbering turtle. Alongside ran black children, gesturing in silence, their sad eyes begging for food. Their teeth shone "white as the wolves of the night" but he could not grasp a word they uttered. Stunned as he was at this poverty, the Reb was even more shocked to encounter his flock. The old ways of the shtetl had become distasteful to them. They foreswore Yiddish in favor of English, they laughed at his beard and black frock coat, and they spurned his orthodoxy. Reb Yehuda stood it for over a year and then decided to go home. But despite his fierce criticism, his sponsors had grown fond of the clever little man. They begged him to reconsider, and eventually reached a compromise: the Reb would leave the goldfields and settle in Cape Town as a ritual slaughterer and cantor. What was more, his family would join him there. For the Reb was in no way a refugee. Despite all his strange clothes and his passion for learning, he was a man with a purpose.[3]

In short, he was a colonist.

Cape Town lies at the tip of Africa, cradled in the belly of Table Mountain, as it slopes into the sea at the Cape of Good Hope. Rollers fetching up from Antarctica, crash against the back-gray mottled rocks and foam up the white sands. This was once the land of the earliest true people, who ranged along its shores for fish and penguins. Millennia later, when Europe yawned and stretched its way across the globe, the Cape had become a land of herders, hunters, and beachcombers, who held sway until 1652, when the Honorable Dutch East India Company made a way station here to provision the ships of their Indies trade.

Written history began at the Cape when the guttural demands of north Europe met the clicks and hisses of the native Khoikhoi people. Soon war and displacement forged a new society. Dutch soldiers became settlers, and Khoikhoi herders became serfs, though many were treated as slaves. European masters from Holland, Germany, and the Baltic states dominated the lives of their Hottentot servants, drawn from the lands of the Great and Little Namaquas, of their Muslim slaves from Bali and Ceylon, and of their African slaves from Madagascar. Free and bonded people dived deep into a common biological pool, rising later, to surface with names like Anna van der Kaap, born at the Cape of a slave woman and a Dutch father, intended wife of a farmer from Danzig; Jan Tamboer, fish vendor on the wharf, named "tamboer" for the drum beaten by his Khoikhoi mother, and "Jan" for his father's Dutch owner, who won him in a wager in the Straits of Macassar; and Scipio, a farm worker, purchased from Arab traders in the swamps of Mozambique, and shipped south, not as he imagined, to be eaten alive, but rather to be worked to death.[4]

Confusing for some, but perfectly intelligible to the denizens of the new Cape Colony, wrested with considerable perfidy and deception from Holland by the British in 1795. The Dutch East India Company

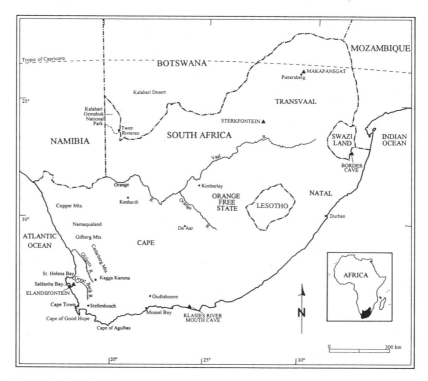

Fig. 1. South Africa

had collapsed in financial ruin the previous year, leaving this plum ripe
for the taking. In December of 1794, Revolutionary French armies swept
into Holland, ousted Prince William V of Orange, and proclaimed the
new Republic of Batavia. At other end of the globe, the commander of
the Cape garrison, Robert Jacob Gordon, descended from Scottish ancestors who had settled in Holland a century earlier, epitomized divided
loyalties. A scholar and a gentleman, Gordon traveled widely, journeying
into the northern desert, and east, toward the realms of the black kings.
At home, he amassed a cabinet of curiosities including a stuffed giraffe.
Euphorbias and aloes were transplanted to his garden on the slopes of
Table Mountain, and Hottentot songs enlivened his dinner table.[5]

His erudition notwithstanding, Gordon's divided ancestry made him
easy prey for the British force that landed at the Cape in the winter of
1795. The expeditionary party under Major-General Craig assured him
that his loyalties to William of Orange would be well served by welcom-

ing the prince's current protectors to the Cape. Craig's reassurance worked for Gordon, but many of his men preferred the new French regime and wanted no truck with the British at all. They mistrusted the invaders and resented their easy access to a Dutch preserve. Events culminated in the courtyard of the old Dutch castle, set on the beach at Cape Town. Gordon urged his command to surrender to the British troops, only to see his own soldiers jeer and spit their contempt. Craig and his troops watched carefully, and pretended not to see. The commander paled. He reeled home and sank into depression. Six weeks later, a shot rang out in his garden, and Gordon's brains splattered the succulent desert plants.[6]

A century passed. The Cape was now a well-established colony of the British Crown. Merchants, builders, farmers and servants built their homes on the slopes of Table Mountain. Far inland, new territories housed descendants of resentful Boers who had trekked away from the oppression of Cape rule. Their trails bisected Iron Age kingdoms, engendering burned wagons, slaughtered children, and whooping armies. But spears being no match for guns, the settlers eventually prevailed in the hard, hot, land. Even as they scrabbled for a living, they recognized that it would yield more than withered crops. Diamonds tumbled from the banks of the Orange River, and a fabulous reef of gold appeared in the Transvaal. The economic, administrative, and social, core of the land swivelled north, and the Cape itself became a conduit for thousands of European immigrants bound for the diamond and goldfields of Kimberley and Johannesburg.[7]

Among them were stunned cargoes of Jews headed for the end of the world. Abraham, Isaac and Jacob, Sarah, Malka, Pesha too. Meyer, Max, Solly, where is Hirschele, where did he go? Reeling on deck in their frock coats, women bundled in shawls, walking in pairs in the teeth of the Biscay gales, whispering intimacies to guard against the distance and the time away from the ones they left behind. On Friday they unpack two small candlesticks and set them precariously on the edge of the shelf between the bunks. Mama lights them, swaying with the rolling ship as she covers her eyes and prays. A bell shrills: almost to the south pole says the captain, we will stop just short of the icebergs and Tristan da Cunha, before we turn eastward to the Cape.

Table Mountain towers gray-blue against the clouded sky, flanked on one side by the Lion's Head, and on the other, by the jagged-toothed Devil's Peak. Their cliffs are drenched with water, dark green forests blanket the lower slopes. The dock is a wooden pier, where black men haul and strain against the ship's ropes, and customs men, cold eyes crossing from trunk to trunk, wait impassive at the shed. Gales howl, pungent with salt and the smell of dead fish piled against the dock. Gulls wheel and screech; a cart waits patiently for its load. Sailors reel to their ships, and Malay vendors teeter by with trays of curried pasties. Up the slope of the mountain, Jewish houses huddle close together, their back doors opening onto cobbled lanes canted to a central gutter.

The servant, a small girl with high cheekbones of the Namaquas, sweeps the red polished veranda until it shines in the morning sun. A ginger cat slithers into its corner to sleep the day away. Mother washes and cooks. She skims the chicken soup, glancing through the window every now and then, at the white cloud that piles down the mountain in the southeast gales on Friday afternoons. Father walks each day to the warehouse, counting bales of cloth, parceling out those for the people, as opposed to kaffir cloth for the *schwartzes*. Across the road, between the castle and the slopes of Devil's Peak, sprawl the slums of District Six, named by the British long ago and crowded with old close-packed houses and stores. Tin horns sound a nasal proclamation of three fresh catches for sale. Muslim women hurry home, their translucent veils tossing in the hot wind. The sharp smell of fish mixes with salt air, tinged with cardamom, cumin, and turmeric. Dusk scatters the children to their homes. New women walk in the street. Their cheeks are rouged, their lips vermilion. They wear no veils, and their smiles are black with the absence of their front teeth. Some say this marks their slave ancestry; others, more carnal, say it advertises their erotic skills.[8]

A lad leaves his house. His shoes click on the steep cobbled street leading down to District Six. Entering the alleys he glances nervously around. A woman beckons, baring her gap-toothed smile. He should resist, but dares not. He despises those who talk of hot meat and black velvet, but the heat in his groin speaks louder than his fear. The woman smiles again: she knows him well. Here is no dance of pursuit and retreat, no subtleties and nuances of skill. Heat, pulse, jet of fire: he gasps. She smiles, wipes her lips. He reels into the street. She laughs, points, and calls after him: "*Jou ma se moer!*" she shrieks. "Your mother's womb!"

She will name the child for him, and he will pay for this. A small amount, that's true, but with patient regularity, nevertheless.

None of this entered the life of Reb Schrire, certainly not in his writings, nor in any aspect of his daily existence, and certainly not on that

day in 1894, when he limped through the town to the harbor. It was a
Saturday, and he would normally have been leading the prayers, but today
he had canceled his duties to greet the boat bringing his family to their
new home. High on the deck stood his wife Gella, face framed in a dark
shawl, clinging to the arm of their daughter Annie. The boys, Max and
Sam, capered around her legs, their fresh, wide faces, red from the sun
and spray. Far below they noticed Reb Yehuda. Outwardly he waved his
stick in greeting, but in his heart, he wanted to "coo as a dove to those
four souls." The boys broke ranks, tore down the gangplank into his
arms. He stumbled a little at the onslaught but held his ground. He whistled for the Colored men who stood watching, and they piled the trunks
onto a horse-drawn cart. Soon there was no more room. The family
gathered the rest of their bags, and walked through the town to their
new home, right next to the soldiers' barracks.[9]

Here was his library, his matched sets of prayer books, his published
novel, and ledgers with his musical compositions, poems, and stories.
The children scampered like deer from room to room, hurtling outside
to play with hoops in the cobbled street, or to shoot catapults on the
grassy slope behind the house. Visitors came to study, to learn, and to
play chess. On occasion they came to argue. Reb Yehuda prospered. He
bought houses, and rented them out, and he helped establish a Hebrew
school, and a ritual bath. But try as he might, he remained uncertain of
his new home. He knew a world beyond the basin of the town, and
needed to be certain that he did not want to live in Europe. Leaving one
son, Max, to work as a photographer in De Aar near the Kimberley
diamond fields, he took the rest of the family to London and Frankfurt.
While he was gone Max met up with one Israel Mauerberger, who was
the local representative of his father's London shipping business, and together they started a small import house. It was only courteous that Reb
Yehuda should call on the Mauerbergers in London. There he met the
widowed father Joseph, and his five children. The Reb noticed the eldest
girl Rebecca, small, with bushy, black hair and a determined set to her
chin. She was corresponding with Theodore Herzl, the founder of Zionism, about the prospects of a Jewish homeland. Reb Yehuda felt a strong
affinity; after all, he had founded the first Zionist group in Africa a few
years earlier. A bargain was struck and Rebecca married Max. She named
Reb Yehuda's first grandson for Herzl, though no one would ever call
him "Theodore."

He was my father, Toddy.[10]

Fig. 2. Reb Yehuda Leb Schrire and his family, Cape Town, ca. 1912. My father is the boy standing on the right.

But enough of genealogies and on to detail. The family home stood between the mountain slope and the sea. Downstairs was the kitchen where Gella cooked great pots of soup, noodle pudding, and carrot stew, replicating all the heavy peasant cuisine of wintry Eastern Europe, under the broiling, southern sun. On occasion, her husband drew on his former skill as a baker and made pastry, candy, even a spun-sugar model of his birthplace. His private domain was a small workroom upstairs that looked out across the town to the glittering sea beyond. The workbench was cluttered with nails, screws, chisels, screwdrivers, watchmaker's tools, wires, and cardboard. Here he mended and polished, refurbishing old tools until they shone like new. Here he carved pictures memorializing Jerusalem, Herzl, and lesser folks, like Rebecca's mother, Sarah. He fashioned lead tops to spin at Hannukah, the Feast of Lights, but he saved his most inventive toy for Purim. This Feast of Lots marks the time that Esther, the Jewish queen of Persia, intervened on behalf of her people to save them from the evil intent of Chancellor Haman. Reb Yehuda commemorated their redemption with a mechanical tour de force. A series of lead figures was cast, and placed in position. The king and queen watched as Haman kneeled at their feet. The executioner raised a tiny axe. The Reb wound the spring of the box and a gay tune tinkled forth.

Suddenly the switch tripped.

The music stopped.

Down crashed the axe and Haman's head rolled away.

The children clapped and cheered. And why not? Nothing could have prepared them for the prophetic overtones of the ancient events that engendered this ingenious toy. There was no precedent in Jewish history to prepare them for the scale on which our relatives in Europe would be singled out for execution thirty years later, with no Esther to mitigate the atrocity. Furthermore, although a long history of pogroms had prepared them for the undercurrents of anti-Semitism in South Africa, Jews here were protected in that they were unmistakably white. So although anti-Semitism was present, it tended to overlap with a more general anti-alien stance by whites in this stratified society, where the phenotypic badge of skin color defined rank. Viewed in this light, it serves to explain how Jews were able to get around certain restrictions, such as those that might have followed on the proclamation of the Immigration Restriction Act of 1902. The act demanded that newcomers show an ability to write in English characters before earning entry to South Africa. Allegedly designed to exclude Asiatics, it might equally well have restricted Yiddish speakers who wrote in Hebrew characters. Influential Jewish leaders now asserted their priority over people of color, arguing that Yiddish was a European language. The barriers were relaxed and the *London Jewish Chronicle* praised the compromise as a tribute to the cooperative humanity of the Jewish race . . . [and] the sense of justice of the Cape Government."[11]

But fine words could not mask a certain distaste for Jews. Cartoons left little doubt about the English view of immigrants like Reb Yehuda Leb. They were depicted with hooked noses and mean eyes, disembarking in Cape Town as "British" colonists under the banner of "The Coming of the Scum," or laying bets both way on the outcome of the Anglo-Boer War. In Johannesburg they became the swarming "Gold Bugs" of "Jewberg," with "Hoggenheimer," a British musical comedy character, encoding all the Semitic greed that would later be foisted on the Oppenheimers of Anglo-American De Beers. Most immigrants did not become millionaires, but merchants, storekeepers, and traders who carried the artifacts of civilization across the frontiers to the rural communities. The peddler, or *smous,* evoked resentment for his prices, his goods, and his origin. As a new class of poor whites rose up from urban poor and landless farmers, many grew to view all undesirable aliens as a cause of their misfortune, and none was more reviled than the ubiquitous peddler, who crossed their path again and again, like a fabulous turtle, with his wealth and power jolting beneath the canvas wagon roof.[12]

But if the South African family could not foresee the great fire storms of Europe, even more could they not imagine the analogy between Reb Yehuda's toy and his own death. In 1912, on the eve of the Jewish New Year, the little Reb limped outside to slaughter a fowl for the pot. Like his mechanical executioner he raised the knife and struck! He did it ritually, mercifully, letting the blood run into the ground, dust unto dust Finishing up, he cleaned the knife, putting it carefully back in its case. He stretched, smiled, inhaling the fragrance of cinnamon and chicken soup that wafted from Gella's kitchen.

He fell to the ground.

The clatter brought his youngest son Harry rushing to his side. Ten thousand kilometers away in London, my grandfather Max suddenly grew uneasy. He cabled home; was Father well? The Morse code operator tapped a dirge out in reply. Max gasped. Across the ocean, in Cape Town, the cortege went from synagogue to synagogue, past the closed stores of Jewish merchants, and out across the sand dunes to the cemetery on the Cape Flats.

I was born in Cape Town in 1941, the second of a string of four girls that my mother produced at regular two-year intervals. My father, a surgeon, wanted a son who would say his kaddish—the ancient Aramaic prayer for the dead—when he died. Being a scientist, he figured out his chances with some persistence, but the laws of probability being what they are, he clearly needed more than four throws of the metaphorical coin. This he would not do. After four daughters he gave up. Not so his mother. Half a century in Cape Town had dampened none of Rebecca's fire, and since she vociferously expected a wife to produce sons, she placed the blame squarely on my mother's shoulders, signifying the worthlessness of her granddaughters with small, potent, gestures. My mother, Sylvie, awed though she was by her husband and his kin, drew the line at his mother: mutual distaste bordering on hatred colored family gatherings from that time on.

We lived in a large modern house high on the slopes of Table Mountain, fronting a rockery of wild plants, and terraced lawns. Streams from the mountain pooled in the lower reaches. Goldfish flashed among the reeds and lilies and frogs croaked at night. We paddled, threw mud, and swung in the branches over the streams. We gathered tadpoles in glass jars and watched legs spring from their fat, metamorphosing, bodies. Friends seldom if ever came to play. Our house was set apart from its neighbors, and bicycles were out of the question in this steep suburb. Then too, there were the dogs. Papa bred ginger-brown Rhodesian ridgebacks. He insisted that they were the gentlest dogs on earth, yet everyone knew that they were trained as hunting dogs on farms. The dogs roamed outside at will, collapsing on occasion, in sunny corners where they snored and twitched, limbs sprawling as though disconnected. Their narcosis was deceptive: at a touch they would spring up, snarling, and at the faintest crunch of a footfall in the road, they raced, slavering after their victim.

The dogs were forbidden to enter the house. Here my mother held sway. All rooms were cleaned every day. Parquet floors shone in the morning sun, silver and brass were buffed to a dazzle, sheets were ironed shining smooth, and windows squeaked in their weekly wash. Three- and four-course meals appeared twice a day, with father, wreathed in ether from his operating room, presiding at the head of the table. Everyone spoke at once, interrupted only by the small bell which mother rang to signal each new course. Dessert over, the last stragglers watched father sip his coffee, and build pyramids of crackers, cheese, and mustard.

"We live," he would muse, "in Georgian splendor."

Mother sighed, imagining the shopping she would have to do once again, as soon as this meal was over. The rest of us sighed from embarrassment, seeing the disparities that grew more visible each day in this divided country. At home, maids and gardener called my parents "Madam," and "Doctor." Servants were "Colored," as opposed to "whites," "blacks," including Bantu-speaking Xhosa and Sotho people, and "Asiatic" Indians and Chinese. Colored people were defined as being the product of intermarriage or at any event, intermixture, among all of the above, including indigenous Khoisan Bushmen and Hottentots and descendants of Indonesian slaves called "Moslems," or "Cape Malays."[13]

Chief among our domestic servants was Trudie, a tall, rangy woman who moved with fluid ease, cleaning, cooking, ironing, playing with us kids and bathing us at night. Born in the eastern Cape town of Oudtshoorn—the ostrich feather capital of the world—she came to Cape Town to find work. Her two children appeared occasionally, small and shy, their collars pressed to a high gloss, and clutching their grandmother's hand. Selena carried her emaciated frame with willowy dignity. She spoke quietly to my mother, while Trudie inspected her kids. Trudie rolled her eyes at the mention of the word *marriage* and spoke bitterly of her man, Hennie-Boy. He drank, he smoked, he rampaged. Worse, he took her money. Mournfully, arms deep in the laundry tub, she sang "his song":

> You are my sunshine
> My only sunshine
> You make me heppy, when skies are gray

She skittered to the phone when he called. Her voice lifted. She smiled. Suddenly her tone changed. She slammed down the phone.

"Dai onbeskofte ding!" she snarled. "That rude thing!"

Hennie-Boy swanned round every now and then. Immaculately suited, he swayed a little, breathing cheap wine. My mother shrugged, my father roared. He was treating Trudie for repeated miscarriages and intermittent bouts of gonorrhea. Papa's temper, short at the best of times, compressed, on occasion, to hair-trigger proportions, especially when a patient hovered between life and death. His fears expanded in summer when typhoid epidemics swept through the city, cramming the wards of the City Hospital for Infectious Diseases with dying patients. Antibiotics were all but unknown and victims suffered until their ulcerated guts burst open. One of the few to attempt a surgical solution, repairing perforated bowels, left father drained and fearful. He insisted that we boil water, scald our milk, and even boil the butter. Trudie listened, an admonitory finger at her lips, as the phone shrilled with news of another death. She was no stranger to disaster. Her stories were punctuated by deep sighs. Most concerned men she had known, and they all ended badly, as in the case of the woman who persistently bit off the thread after mending her clothes. People said this would bring bad luck, but she went right on, never mind what everyone said, until one day, she bit off the cotton and there was a man with a big scissors: "What?" we yelled, knowing the end.

"He cut off her blerry head!" snapped Trudie.

She mashed the potatoes with venom.

"Out! I have to work!"

Although she cursed us, Trudie relished the chance to exhibit her brood in public. On Saturday afternoons she herded us into the bus heading downtown for tea. We clambered to the top where Trudie announced a concert. Scurrying to the front, we sang and danced in front of the bewildered passengers. Many of our songs concerned bodily functions. White people looked aghast. They stared out of the window, affecting interest in the all-too-familiar scenes. Other maids, faces rouged and powdered for their day off, laughed and clapped their hands. Trudie who had taught us most of our songs, feigned horror, even as she sniggered behind her hand.

No one absorbed Trudie's tales faster, or embellished them with more relish, than my elder sister Tamar. According to her, storm drains were the homes of mythical creatures, and the mountain slope behind our house was dotted with strange rocks that had once been live animals. Her most explicit belief concerned the City Hospital for Infectious Diseases, where my father worked so fearfully in the summer months. A Victorian pile, it faced the glass-encrusted wall of the Breakwater Prison, which had once contained the felons who built the harbor wall, but was now used as government offices. Tamar still regarded it with distaste and saw the hospital as nothing less than a charnel house, from which no one ever emerged alive.

In the summer of 1946 I fell ill. My throat hurt and my temperature soared alarmingly. By nightfall, the characteristic rash of scarlet fever appeared. An ambulance arrived, lights blazing and siren shrieking. My mother sat in the back with me, smiling encouragingly. Father followed behind in his car. I woke the next morning in a strange, iron bed. The sheets were starched and white. In front was a doorway opening on a long stoop that ran the length of the building. Behind the bed was a window. I scrambled free and knelt on the pillow to look out.

Across the road stood the high stone wall of the Breakwater Prison, its broken, glass topping winking in the sun. Instead of being transfixed with terror at Tamar's prediction, I figured that she must be wrong, since I was so patently alive. My parents were less sanguine, and the hospital justified all Tamar's fears. Hot, dark nights were filled with delirious shrieks that tapered into panting sobs. Running feet clattered across the stone balcony, deep voices called out from the wards. I remained quarantined in my room for the requisite six weeks. Mother brought a teacher who sat at the doorway and taught me to read. On my release I looked like a ghost, pale, with a shock of white curls. My parents decided that a holiday would be just the ticket. They rented a villa by the sea. An electric bell hung on a woven silk cord in the dining room, and we swung on it, like Tarzan, until the ceiling shattered.

But beneath the idyll of spoiled white kids, holiday homes, wildness, and nannies lay the inequitable laws of South African society that kept everyone in place. They exploded into view when I was about eight years old. It was a clear autumn morning and my parents had gone out. Trudie was cooking, and Isak, the gentle, stuttering, gardener, was raking leaves. Tamar and I hung about, bored. Suddenly she ran into the garage and came out with two broomsticks.

"I've got a wonderful idea!" she burst out "Let's chase Isak round the house and shove the broomsticks up his bum?" I could hardly wait. Shrieking like banshees we lured Isak from the flower bed, and explained the game. He looked astonished. We prodded, and chased, laughing till we cried. He stood his ground. Trudie tried to catch us, cursing and shouting at us to stop.

The game tapered off and Isak stormed off. We wandered afield to climb trees. Around lunch time my parents car drew up the driveway. Isak buttonholed my father.

"Doctor, DDDDDoctor?"

My father stopped. He held his head politely on one side.

Isak let him have it.

"The children!" he stammered. "The children tried to stick a bbbrooomstick up my . . ."

He paused. My father turned red.

"Up my *tttochis!*" finished Isak.

Everything was encoded in this last word. That Isak used the Yiddish term, *tochis,* with its etymological roots in the Hebrew *tachat,* or "bottom," was not in itself surprising, for he had lived with us long enough to pepper his speech with Yiddish. It was not surprising, but it was agonizing to hear Isak, a small brown man with the high cheekbones and slanting eyes of his Khoikhoi forebears, reproach us in our own terms.

My father went inside and took off his jacket. He took the whip from the coat rail in the hall. He came outside. Calling Trudie and Isak, he invited them to watch. First he apologized that he had raised such children. Then he apologized for our behavior. Then holding us firmly by the hands he whipped our legs with a four-tailed leather strap. After an initial feeble effort to run away, Tamar and I gave up. Trudie wiped her eyes on her apron, Isak stared. After the first whipping Papa let us apologize. After the second, he sent us to sit on a great granite rock in the garden, to think about what we had done. For good measure he sent our younger sisters, Sharon and Gail, to join us. The insult to Isak grew with each moment. Occasionally, Tamar or I said we hadn't meant anything more than to have fun, but the two younger girls said nothing. Sharon wept great tears that coursed down her face and dripped off her chin. Gail watched, a small frown of bewilderment on her face. As the day waned, my father called us back inside. Words like respect, dignity, and kindness punctuated his talk, but all I could see was Isak's small, slanted eyes, deep and wet.

Once it became clear that there would be no sons, my father settled for what he had. I loved encyclopedias, especially those on biology, and these were brought each week and piled on the floor by my bed, where I devoured them for medical disorders, especially those afflicting young children. Father never discussed his work. He thought of surgery as a skill, as opposed to anthropology, travel, mythology, and adventure, whose pursuits he regarded as pure pleasure. I struggled briefly with the mythology of ancient Japan to understand his large collection of ivory netsukes, but gave up when I couldn't tell one name from another. I wrestled with the history of Mexico and Peru, and dropped that too. My father quoted Dickens on occasion, and I waded through a few novels but disliked their gloomy tone. My tastes ran to medical fiction, to W. Somerset Maugham's Southeast Asian stories and to the adventures of Richard Halliburton, who had climbed the pyramids, swum the Helles-pont, and interviewed witnesses to the slaughter of the Romanovs.

My parents led a regulated social existence. Patients permitting, each night was scheduled for a different purpose. There was the symphony concert, the photographic society, and a group of Jewish intelligentsia, handpicked by their stern leader, with a tacit understanding that wives did not speak. There was also the monthly meeting of the South African Archaeological Society. My mother had long since given up the hope of frivolities, like going to the movies or eating out, and she contrived to make such things a treat. The Archaeological Society met in the icy rooms of the Athenaeum. A collection of curates and ex-Indian army types, veterans of the war in the Western Desert, and dry donnish men from the university, with their equally serious wives in tow, sidled in. Seated on folding chairs, they listened to reports of Greek statues and Japanese martial weaponry. Mostly they heard about African archaeology. South Africa was famous for two things: It was the birthplace of early hominids, whose shattered bones were fossilized in the limestone caves of the Transvaal, and its rock shelters and caves were covered with the art of Khoisan people. Lecturers speculated on human origins and on the beliefs underlying great vistas of painted animals. The audience nodded and yawned, rousing themselves at suggestions of ancient violence and modern ritual. Suddenly the lights came up. Polite applause and desultory questions were followed by blueish tea in thick white cups, a hard biscuit, and subdued good nights.

Driving home, windshield wipers hissing against a dark drizzle, we discussed what we had heard. I racked my brain for questions: What did sailors eat? How did Phoenicians row their ships? The more interest I showed, the more likely Papa would let me come along when the society took its field trips to ancient sites. There the mysteries deepened. Experts described the rise and fall of seas during the great Ice Ages, pointing to layers of round pebbles that marked the position of ancient raised beaches. They led us into dank caves and up steep, coastal middens, where millions of seashells attested to former meals. I crouched in the dusty holes, wondering how many other children had shivered in the winter rains, thousands of years before.

In grim counterpoint to these exciting imaginings was my formal education. We were the third generation of daughters to attend the Good Hope Seminary, a local government girls' school where admission was restricted to white girls, most of whom were Jewish daughters of immigrant parents. Its dim cool halls with their red stone floors and dark green walls smelled of institutional floor polish, chalk, and the insides of several hundred lunch boxes. Tight-lipped teachers taught the state syllabus, with no deviation from the six prescribed subjects, which included Afrikaans as a second language.[14]

The diminutive principal was a strict disciplinarian with a passion for Shakespeare and the Old Vic. Large photographs of John Gielgud lined her office walls, his penetrating stare affecting profound intimacy. She strode onstage each morning in her academic gown and with a tiny gesture initiated assembly. "Our Father," prayed the girls, most of whose mothers murmured their litanies in Yiddish, "Which art in Heaven, Hallowed be thy Name." The daily hymn came from the Book of Common Prayer. The gym teacher, stolid as a sumo wrestler, pounded out the chords on the piano. Jewish girls were advised to remain silent when the Trinity cropped up. Prayers done, the principal read aloud the names of girls given detention. I hated the school most of the time, but I was not actively unhappy, because distaste lent a sense of purpose to the daily round. I fidgeted, cheated on tests, chewed musty fruit gums at every opportunity, and teased my classmates. In return they tormented me for my size and for my patent failure to show any signs of adolescence. The last girl in the entire grade to wear a bra, and the very last to menstruate, doubts were easily cast on my femininity, and indeed, on the very question of my gender.

In addition to regular school, Hebrew classes occupied two hours a day, every day except the Sabbath. Our devotion sprang less from orthodoxy than an insistence that we study our own traditions. Papa practiced a unique brand of self-defined Jewishness. Neither parent ever went to synagogue, yet at home we observed every Jewish ritual. Mother lit candles on Friday night, and recited special prayers at Sabbath's close, yet we never rested on this, the holiest of days, but drove, cooked, and went to the movies. On Passover, we marked the liberation of Jews from Egypt with a ritual hunt for the unleavened bread followed by a perfect Seder, yet the house was never ritually consecrated. The long Jewish sojourn in the desert was commemorated by building a booth or Succah, complete with branches on the roof through which to see the stars. On Hannukah, the Feast of Lights, my father made lead tops using wooden molds exactly like those carved by his grandfather Reb Yehuda Leb. But on the Day of Atonement, the most solemn in the Hebrew calendar, when every observant Jew fasted as prescribed, Father ate a good lunch.

The paradox puzzled everyone, except my father, who had no doubts whatever about his affiliation. He watched as Jews vanished in the Holocaust, waiting anxiously for word of his favorite youngest brother, Isch, who spent five years in captivity in places like Colditz, after being captured by the Germans behind enemy lines in France. When Isch was liberated Father hoisted the Union Jack on a flagpole atop the rockery and played Beethoven's Fifth Symphony full blast. In 1948, when the State of Israel was proclaimed, he flew immediately to Haifa to serve as a surgeon during the War of Independence. His allegiance was crystal clear, but his lack of orthodoxy set him apart from other parents. For him, ritual was performed out of a sense of tradition rather than belief. This rationalization irritated my mother, who wanted the entire package. She dreamed fondly, if sentimentally, of a protected social existence in the European shtetl. She longed to stroll down the oak-lined avenue to the Great Synagogue. She yearned to sit in an allotted seat and smile down on the shawled men below, seeking out her husband in his dark suit and listening to the women in their Chanel suits and furs.[15]

But Father would not have it, and she would not attend a social event without him.

His inconsistency puzzled our teachers too. The Hebrew School,

founded by Reb Yehuda Leb back in 1899, stood near the Good Hope
Seminary, directly opposite the squat classical facade of the Zionist Hall.
Students spent hours there, practicing and translating the Hebrew script.
I never curled my tongue around the words and never learned to speak
the language. Instead, I concentrated on a large clock that hung above
the teacher's desk, holding my breath as the seconds slid into minutes
and finally into the requisite two hours a day.[16]

Mr. Rosen, an elegant gray-haired man with pale blue eyes, wore an
impeccable dark three-piece suit. He dragged his students through ten
verses of the Book of Kings each day. We responded with lethargy bordering on coma. Mr. Rosen might have preferred outright revolt, but
knowing as we did that most of the teachers were refugees from Hitler,
our protests were tempered with mercy. We yawned and asked repeatedly
to leave the room. Mr. Rosen took it philosophically most of the time
though on occasion he snapped. Stalking stealthily toward a dozing student, he slammed his fist on the desk:

"Look it in the book!" he shouted.

The student leaped up, trembling with shock.

"What do you want to end up, a goy in the street?"

Strictly speaking, *goy* means "nation," or, in the parlance of today,
"Other," as opposed to Jew, but Mr. Rosen did not use the word in this
exalted sense. We knew exactly what he meant. A few blocks down the
road was a pool hall. Men loitered at the frosted glass door, reeking of
beer. They smoked, laughed, and whistled at the schoolgirls walking in
clumps down to the city. Occasionally one sat on the sidewalk, with his
head between his knees. Once, one vomited on the pavement as we
passed. Some dismissed them as wastrels, but we schoolgirls thought they
were powerful and terrifying.

The day Mr. Rosen encountered the paradox of our family's religious
life began much the same as any other. Midway through the class came
a knock at the door to announce his daily cup of hot milk for his ulcer.
Mr. Rosen brightened up as the steaming cup was placed before him.
He marked his place, removed his wire spectacles, and rubbed the marks
on his nose.

"Tell me," he ventured, "how do we kill it the chicken?"

I brightened up. Here at last, was something I had actually seen.

I raised my hand,

"Isak the gardener takes it to the chopping block and chops the head off. Then he lets go. It runs around in circles. The blood . . . it's a chicken with its head chopped off!"

I laughed, yelping with excited pleasure at the recollection.

The room was silent. Mr. Rosen stood up, his face a mask of disbelief. "Excuse me?" he stuttered.

I hurried through the description leaving out the running around.

Mr. Rosen's grayness flushed florid. He sat down.

"Your father . . ." His voice trailed off "Your father gets the *gardener* to cut the chicken's head off?"

He could not have put more horror into "gardener" had it been the "Antichrist."

I was nonplussed.

"Well he can't do it himself. He is at the surgery in the afternoons . . ." I trailed off.

Mr. Rosen walked over to the window and looked out. Across the road the whitewashed Zionist Hall gleamed pink in the setting sun. He sighed.

At dinner that night the maid served soup. Mother flourished the ladle and filled the plates. I repeated the tale of the chicken My father took no notice. He continued spooning his soup as though nothing had been said. At last he sat up, patted his lips with the napkin, and held his plate out for a refill. He looked around.

"Mr. Rosen is there to teach Hebrew." His voice was very soft and calm. Then the tone changed a fraction, segueing into menace. "Let him worry about *his* chickens, and I will worry about mine."

There was a deep consistency to his inconsistency. It was just a matter of rules. It marked our little family off as strange, but we were so well insulated within the close confines of the Jewish community that I was six years old before I realized that most people in the world were not Jewish. In 1947 Britain graced its colonial possession and its leader, General Smuts, with a royal visit. King George, his gracious queen and the two princesses, Lillibet and Margaret, came to Cape Town. The local newspaper proclaimed the day of their arrival as the "Proudest Day in the City's History," noting moreover, that "Not since the day that Antonio de Saldanha first scaled its heights just 444 years ago has the mountain provided a more sublime setting for the second oldest city in the Empire." Mother hatched a plan to get a first-class view of the occasion by intercepting the White Train in its royal procession to Johannesburg. We drove to a small siding on the sandy Cape Flats outside the city. Standing at the barbed-wire fence that lined the track, we strained for the whistle of the approaching train. Mother straightened her Swiss Hanro suit, patted our hair straight, and warned us about the barbed wire.[17]

"What do they look like?"

My mother gazed down the track.

"Lovely!"

"Do they look Jewish?"

My mother looked amazed.

"Of course not! What on earth made you think they would?"

"You mean? . . ."

Tamar began to laugh.

"Carmel thinks the whole world's Jewish!"

I elbowed Tamar aside. She stumbled against the fence. Suddenly, a roar filled the air, wind funneled down the track, and the train barreled past. Several small figures waved dimly from the windows.

"Look! Look!"

My mother leaped up and down in a frenzy of excitement.

The roar faded. She turned to us.

"Wasn't it marvelous?"

I stood sulkily. A faint moan broke the silence. Tamar hung suspended on the fence, the hem of her dress tangled in barbed wire. Her voice rose plaintively:

"Have they come yet?"

So there we were. A minority within the larger white group, living in a land intent on entrenching inequality in its constitution. By the end of the Second World War, South African Jews had survived renewed attempts to curtail immigration from Eastern Europe through the Quota Act of 1930 and had endured the persistent effort of certain factions to ally with the Nazis, in spirit if not in fact. True, major leaders of the trade union movements came from the ranks of former denizens of Eastern Europe, earning their derogatory sobriquets of "communist" and "liberals," but in this stratified caste system, where skin color overrode ideology, the Jewish population cashed in the chips of their appearance.[18]

Smuts's sponsorship of the royal visit of 1947 was his last high point. He was ousted by the Nationalist Government that swept into power the following year and set about implementing every offensive detail of a policy of apartheid. Outwardly the daily lives of bourgeois Jews seemed similar to those elsewhere in the West, but within, social constraints were tightening up. The Population Registration Act of 1950 defined three phenotypic categories of Whites, Africans, and Coloreds. The Natives (Abolition of Passes and Co-ordination of Documents) Act of 1952 controlled the movements of Africans with reference books that had to be produced at all times. The Natives (Urban Areas) Consolidation Act of 1945, restricted African residence and movement in cities. The Group Areas Act, first enunciated in 1950 and reiterated repeatedly till 1969, defined where people of each group might live. The Suppression of Communism Act of 1950 restricted what people might think, or if that failed, what they might say aloud.[19]

In 1952 the rulers proclaimed a tercentenary to commemorate the arrival of Europeans at the Cape three hundred years earlier. The Van Riebeeck Festival marked the landing of the first fleet of the Dutch East India Company at the Cape. Hindsight has since advised would-be celebrants to regard such anniversaries with trepidation. In 1988 Australia's Aboriginal people marked their bicentennial year of colonization, by leaping, almost suicidally, into Sydney Harbor in front of Prince Charles's royal entourage. Four years later, America's quincentennial moment involved an orgy of apology to indigenous people, certain women, and descendants of slaves on Columbus Day. South Africa missed the point, until 1988, when they tried to celebrate the quincentennial landing of the first Portuguese caravel on the beach at Mossel Bay. Organizers, unable to recruit a single person of color to represent some of their very own Khoikhoi ancestors, hired white actors, who blackened their faces with shoe polish, and stumbled ashore. Crowds of disaffected people booed their landing.

No such sentiments intruded openly on the tercentenary of 1952. Overnight, a village of booths and stores sprang up on the reclaimed foreshore. Jan van Riebeeck was immortalized in medallions and stamps, and the five-bastioned castle built by his successors became the tercentennial icon. A replica of Van Riebeeck's home town was peopled with actors wandering about about in seventeenth-century dress. Although the majority of the city's population were descendants of the earliest colonists and natives, Bushmen were trucked down from the Kalahari Desert to present a more authentic representation of the Khoisan greeters of that first fleet. They were no strangers to scientific inquiry, having been drawn, measured, and even live-cast by curious scientists for many years. Now they built grass huts and fires in their enclosure, made bows and arrows, and smiled shyly through dangling fringes of ostrich eggshell beads at the crowds gaping at this most popular of all the tercentennial exhibits.[20]

The girls of Good Hope Seminary were part of the show. Textbooks were altered to incorporate the event and children were drilled to parade on the original landing place in Table Bay. We were recruited to sing two songs: The first was the Afrikaans national anthem, the second, an Afrikaans praise song, celebrating the birth of a "Volk," whose awakening made hearts swell with praise. It began softly, asking if you could hear the mighty drone coming over the veld as the nation awoke:

> En hoor jy die magtige dreuning?
> Oor die veld kom dit wyd gesweef.[21]

In later years these lines would be invested with irony to ask whether one could hear the mighty drone of the masses who were beginning to stir under the jackboot, but in 1952 such subtleties evaded most people. Uniformed in green and navy, the girls of Good Hope lined up, six to a row. Dust coated our tongues in the dry heat. Small and untidy, I was placed in the middle. I strained to see, to be seen. Suddenly, there was a commotion in the front row. A girl had fainted. Porters carried her off, and the teacher looked around for a substitute. I leaped up, hand waving.

"I'll walk in front," I called, "I'm ready!"

"No!"

The teacher looked particularly cross.

"Miss Carmel Schrire!" She spat out my name as one would a peach pit. "Why do you always try and take advantage of the misfortunes of others?"

I slunk to the back of the line, where the most dissolute girls giggled and fidgeted. Rumpled and bored we scuffled through the dust, bellowing a song of white ascendancy.

Four years later everything changed. In 1956 my father was fifty years old. Years of study, coupled with the courage to take calculated risks, had swelled his reputation as a bold and successful surgeon. His most recent triumph was the repair of a young lad's ruptured liver. The child's family were effusive in their gratitude, and they insisted that he attend the boy's bar mitzvah a few months later. My mother pounced on the opportunity to wear her new dress of shot-silk taffeta, whose tiny knife pleats flashed purple and red tones as she moved. There at the Zionist Hall they sat, honored and glowing. The boy made his speech, and people began to dance. But as the familiar tunes of the shtetl boomed out, my father felt a tingling along his left side. He stamped his foot, impatient at first, then deeply afraid. Pulling my mother to her feet, they stumbled out. They sank onto a bench beneath the picture of Herzl, and as the ambulance siren approached, a massive stroke slammed through his brain.

At that instant, our lives faltered and changed course. Papa's left side was paralyzed. He wore a splint to help him walk and used a stick as he limped along. His left hand dangled useless by his side. Surgery was a thing of the past. Mother rose, as though her entire life had been choreographed for this occasion. With insistent clarity she pulled us together. Father would always be the head of the household. Deferring to his design, his will, and his opinion, she rode through the despair, poverty, and shock to forge a new existence. After many months' rehabilitation at Queen's Square hospital in London, he returned to run the Casualty Department at Groote Schuur hospital and to study Jewish mythology and mysticism. Trajectories of recovery read smoother than they live, and the family blundered through the catastrophe, buffered by demands of children and daily routines. We coated our pain in black humor, presenting such a unified front that people on occasion would say how much they envied my father having all that time to write.[22]

Two years later, I matriculated and fell into the highbrow halls of the University of Cape Town. The college stood on mountain side, land donated a half-century earlier by Cecil John Rhodes to exemplify and encompass his visions of imperial excellence. Ivy-covered buildings rose in a majestic procession up the slopes of Devil's Peak, culminating in a white-pillared Greek temple. This was Jameson Hall, named after Rhodes's lapdog, the duplicitous Dr. Leander Starr Jameson, who had inadvertently sparked the Boer War when he spearheaded an unsuccessful putsch designed to wrest the goldfields of the Transvaal from President Paul Kruger.[23]

The university epitomized the Oxbridge tradition. Many teachers were British, or else they had been educated in places like Kings, Trinity, and Balliol. Swooping across the campus in academic gowns, they forbade any interruption as they lectured to large, intimidated classes. The student body was mainly white, though a few Colored and black faces swum into view occasionally, especially in the Department of African Studies. This was not entirely due to their intrinsic fascination with their own culture but rather a direct consequence of the politics of separate education. From its inception in 1948, the Nationalist Government planned to provide separate universities for different racial groups, and they promulgated an escalating series of laws to control admissions and appointments. Up to 1959, only the "open" universities of Cape Town and the Witwatersrand accepted nonwhite students in mixed classes, though even here these students were segregated with regard to residential, sporting, and social activities. In 1959, the Extension of University Education Act set about tightening the separation of educational facilities, and the following year a proclamation explicitly banned Africans from registering in many departments at the open universities, including the African Studies program at the University of Cape Town. There was one small loophole, however, and that lay in the fact that if there were no other program available to them, students of color might, with special pleading, cross the Great Divide and enrol in a specialized and unique program at an open university. Since the African Studies department was one of a kind in the Cape, it was therefore able, on occasion, to admit a phenotypically more varied student body than might gain access to the rest of the university. Not unexpectedly, this loophole soon proved to be a noose when in 1968 the University of Cape Town was forced to rescind its offer of a post in social anthropology to one of its most esteemed black graduates.[24]

It was in this context that I enrolled for courses in the Department of African studies. The program included social anthropology, African government and law, Bantu languages, and archaeology and ethnology. It enjoyed widespread acclaim, having numbered among its chairs A. R. Radcliffe-Brown, the founder of the British functionalist school of anthropology, and the ethnographer Isaac Schapera. In 1960, Professor Monica Wilson held the chair. Her roots ran deep in the liberal tradition, farming on the eastern frontier in the heart of Pondoland and teaching at the black university of Fort Hare. She had studied at Girton College, Cambridge, and her fieldwork among Bantu-speaking people ranged from Pondoland to Tanganika. Rangy and handsome, with pale blue eyes, it was difficult to decide whether her intellect, her calm, or her arresting stare inspired most terror. But Monica Wilson had more important things to handle than her intimidated students. By 1960 liberal elements in all universities were locked in a deadly struggle with the government's unequal education system. The principal of the University of Cape Town remained inscrutably silent and aloof. It fell to individuals to orchestrate a response, and foremost among these were Monica Wilson and her colleague Jack Simons, a self-proclaimed communist who was the professor of African government and law. It was a worthy cause but a lost one. Students massed and protested, but government agents infiltrated the classrooms, police monitored demonstrations on campus, and eventually protestors marked the passing of the separate universities act by extinguishing a symbolic torch of academic freedom at the Houses of Parliament.[25]

Astley John Hilary Goodwin was the professor of archaeology. A Cambridge-trained man, he joined the university as an ethnologist in 1923, and he remained the only full-time teacher of archaeology in the subcontinent until he died in 1959. A world expert on stone tool technology and prehistoric chronology, he alternated between teasing, coaxing, and threatening his students with failure unless they could memorize the sequences. Some said he was a disappointed man; others said he was entitled to feel that way. His favorite daughter had died young, and his only son was brain damaged. His brilliant insights were snatched from his grasp by his mentor, Miles Burkitt, the genial and well-loved teacher of archaeology at Cambridge, who visited Goodwin in 1928, saw his sites, heard his opinions, and then sailed home to publish it all under his own name. Goodwin, realizing what had happened, raced Burkitt to the finish, and lost, leaving him with the bitter realization that he was nothing but a colonial, working in the field, for the greater glory of his Cambridge betters.[26]

In the winter of 1959, Goodwin, his student Glynn Isaac and I drove north to the snow-covered mountains to look for ancient sites. High up on a mountain pass we found trilobite fossils marking the passage of a 400-million-year-old Devonian sea; down in the valley we gathered pear-shaped stone handaxes made by people a mere million years ago. At night we stumbled into a caravanserai of Jewish peddlers, the Grand Levine's Hotel. Its gloomy lounge, with maroon plush chairs and lace antimacassars, was hung about with ferns, and sepia portraits of Victorian ancestors. Goodwin could hardly wait. Wheezing and coughing from the cancer in his lungs, he lit his first cigarette of the day. He inhaled and turned blue. Glynn and I leaped to our feet. Goodwin waved us away, gasping.

"Too bloody late!"

The new academic year of 1960 found the small senior class with no professor of archaeology. Glynn Isaac had a few months to spare before leaving for Cambridge, so he was seconded to teach. He plowed right into sequences and dates, and we took notes as though our lives depended on it. In March, he handed the baton over to another Cambridge man. Brian Fagan, the curator of the Rhodes Livingstone Museum was in his early twenties, with floppy brown hair and an enthusiasm and energy that enervated his audience on sight. His interests in prehistory seemed peripheral to general departmental concerns. In March the Sharpeville massacre splattered images of shattered black children on the front pages of the world's newspapers. Some said the bloodbath had begun. Joe Jordan, professor of Xhosa, was assaulted by police on his way to work, and Jack Simons waited daily for the knock that would announce his house arrest. Professor Monica Wilson, serene in her belief that good must triumph in the end, spoke out against the government at every opportunity. About a week after Sharpeville, a mile-long crowd marched behind the twenty-one-year-old University of Cape Town student Philip Kgosana to demand justice from the police.[27]

The newly appointed Senior Lecturer arrived for the last term. Ray Inskeep was compact, with a mop of curly hair. He sounded like an English schoolmaster, which is exactly what he had once been. He listened to what we knew about archaeology and his lips whitened. Drawing a deep breath, he told us exactly what he expected us to learn. We wrote it down. He said he would take us into the field to show us what we were reading about. Inskeep promised to teach us how to dig, how to analyze collections, how to do research.

Inskeep's lectures were models of clarity. Each site was located on a map, its sequence was drawn, and it was fitted into a broad master plan of climatic and cultural change. We were introduced to the realization that all sites were not of equal importance, that all excavators were not of equal reliability. He listed alternatives with clarity, reconstructed changing landscapes with verve. His sketches of the East African lakes tipping out their contents to produce a semblance of aridity made the pluvial–interpluvial muddle there into child's play. He had, after all, been to all the sites, even to Mount Carmel, where he served with the British forces in Palestine during the Mandate.

"Tell me!" I begged.

Palestine was not his favorite memory. A young soldier, he was seconded to turn away a shipload of refugees from the Nazi death camps. He tore off his stripes and stamped them into the wharf.

"Bastards!" he declared.

Instant demotion followed.

I thought he was wonderful.

We started fieldwork that spring at Elandsfontein, near Saldanha Bay in the southwestern Cape. The archaeological site had once been a swamp, but major climatic changes had since left it dry and barren. White dunes shifted to reveal patches of ground littered with dark brown fossilized bones and occasional sharp stone tools. Several years earlier, fragments of a human skull dating from about 500,000 to 200,000 years ago, had been found, but not another trace of a human fossil had appeared since the discovery of this Saldanha Man. Inskeep and Ronald Singer, the professor of anatomy, hoped to find more remains. Singer prowled around the dunes and Inskeep dug long trenches, watching as the wind blew first small holes, then caverns, in their walls. He measured and plotted, but was eventually forced to conclude that the concentrations of tools and bones did not represent the actual campsites of prehistoric people. Rather, they seemed to be a product of deflation and sinkage, brought about when heavy objects that had fallen on the sands at various times migrated downward to congregate on a single surface.[28]

The final exams were over. Summer lay ahead. Inskeep asked if any of us would like to go with him and Ronnie Singer to visit the great Australopithecine sites in the northern Transvaal. I raced home. My father looked skeptical, but he had taught Singer and had served as co-editor of the *South African Archaeological Bulletin* with Inskeep. He agreed. Our arrangement was to rendezvous at noon at a cafe in Pietersburg, 1,600 kilometers away in the northern Transvaal. Inskeep and Singer would drive up from the Cape, and the other scientists, including archaeologists Revil Mason and Berry Malan, and paleontologists Raymond Dart and Phillip Tobias, would come in from Johannesburg. I traveled alone from Cape Town by train, clutching my new checkbook. The other passenger in the small compartment was an elderly lady with tight curled white hair. Barely out of Cape Town, she stared pointedly at my shorts and told me to cover my legs. Later that night, she prayed out loud asking God to forgive them, to redeem them and to show them His light. "They" featured prominently in her entreaties, recounting as she did, more the sins of others than her own. Next morning she announced that I was no better than a Red Kaffir. She claimed to have some familiarity with the darker side of such folk, dating from the time when her husband ran a trade store on the Natal coast.

We reached Pietersburg at daybreak on the third day. The air was already dusty and hot. There were two cafes. I made for the one with the "Europeans Only" sign. Inside, a juke box played Buddy Holly. I read comics and waited. Nearby a mustached man sat staring at the door. Four hours dragged by.

"Poor bugger," I thought. "Doesn't he have a job?"

Around midday a landrover skidded up. The cafe door swung open. Ray Inskeep and Ronnie Singer burst in. Rushing past my outstretched arms they enveloped the stranger.

"Phillip, how wonderful to see you!"

For two weeks we toured the sites. The archaeologists decoded the sequences at Makapan, Sterkfontein, and the banks of the Vaal River, and speculated about broken bones in the Transvaal Museum. Forty years earlier Raymond Dart had discovered the first australopithecine, or "Southern Ape," whose ancestral humanity made Dart's name and established South Africa as a birthplace of humanity. Dart devoted a large part of his life thereafter to classifying fossil hominids and trying to reconstruct their behavior. He focused his attention on the innumerable fractured animal bones found in these limestone caves, and speculated that they might have been the weapons of the earliest carnivorous killer apes. Others demurred, especially Bob Brain, who figured that they represented the crunched-up meals of hyenas and other animals. Dart's former student and current heir, Phillip Tobias, could scarcely stand still. He was brimming with excitement about mysterious new hominids from Olduvai Gorge, in Tanganika.[29]

Leaving the limestone caves behind, we set off for the south coast. Lunches were small celebrations that culminated with both men sipping brandy as they puffed on cheroots. I proudly attended to the bills with my new checkbook. We finally reached a small motel on the beach, where late at night I lay resentfully listening to Singer's famous snores several doors down. Suddenly there was a scratching on the door. It was Ray.

"Asthma!" he gasped.

"You never had it before?"

"Always!"

He looked awful. I followed him back to their room, and shouted in Ron's ear to wake him.

"What shall we do?"

"God knows," said Singer.

For a medical doctor he seemed alarmingly uninterested.

I called the desk. A half-hour later a stout district nurse trundled up on a bicycle. Her wheezing made Ray sound like an athlete. He eyed her nervously. She snorted and struck him a hearty pat on the back.

"Adrenaline," she declared, "straight into the chest."

She rummaged in her bag. Ray rolled his eyes and held his breath. Ron lit a cigar.

"No," I said. "He's better."

Ray fell onto the bed.

Ron looked at his watch. It was 6.30 A.M.

"Let's eat." he said. "Right now!"

We had an early start for the Tzitzikama caves at the mouth of the Klasies River. Our map was old and crushed, but there was no missing the black holes dotting the dense bush on the slopes. Archaeological deposits drooled from their mouths. We panted uphill and strode into the darkness where dripping water ticked monotonously. Peering into the gloom we felt a draught suggesting that a passage was open through this cave into the one next door.[30]

"Carmel first," said Ron.

Ray laughed.

I was fast as a rattlesnake.

"He's smaller," I countered.

"But you," said Singer, cigar clamped between his teeth, "you are the student."

The deposits in the Klasies River Mouth cave had been eroded by an ancient high sea to form a vertical cliff. Creamy white ash alternating with layers of black charcoal lay packed with sharp flints and bone splinters that protruded like daggers from the face. We scrambled up the hillside into the cave, and looked out over the cliff. Ray chuckled with delight. I turned, stumbled, and fell backwards, down the exposed face. Prehistoric bones and flints ripped my chest and thighs as I clawed for purchase. I crouched at the bottom of the cliff, hoping they would not fall in their haste to reach me.

There was no need for concern. Both men were riveted to the section, mentally estimating how many millennia of human behavior must be stratified in the stacked levels.

I got up. Blood was starting to seep through my shredded shorts and shirt. I walked straight into the sea, staring at the horizon. Their cries of excitement carried on the wind. I turned. Huge smiles wreathed their faces.

Smiles faded a few weeks later at my father's expression when he saw the state of my new checking account.

"What the hell did you eat?" he asked.

"Ronnie Singer ordered the meals."

My father remembered Singer well as a medical student.

"Bloody mastodon!" he roared.

With Monica Wilson's endorsement in hand I applied to her old Cambridge college, Girton, in September. Inskeep's long association with Cambridge was also brought into play. I felt then that I could not have chosen better mentors, but I might have been less sanguine had I seen a private review of his students penned by Fagan to Inskeep a year earlier: "Schrire (Carmel, Miss, c. 18). A Jewess, and a curvaceous one. Local secretary of the Society, but not active enough. . . . Her interest in archaeology is somewhat superficial—she is at heart a Social Anthropologist. Not interested in the practical side, except perhaps paintings. Works hard. Boy friend (steady) in Jo'burg. Ardent liberal."[31]

Cambridge was cold. It took a half-hour to cycle the five windy kilometers from Girton into town. Darkness fell shortly after midday, and by late afternoon a white moon shone coldly through the sodium glare in the wet streets. I could only read English and Afrikaans, and the archaeological literature was largely in French. A course in Russian archaeology was scheduled to be taught, but neither the teacher nor the students could read any of the reports. Inskeep's tutelage meant that I knew more about stone tools than my fellow students, an advantage that the teacher proclaimed to the class. The men shot looks of undisguised hatred in my direction.

At Cambridge, men outnumbered women ten to one. The disparity was enhanced by the unequal treatment of women students in the archaeology department. St. John's College men were wined, dined, and educated by Glyn Daniel. Charles McBurney handled the Corpus men, and the Disney Professor of Archaeology, Grahame Clark, presided over a long tradition of archaeological students at Peterhouse. None of the women's colleges, including mine, boasted a resident archaeologist to tutor the students. On Inskeep's advice I went to see Eric Higgs. He was a former stockbroker who had decided to become an archaeologist after meeting Grahame Clark on a dig. He had dug up the bones on McBurney's expedition to Libya, and he now specialized in faunal analysis. A large, bald man, his stoop and omniscient expression recalled a Galapagos tortoise. His lab was crowded with finds. Animal bones hung suspended from a large peg board. An elongated ostrich pelvis dangled beside a fox. A Pekinese skull grinned as if it were trying to fool you that it was a human infant, and the pangolin head seemed to have no holes at all.[32]

Eric sat shrouded in smoke and cunning. He looked like Alastair Sim, the comedian who epitomized the art of one-upsmanship. He sounded like him as well.

"If you are not one up," he intoned, with an upward inflection that challenged you to deny the proposition, "you are one down!"

The world, he said, was divided into clever people and those who did what they were told.

"Chuff, chuff, chuff," he grinned, "put them on the track and off they go, chuff, chuff, never looking to left or right."

Every now and then a specimen broke its moorings. A cow's head crashed down, teeth scattering all over the floor like dice. A tusk dangled precariously over our bent heads. Eric was quite explicit about my position at Cambridge. Although I received no archaeological supervision at Girton, he had no time to supervise me. Moreover, he would not take women into the field because they caused nothing but trouble. Eric seemed experienced on this issue. He had lost one in Benghazi, though another survived a field trip to marry him when it was over.

It took months for the subtle differential treatment of women at Cambridge fully to sink in. The University of Cape Town sported very few female faculty, but Monica Wilson was a legendary force in the field. Ray Inskeep treated all his students as equals. He taught me, argued with me, cajoled, laughed, resented, and insisted, but he never raised gender as a factor in my intellectual life. Cambridge had practically led the world in women's education. It had, in fact, appointed Dorothy Garrod to the Disney Chair of Archaeology in 1939, even though women were not full members of the university at that time! Nevertheless, more than two decades later, a disparity still existed in the Archaeology Department, where women were relegated a subtly lesser role, as helpmeets, rather than protaganists.[33]

What was less clear were matters of class and ethnicity.

It came home to me late one night after a bull session in one of the rooms overlooking the courtyard at Girton. We were discussing the forthcoming Hunt Ball. Scottish students planned to wear long white frocks draped with the tartans of their clan. They launched into an excited discussion about the pedigrees of the men who would attend, the implications of who was who. I asked question after question, evoking a storm of information. Finally one of them asked who my people were.

I explained. Silence fell. I elaborated on origins, immigration, South Africa. The silence deepened. One snickered, whispered, and turned away. Stung, I stared at their polite, closed faces.

"Let's get this straight . . ."

My voice was high and nervous.

They turned, unwilling to listen, but too polite to say so.

"While your people were running around the hills painted blue, mine were writing the Talmud."

There was an embarrassed hush. The room cleared. A friend hustled me to the door and set off down the cold corridor at a fast lick. We rounded the corner. She pulled me into the Gyp room, where the daily maid washed the cups. The small tiled recess smelled of disinfectant and boiled cloths. Her eyes blazed.

"Tell me," she spat, "who are you?"

"I'm from South Africa . . ."

She cut me short.

"No!" she snapped, "Who are you?"

I began again.

She whirled around.

"Listen!" she hissed. "You're not only a wog, you're a Yid, understand?"

I stared.

"A wog and a Yid!" She paused. "And don't forget it."

I graduated in June. In the long, sunny days we sat around wondering what to do, where to go. Suddenly a call came from the Indian expert in the department, offering my fiancé a position as archaeologist in Peshawar. He was no fool. Boldly he asked them what I might find to do there?

The expert smiled kindly.

"We wondered if Carmel might teach needlework to the girls?"

My fiancé swiveled toward me. I read a certain hopefulness in his gaze. I wondered how I might tell my father, Monica Wilson, or Ray Inskeep, of such a plan.

"Nope." I said. "I won't!"

Around 1962 the Australian National University in Canberra recruited a Cambridge man, Jack Golson, to initiate its research program in archaeology. Born into a working-class family in Yorkshire, Golson was a conscientious objector who fulfilled his wartime service as a coal miner. At Cambridge he joined the Communist party, an action that earned him rich retribution later, when he was repeatedly barred from entering the United States. He yearned to specialize in the Dark Ages, but instead Grahame Clark dispatched him to teach archaeology in New Zealand. Here his excavations of ancient Maori hill forts revealed patterns of colonization, defense, and survival that echoed medieval settlement. Golson's ability to draw these broad analogies drew such professional and popular acclaim that when the time came he seemed the obvious candidate for the Australian job.[34]

In the early 1960s the prehistory of Australia was just beginning to emerge. Not much was known about where the First Australians came from, what they looked like, what routes they took once they reached land, or what their impact on this huge unpeopled land may have been. A handful of radiocarbon dates suggested that people had come there about 10,000 years ago. Golson needed students, and where better to recruit them than at his Alma Mater? I was at a loose end. I had already received a series of curt, negative responses from Israeli archaeologists, and their disinterest contrasted strongly with Golson's enthusiasm. Moreover, he could back up his excitement with offers of stipends and field support. By the end of the year, a number of us had decided to try our luck in the Antipodes.

The ancestry of people who hunted and gathered their food on its shores when Europeans first colonized the Australian coast 200 years ago was unclear, but the Aboriginal inhabitants were some of the best-documented Stone Age people in the world. In 1964 the new buzzword around the Cambridge department was *ethnoarchaeology,* the study of living people as models of the past. Elsewhere original contact populations seemed to have been absorbed into the wider pluralistic society, but in Australia hunters and gatherers still lived off the land. They performed ceremonies, traded, and made stone tools. Some even said there were tribes in remote reaches of the land who had never been seen by Europeans. It seemed an ideal place to try to link past and present by observing living people as we excavated their past.[35]

Cambridge graduates and their Australian colleagues began to generate a distinct school of Antipodean archaeology. John Mulvaney excavated classic sequences along the Murray River near Melbourne. Rhys Jones's stylish work in Tasmania foreshadowed the antics of his eponymous hero Indiana Jones. He showed that Tasmanians were Australians who were cut off from the mainland by the rising postglacial sea about 12,000 years ago. In New Guinea, Peter White watched remote native people carving bows and arrows with stone tools and used what he saw to interpret prehistoric artifacts. Richard Wright related his study of Cape York painted caves to Aboriginal interpretations of the rock art. Jack Golson was working in north Australia, and since I was anxious to find a field location, he agreed to take me along to find a project there.[36]

The Northern Territory was an endless outback. Farms, missions, and small towns were beads on the thread of the Stuart Highway, a tarred ribbon that bisected the continent from Darwin to Alice Springs. Golson's party camped in a shed on a research station outside the town of Katherine. Here, as elsewhere in the Territory, Aboriginal people lived on the urban fringes in a spiral of unemployment, alcoholism, and desultory violence. No signs proclaimed their rights, no "Whites Only," "Non Whites," or "Natives," such as demarcated existence in South Africa, yet custom ruled that they never frequented pubs and cafes. They squatted in the dust, shooting longing glances toward the hot, beery interiors. They worked for a pittance yet seemed to have a rich communal life in their camps, where singing and clacking sticks broke the darkness at night. They wore shorts and mission dresses, yet they also organized ceremonies, journeys, and marriages according to the dictates of their own rhythms and custom.[37]

Golson was immersed in a thick dog-eared book on the Thirty Years' War and seldom crawled under his mosquito net until long after midnight. Since he could not begin the day without a solid English breakfast, we generally reached the dig around midday. At sunset Golson turned the landrover toward the hole and worked on by the glare of its headlights. Finally we decamped to town. Katherine straddled the highway 300 kilometers south of Darwin, a net to snare transients as they trawled up and down the width of the continent. No one was too old or too dull for a conversation. In Canberra, my accent pegged me as a despised South African racist, but in the Northern Territory conspiratorial nods and nudges greeted my every word. I felt familiar yet hostile. For whereas overt racism in South Africa was bolstered by the fear by whites of an overwhelming black majority, here white antipathy to Aboriginal people seemed utterly gratuitous. Fuming with beer, talk ranged from history to metaphysics, from party politics to mining, reverting to sex, race, and abuse as the night wore on. Mostly it was about women, gins, lubras, bitches, and worse. Even the barmaid was suspect.

"Take a look," said one raddled drunk leaning on the bar. His voice dropped to an intimate leer. "You can tell, can't you?"

"Tell what?"

"She's the town bike, you arsehole!"

A long pull at his beer. His smile brought to mind the look on the face of a scholar expounding some convoluted theorem.

"Bloody idiot! You can just tell!"

It was clearly no place for me, twenty-three years old, all but teetotal, and dreaming of caves like Mount Carmel or of the Libyan cliffs at Haua Fteah. We headed into the remote outback, to the Arnhem Land Reserve. The cliffs were pocked with rock shelters, and low shell mounds dotted the plain. At Oenpelli, the chief missionary had no interest whatsoever in research, and he felt deeply opposed to having a young white woman, wandering around on her own. The problem was solved when an Aboriginal man found us struggling to open a gate and declared himself as our guide. Frank Gananggu shepherded me through two field seasons, through interactions with Oenpelli Mission, and with the Aboriginal people, who would later be declared to be the traditional owners of the very sites we dug. Very little surprised him. Not the persistent antagonism of the missionaries toward archaeology, nor the unwillingness of Aboriginal men to work for a woman. The only thing that overwhelmed him was the liquor that poured into Arnhem Land a few years later, when the reserve was declared Aboriginal land. Mines were dug, roads were tarred, tourists appeared, and Aboriginal people were caught up in decision making, cash flow, fast cars, and booze.[38]

But by then I had left Australia for Canada and the United States. For ten years I stayed there, teaching and raising children, and by the time I returned to Arnhem Land in 1980, it was clear that a new consciousness dominated Australian archaeology. Here, as elsewhere in the former colonial world, the new Land Rights movements, represented an effort to incorporate aboriginal people more equitably into the nation-states that encapsulated them. In Australia, landmark legislation was encoded in the Aboriginal Land Rights (Northern Territory) Act of 1976. Up to that point, Aboriginal people were not considered to hold legal title because the land was seen as having been ceded by the natives, rather than conquered by Europeans. In a stunning reversal of policy, the act now

declared that Aboriginal people might lay legal claim to land lying outside their former reserves, provided that it was not held by the Crown.
Traditional landowners might file their claims by presenting evidence of
a spiritual affiliation and prior use of specified tracts and landmarks. A
welter of claims followed, and many anthropologists used their academic
knowledge of prehistory, anthropology, and traditional life to explore
these practical issues, and to champion indigenous people in the court-
rooms.[39]

Even the most narrowly focused archaeologists were drawn into its
ambit. It became imperative for them to negotiate not with their own
officials but with the newly declared traditional owners. Aboriginal
people could, and on occasion did, refuse access to would-be excavators.
Intrigues abounded to such an extent that one archaeologist was moved
to wonder whether politicians were giving the past to the Aborigines
because they were unwilling to give them a future! For all the misgivings,
a new richness emerged in the public perception of Aboriginal land use
and beliefs, but at the same time the changes spelled difficulties for someone like myself, living as I did outside Australia, beyond easy access to
the negotiating parties. I joined a project aimed at assessing the effects of
uranium mining and royalty payments on formerly isolated communities.
Watching miners, politicians, traditional landowners, and academics trying to reconcile profits with a sense of preserving the past, I began to
understand how the earliest mercantile expansionists must have watched
the world into which they stumbled fade and change. I began to feel
what it was like to witness, even perhaps, to preside over the transforma-
tion of indigenous societies.[40]

The longer I watched, the more grew the desire to explore the concrete expression of such change. I wanted to taste dispossession in the
material elements of invasion, the clay pipes, stone flasks, and bottles. I
wanted to stumble through ruined outposts, where north European
bombast once boomed over the sharp, soft clicks of aboriginal opinion.
I dreamed about lancing old middens and retrieving the garbage of settlers and indigenes. I wanted to run my fingers through the very same
beads, pipes, and coins that once lubricated the loss of land, and to pore
over the documents announcing the hegemony of the European enterprise.

What was more, I wanted to go home.

In 1983, I began a new project aimed at digging into the actions and
consequences of colonial-indigenous interactions there. I renewed my

links with the University of Cape Town and strengthened my ties with friends and family, so that what set out to be an exploration of other peoples' history became a window into my own.

I returned to Cape Town for my regular annual visit in 1992. My father had died the previous year and we needed to raise a tombstone in his honor. My mother canvassed all four daughters about inscriptions. Some wanted curlicues, others settled for a plain Star of David. One suggested a biblical verse, another wanted his professional identity inscribed. The stonemason insisted that the three generations he had sired should all be noted. We studied the memorial plaque carved by Reb Yehuda Leb eighty years earlier, wondering whether to copy some of its designs. Final decisions were made and a date was set. A crowd gathered on a clear winter day. More than twenty-five years had past since the death of the grand architect of apartheid, when a parliamentary official stabbed Verwoerd dead. Father had reached the hospital just in time to certify the death. Verwoerd's passing accelerated the enforcement of apartheid, forcing the country into an isolationist cocoon, surrounded by world hatred and contempt. It took decades until the minority government could tolerate economic and social sanctions no longer and capitulated in small part in 1990 by releasing Nelson Mandela to herald the postapartheid society of a new South Africa.[41]

Old friends, Professor Jack Simons and his wife Ray Alexander, stood at the grave. Rooted out as communists, they had spent twenty years in exile in Zambia. In February 1990 Ray listened with half an ear to the news as she prepared lunch. A breathless voice announced the release of Nelson Mandela from jail. She hurried to the door and called for Jack. He was pruning a riotous bougainvillea at the gate.

"Jack!" she yelled "Quick!"

He turned.

In her excitement, Ray's babushka had slipped down over one eye. Impatiently, she pushed it straight.

"Jack! To the embassy! We're going home!"

Tumultuous crowds greeted them at the airport when they returned. Within days Ray marched to protest the rising price of milk.

The cemetery lay on the sandy flats, that linked the mountainous peninsula to the hinterland. Alongside ran the railway line where Tamar was impaled during the royal visit. Over to the west stood Table Mountain, its flanks ringed with skyscrapers that sprouted where our colonial ancestor once hurried to greet the steamship bringing the family to the Cape.

On either side lay the oceans, and to the east rose the gateway of the Hottentots Holland Mountains, now a conduit for a million people who swarmed down to the shantytowns of the Cape Flats in search of work.

The rabbi stood by the grave flanked by two other priests, forming a full contingent in recognition of the respect they felt for the family. He intoned the kaddish, his voice clear and confident. It was fitting that he should do so, since my father had no son to pray for him. Tamar met my glance. We nodded at each other, and joined in the praise song, our voices rising firm and loud, drowning out the disapproval in the rabbi's cadence.

Our chant circled the grave and rose into the clear winter air. It bounced off the mountains and mingled with the smoke from the shantytowns that drifted between the oceans at the Cape of Good Hope.

Chronicles of Contact

Documents abound on the spread of European mercantile capitalism. They tell almost the entire story, as we know it, starting about a thousand years ago, when European navigators, using vessels that one might hesitate today to employ for a brief ferry ride began to colonize the world. For thousands of years navigators puzzled over how to see the world and how to map its curves. They had to understand the winds and currents in order to discover, and then bring back, the knowledge they had gained. Returning crusaders brought the news that magnetic north could be found by a pointing needle, and Arabs pioneered the stern rudder and the lateen sail. Hundreds of years before Columbus sailed west, or Prince Henry the Navigator sponsored the circumnavigation of Africa, Arab fleets criss-crossed the Indian Ocean, trading in a multiplicity of goods, even to the point of ferrying giraffes to the Chinese court. But then, in 1433, the Chinese stepped back and closed their doors, and the Arabs (being, so some say, exactly where they wanted to be), explored no further. The focus of marine exploration now swung across to Europe, where Viking seafarers had already crossed the Atlantic Ocean from Norway to Newfoundland. In the late fifteenth century, the maritime nations started to make significant moves that would culminate in trade and settlement. Staging points appeared on the Atlantic islands, in the Cape Verdes and Madeira, and fleets were launched westward to America, and south, down the African coast, to enter the realms of the Arab and Chinese traders in the Indian Ocean.[1]

Many scholars have contemplated the impact of the spread of mercantile capitalism worldwide. Boorstin's magisterial history of conquest draws on an escalating series of scientific discoveries through time. Alfred Crosby's global ecology sees the creation of new "Neo-European" states as a process that cobbled together the seams ripped apart by continental drift 180 million years ago. Marx and Engels defined new world systems in the light of this process, and recently, Wolf drew on exotic Oriental and Arabic sources to document the pre-European history of the so-called savages of the world. The historical archaeologist Jim Deetz likens the spread of English ceramics worldwide to a tin of paint emptied over the globe that blanketed the world in an inexorable viscous flow.[2]

Whatever image serves best, the arrival of Europeans in four relatively new continents came as a considerable shock to all parties.

Consider this analogy: A spaceship lands in a shopping mall plaza. Bipeds emerge, their reptilian skins gleaming in the reddish, late afternoon sun. They reach into pouches in their bellies and distribute diamonds as if they were candy. The Anglo-American cartel, which has dominated the diamond market for a century, tries to control this generosity. One magnate recalls how once, around three centuries ago, a party of shipwrecked Siamese ambassadors offered rough diamonds to their Hottentot rescuers on the African coast, only to watch in open-mouthed astonishment as the natives tossed the stones into the dust. His historical musings come to nothing, for today's women are not yesterday's Hottentots. Tossing their zircons to the ground, they pounce on the diamonds, whooping with joy.[3]

The invaders (for no one thinks of them as visitors for long) also hand round narcotics that make a cocaine rush feel like a light sneeze.

They are irresistible.

They ask only one thing.

They want to buy the sky.

This is the moment that every con man in the world has been waiting for, finding a buyer who wants to buy something that doesn't exist at the highest imaginable price. Everyone from congressman to crack peddler climbs into the act. Agencies and task forces articulate rules to negotiate the sale of what everyone knows cannot be sold. Bankers, taking time off from robbing the poor, under the guise of looking after their life's savings, turn to cheating the invaders. After all, the sky is "commons": the air is there for all. But the invaders are so rich and ignorant that their demand brings a heady seriousness to the negotiating tables. Agreements are reached whereby every individual on earth is recognized as holding the deed to that section of the sky above his head, and a price is set, which relates the net worth of each person, to the estimated worth of his sky.

Dealers rock with suppressed laughter as the consultations proceed, recovering now and again to adjust the prices upwards in response to bribes and payoffs.

At last, with many side glances and snide comments, the deals are cut.

Four days later, people wake to a strange sense of compression. It is hard to breathe and tiresome to stay awake. Limbs are slow and torpid. Forcing their drooping eyes upwards, they notice that the sky has changed. An expanding mosaic of black squares shimmers above each person's head, like tiles set uncertainly in a bowl of blue jello. Only a few Turkana herdsmen, who could not be reached because they were observing a ritual seclusion continue to breathe easy. Tiny squares of clear sky follow their movements, illuminating their heads like medieval halos.[4]

Colonialism is a chronicle of betrayals. First landfalls were often the outcome of prolonged and serious planning at home, but on the alien shore invaders splashed ingenuously through the shallows, smiles weighed down a little by their sodden clothes. Responses varied. When Capt. James Cook sailed into Botany Bay in 1770, he noticed that Aboriginal people fishing in a nearby canoe kept their heads down. He thought they were outwardly fixated on their "business or sport." Later scholars conjecture that they were probably dying inside, as they watched their worst nightmares come true. For them, the British might have been bloodless men from the Land of the Dead at the end of the horizon, and the smoke from their ships, confirmed this fear, because it was like the sand thrown up by crabs when they bury themselves, as if they were dead. A world away Inuit people ran along the high Arctic beach to watch a house with smoking chimney materialize out to sea. Hawaiians, on the other hand, mistook the invaders for gods. They welcomed their long-awaited God, Lono, even though he was disguised as Captain Cook. Later, as some believe, having already accommodated him into their wider mythology, they incorporated him even deeper into their lives by eating his corpse. Whatever the symbolic interpretation put upon these encounters, many had the same practical outcome. Spears whistled through the gut of the invader and bullets smashed the face of the indigene.[5]

But finally, always, when the initial shock waves of recognition receded, it was time for business.

Both sides had something to offer. Goods were spread upon the smooth sand. On one side, the local treasures: corn, peas, beans, fish, a cow, a sheep, even a goat. Skins, feathers, tusks, a node of green copper, and crystalline rocks glittering with promise. Metals, jewels, pots, gum, and heavy, dark wood. Spices, like pepper to burn the tongue and a prickly clove to scent the breath. Lined up against this, the wares of the West: iron knives, hoes, and pitchforks, strings of beads, red, green, blue, and sparkling crystal. Whistles and bells, flasks of spirits, cloth, rolls of tobacco, and a box of pipes. Most intriguing of all, mirrors to reveal the "Other" to himself, evoking such astonishment, that one observer, compared the native reaction to Narcissus preening and cavorting at the waters' edge.[6]

Around 1700 every European knew that a cow was worth more than a mere knife and two strings of beads, but, likewise, every Indian, Hottentot, and Tierra del Fuegan knew equally well that red beads were far more valuable than blue. In this respect, everyone was profiting at the other's expense, except for one thing. The exchanges were a mere preamble to the big takeover, namely, the loss of native land, labor, reproductive capacity, and power, in exchange for nothing at all.

Well, perhaps not quite nothing. For after all, there was the exchange of pathogens between parties—air-borne viruses and semen-borne bacilli, tick-borne fevers, and rat-borne plagues. The effects on the indigenous populations were striking. Whole villages succumbed. People grew feverish; they swelled, festered, writhed, and died. Travelers reported corpses felled abruptly in their tracks. Their memoirs evoke Pliny's description of the eruption of Vesuvius 1,600 years earlier. It is, of course, a matter of conjecture as to whether these reports were strictly accurate or whether they were embellished to mask more direct extermination of the natives, but some accounts are so graphic that they leave no room for doubt. So devastating was this one-way onslaught that one is tempted to cheer at the theory that the natives of America got even by infecting the sailors of Columbus's fleet with syphilis.

Most certainly, its debut at the Siege of Naples in 1495 was nothing short of sensational.[7]

In the heyday of mercantile colonialism, when Europeans captured land and commodities from Biscay to Bombay, the people of Holland—that miserable low-lying Netherlands—wriggled free from Spain and declared themselves to be the United Provinces. They set up two trading companies. The Dutch East India Company, or VOC (Verenigde Oos-

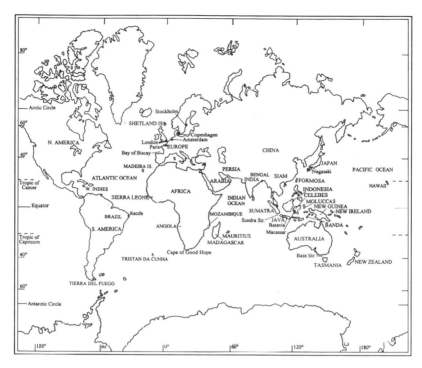

Fig. 3. The realms of the Dutch East and West India companies

tındısche Compagnie), was the largest commercial operation of ancien-régime Europe, employing almost a million men in the course of its 150-year operation. Chartered in 1602, its influence extended from the Cape of Good Hope to Japan, ousting the Portuguese, to claim the spices, fabrics, tea, copper, silver, and porcelains of the East. The West India Company, chartered in 1621, claimed hegemony from west Africa to America and shipped slaves to the sugar fields of the Caribbean and Brazil. Both outdid the Dutch Parliament, or States General, in power and effectiveness, commandeering private armies to make war, negotiate peace, to take land, to import slaves, and to hold on to everything they possessed.

In all these realms it was policy, above all else, to trade. The outward-bound fleet of the VOC carried gold and silver bullion for general trade, textiles, wine, a little mercury. They picked up ivory, on the African coast. In Asia an early concentration on pepper and spices yielded later to more varied cargoes. They took cloves and nutmeg from the Moluccas pepper from Sumatra and west Java, textiles from India, silk from Persia and China, tea, sugar, and coffee from China and Java, silver and copper from Japan, porcelain from China and Japan, and indigo, sandalwood, benzoin, and musk from tropical forests between Arabia and Indochina. VOC traders marketed these commodities throughout an inter-Asian network and then set sail for home. On the west African coast, they traded cloth from India and cowries from the Maldives. Then, hoisting their sails, they headed for home, to deliver their goods to European contractors. Outbound ships used bricks for ballast, and homebound ones used rattan mats to sandwich pepper, cowries, and textiles on top of each other. Today, shipwrecks all along the routes, confirm these practices, in finds such as eight thousand bricks on the outward bound *Vergulde Draeck,* wrecked on the west Australian coast in 1656, peppercorns cemented to porcelain dishes on the wreck of the *Witte Leeuw,* sunk off St. Helena in 1613, and mounds of cowries on the *Oosterland,* wrecked in Table Bay in 1697.[8]

The VOC established factories on islands, headlands, deltas, and rivers, as close as possible to the trade routes, and defended them with guns. They generally left the hinterlands to themselves. Their purpose was neither to rule, nor to tax, nor even to bring Light to the Darkness of the heathen. The Dutch closed down their missionary training school in Leiden in 1632, twenty years before they ever settled at the Cape, in the firm understanding that although they were happy to covert Catholics to Calvinism, in their colonies Mammon came long before God. Indigenous peoples who fell under Dutch rule all had different tales to tell. Some were enslaved, with Indonesians shipped from island to island and thence to the Cape of Good Hope, and Africans transported to the Caribbean and Brazil. Bengali women stirred curried fish in Cape kitchens, and Balinese men trampled out the vintage in the lee of Table Mountain. West Africans sweated in the sugar fields of Surinam, cutting the cane in the heat of day, then boiling it down in steaming cauldrons to make molasses and rum. Absentee owners grew fat in Europe, whilst the teeth of poor folk rotted early on the cheapest possible diet of bread and molasses. Cries broke the warm tropical nights as slaves writhed for freedom, dreaming of their village in the Gambia: overseers watchful of riots, beat them back to work.[9]

In the southeast Asian archipelago, good sense and Dutch law held that unless a monopoly could be kept on certain commodities, one might as well go back to Amsterdam. The Dutch East India Company came on heavy in Formosa, to ensure clear access to the skins of island deer. In order to maintain a monopoly over nutmeg, the Banda Islands were depopulated of natives and restocked with slaves. In the Moluccas, raiders from the sea launched periodic attacks on illicit plantations, to ensure a monopoly on cloves. It was less easy to monopolize pepper, which had ceased to be a luxury and had become an absolute must for northern European housewives trying to disguise the saltiness of preserved meat, but even though the Dutch never cornered the market for themselves, they remained major players in the field. Only in China and Japan were the tables turned on Dutch control, and this, because they were fools for porcelain.[10]

"China," said a German statesman, punning with pain at the sight of his depleted treasury, "is the bleeding-bowl of Saxony." Europe salivated for the blue and white dishes and cups that emerged so sparkling clean, no matter how many times they were used and washed. The calligraphy was on the wall in 1644, when war broke out in China, followed by a ban on Dutch-Chinese trade in Formosa and their expulsion from that, their last Chinese foothold, in 1662. The Dutch now concentrated on Japan, letting profits outweigh dignity, whatever the cost. No matter that they had to raze their buildings at Hirado to the ground when their ostentation became offensive to their host, or that they had to help the emperor root out Christianity. Or even that they had to decamp, in 1641, to Deshima, to live in virtual imprisonment on this tiny spur in Nagasaki Bay, crossing to the mainland only once a year, before returning to their sodden home. It was all worthwhile. Japanese kilns boomed, producing a variety of vessels for the European market, that wedded the Orient to these distant tastes. Beer jugs, ewers, and chamber pots decorated with old Chinese motifs were embellished with tulips, Persian metal mounts, and even the Company monogram itself. A bold *V* encircled with an *O* on one arm, and a *C* on the other gleamed out among dark blue chrysanthemums, horses, and dragons, disporting on a field of purest white.[11]

The ways in which the Company put in the boot in the islands, and licked their masters' boots in China and Japan, contrast with their enlightened vision in another Dutch colony half a world away. Between 1637 and 1644 the Dutch were represented in Brazil by a royal governor general in the person of Prince Johan Maurits of Nassau-Siegen. He led the Dutch troops against the Portuguese and held them at bay until they capitulated in 1641. Over and above his military skills, this "humanist prince" engaged teams of scholars to study the exotic colony in a manner that would not be repeated again until Captain Cook's voyages in the Age of Enlightenment. Johan Maurits brought draftsmen and artists, scientists and poets, even Jews to study and to celebrate this strange new land. The German scientist Georg Marcgraf made a remarkable study of the plants, animals, geography, weather, and ethnography of the region, and Willem Piso, the prince's physician, wrote a tract on tropical medicine and discovered ipecacuanha, an antidote to poison, that remains a standard remedy today.

The artists Albert Eckhout and Frans Post drew sugar mills, settlements, strange plants, and curious animals. Johan Maurits shipped these back home to the Mauritshuis in The Hague. It was furnished with Brazil wood and swathed with Gobelin tapestries of exotic lands, dubbed "peintures des Indes." Some of these treasures may still be seen there today, including Eckhout's tortoises, their glazed umber and black carapaces confronting each other with a ferocity unusual in reptiles such as these. But the most striking paintings are strangely absent, for Eckhout's luminous oils of Brazilian farmers and hunters hang in the Royal Copenhagen Museum in Denmark. There, Tupi agriculturalists wear demure cloth skirts. A farmer stands armed with bow and arrows above the stream where others are gathering crabs. At his feet lies a huge, cultivated tuber. His bucolic female equivalent stands under a banana tree, above in a neatly planted field, holding a basket of food on her head, and a docile baby on her hip. In contrast, the Tarairiu or Tapuya hunters inhabit savage landscapes. Bone points bristle like tusks from the pierced cheeks of the hunter. His penis is encircled with a desultory string, and a serpent writhes at his feet. His woman bestrides a pool, gently accommodating a snaggle-toothed carnivore lapping at the pool between her feet. The sweet set of her Cupid's-bow lips contrasts with the fearsome implications of a severed human hand, held in her own, and a dismembered foot, protruding from the basket on her back.[12]

These, the greatest of Eckhout's portraits—"the first full-length paintings of exotic people in European art"—are no longer in Holland, for good reason. Prince Maurits was miffed at what he regarded as his premature recall from Brazil. By then his backers at the West India Company were beginning to lose their grip on a shaky economic venture. Brazil, for its seeming prosperity in sugar, dye woods, and imported slaves, could not export enough to cover the huge cost of its imports. The prince ignored their first summons. He shuffled his papers, and left his mail unanswered, but in the end, he had to go home. In May of 1644, he left Mauritsstad, the town he had built on the island adjoining Recife, and rode to the harbor. Trumpets sounded the old "Wilhelmus Van Nassouwen." Weeping burghers lined the track, reaching to touch him as he proceeded shorewards. Suddenly, out of the forest, burst a horde of Indians, sent by their chief, Nhandui. Hoisting the prince aloft, they bore him through the waves. A cynic might say they were eager to assist his departure, but it is just as likely that Nhandiu, who had helped the Dutch against the Portuguese in the field, was loath to see his backer leave.

So moved was the prince that he offered six of the Tapuyas a trip to Holland. There as guests in his palace in The Hague, they were presented to the States General and informed of their rights. For all its exotic furnishings, the Mauritshuis was a far cry from the shores of Brazil, with its formal garden out back and an icy canal alongside. Nostalgia must have colored the performances that the prince orchestrated, where the naked visitors did a war-dance in savage, if bawdy, display for the burghers of The Hague.

Some dominies and their *huisvrouws* found the lewdness intolerable, but in the end, the pleasure that the prince derived from shocking his subjects was no compensation for the loss of Brazil. His recall rankled, and, smarting, he gave the great Eckhout portraits to the Danish king.

In exchange, he received the Order of the White Elephant.[13]

Elements of these anecdotes echo in the history of the Dutch conquest of the Cape of Good Hope. Their original purpose was to establish a refreshment station to provision ships and facilitate trade. Native policy was consequently articulated to avoid incurring undue expense for the Company. Thus the indigenous Hottentots, or Khoikhoi pastoralists and beachcombers, were not to be provoked in any way. If they wanted to work, they would be paid, but they were not to be enslaved. They were expected to conform to Dutch law on matters of property, so that their land might be bought for a song, their women for a whistle, and their undying loyalty to Jan Compagnie for a tot of brandy. The trade involved the movement of Dutch tobacco, pipes, trinkets, beads, arrack (rice spirits), and wine in one direction, and Khoikhoi meat, water, veld products such as honey, skins, tusks, and ostrich plumes, in the other (fig. 4).[14]

The exchanges dominate the documents. The Dutch colonies called the Netherlands "Patria," but would better have named it "Matria," bound, as they were, to the ruling Council of Seventeen, by umbilical scrawls of ink. Company soldiers of the pen, put all transactions in writ-

Fig. 4. Exchanges of goods between the colonists and Khoikhoi people at the Cape of Good Hope. The Dutch offer a roll of tobacco, a pipe, iron tools, liquor, and beads, in exchange for sheep, cattle, and tusks. (Kolbe(n)) 1745, frontispiece; Kennedy 1975, K29)

ing, and in return, received detailed instructions about everything, from the color of trade beads to the fortunes of war in Europe. True, a man's opinions might be read in his acts and requests, but still it is difficult to infer the character of individual writers since most dispatches were translated into official language by official scribes. What does emerge is a certain homesickness, an exasperation with the language, manners, and minds of the indigenes. There is a desire to have done with opposition, to take the land for once and for all. The impatience is compounded with a taint of relish that attends some of the judgments of the Court of Justice, meted out here at the end of the world: "First to be brought to the place of execution, next to be flogged, with a ball fired above the head, then to be flayed, then scourged, then impaled whilst drinking arrack, then cut down, then paraded, then dragged through the streets."[15]

What seldom, if ever emerges, are the opinions and feelings of the dispossessed.

It is not that they were silent, these small southern folk, known in the ethnographic record as Khoisan, Hottentots, Khoikhoi, Boshiesmen, Bushmen-Hottentots, savages, or whatever. It is simply that they went unrecorded.

They were, in the very long-term sense, heirs of the earliest modern humans to appear on earth, products of a mutation that birthed us all and in doing so separated us from all other bipeds whose skeletons dangle today from museum stands or lie, deified, in velvet-lined safes. Some say we are all direct descendants of a first mother, a mythical woman whose birth tissues carried the genetic mutation, earning her the label "Mitochondrial Eve." Others, who on the balance of present evidence may be more correct, regard her as a statistical artifact of questionable integrity, who may, or may not have lived any time around 200,000 years ago.[16]

If the South African evidence cannot speak clearly for itself, it certainly has character. Encased in lime and pumice, and crowned with crystal thorns, the two-million-year-old bones of early bipeds lie waiting for the archaeological trowel. Their successors rest high up the mountains at Border cave, and low down at the tip of Africa, sandwiched in layers of ash, charcoal, and shell at Klasies River Mouth cave. Here, around 100,000 years ago, folk ate, slept, bred, and died. They scuffed discarded bone and shells, broken spears, and blunted stone knives into the soft floor of their home. Archaeologists retrieve the droppings for decoding. From superimpositions and isotopic imprints, they figure time. From fragmentary weapons and dietary residues, the getting, eating, and sharing of food; from the curve of a bone and the cusps of a molar, taxonomic status.

But we have not retrieved the DNA of these ancestral people, and lacking that, we do not know exactly who they were.[17]

Two schools of thought abound today. Both call these people truly modern and think that their mutation traveled north, darting, like a flash fire, way up the Rift Valley to Israel, where it diverged to Europe on the west, and Asia on east. Opinion diverges here too. One side imagines that the new moderns replaced all other people in the world, and the opposition argues for integration and admixture with existing groups.

We cannot be sure because the evidence is murky.

In Israel, truly modern folk appear to rest side by side with the more ruffian Asiatic Europeans that we call Neanderthals. But although the taxonomists with their calipers and CAT scans define Neanderthals down to a T, it seems that for all their differences they practiced exactly the same arts and crafts as did the modern folk. In Asia, human fossils all show continuity, rather than betraying any marks of a sudden invasion and takeover by superior Africans. So even if the first mutation engendered a fully modern look, it might have been of little or no consequence where it counts. Neanderthals and moderns seem to have made the same tools, eaten the same foods, and lived in the same intellectual cold storage, making no art, and practicing few, if any, rituals. True, the moderns were standing tall and looking good, but it seems that they were thinking no better than anyone else.[18]

The question is, Who was, and when? Conventional wisdom now holds that the anthropological Rubicon of Humanity is not morphology but symbolic thought. Until people symbolized their ideas in art and burials, they were not fully human. Some apes make signs, but since they are patently not human, this does not count. Where true humans are concerned, when, and only when, they painted on rock walls, carved beads and images from bone, decorated themselves alive and dead, and placed objects into graves can we construe that they, like us, rendered reality into signs and beliefs into action.

But leaving aside our ancestral philosophy for the time being, if the working definition of modern humans rests on inferences such as these, we are trafficking as much in myth as in science. And so, while we are about it, let's go a little further, and trawl the human record right up close. If early modern humans took their genetic baggage from the tip of Africa, north to Israel and Europe, then, when the Dutch landed at Table Bay in the lee of the great flat mountain and began to trade, fight, and live with the indigenous people there, an arc rooted at the Cape some 100,000 years earlier, finally came full circle and snapped shut.

Now for details. Hunters are recorded at the Cape for close on a million years. Their latest heirs, the people of the Later Stone Age, left their garbage in innumerable caves over the past 35,000 years. They probably looked like people we call Khoisan, an amalgam of Khoikhoi and San, with their smallish build, high cheekbones, and wistful, delicate faces. They used spears, bows and arrows, scrapers, and stone knives. They made beads from ostrich eggshell, pendants from mother-of-pearl. They hunted and scavenged big game,shot and trapped small buck, birds, and hares, and scooped tortoises off the land, seals off the shore, and oysters off the rocks. They buried their dead in graves, decorating the bodies with bracelets, pendants, beads, bows, and spears to ease the passage out. They returned repeatedly to the same caves, weighed down with baskets of shellfish, joints of meat, and earth-smeared roots, trudging up the slopes to crouch around fires and sleep on fragrant bushes set in a curve around the hearth. Eagles sailed in the air, swooping down in a rush of wings to pluck a squealing rock rabbit, or dassie, off the slope. Out, beyond the cave mouth, the dusty veld merged imperceptibly with the pale sky.[19]

About 2,000 years ago, some hunters became herders. From the north the technology of breeding fat-tailed sheep percolated south in the minds and bodies of herders and their bleating charges. Stopping and starting, tarrying and traveling, they left a trail of dung in kraals and caves, which constituted a matrix for broken pots and charred bones of an occasional sheep. At the Cape these elements spread into the population of hunters, occasioning endless disputes in anthropological circles. Did hunters become herders, did herders hunt? Did ideological constraints keep hunters bowed over their arrows and herders flocking round their kraals?[20]

I pun for fun. What matters is that it happened. Once herding arrived there were other possibilities for a hunter, and it was just these that were being explored by the indigenous hunter-forager-herders at the Cape, who collected and hunted wild plants and animals and herded sheep and cattle, in differing amounts depending on the season, when the Dutch splashed ashore to found their refreshment station, in the Year of Their Lord, 1652, by the Gregorian Calendar, and by the Grace of God, Amen.

The meeting of 1652 at the Cape was not the first in recorded time. Legend holds that in the reign of Pharoah Necho, around 600 B.C., Phoenicians sailed through Gibraltar and circumnavigated the Cape. History holds that from 1487 onwards, first Portuguese, then English and Dutch navigators, rounded the Cape en route to India, China, Japan and the Spice Islands. Mapmakers used sailors' logs to draw the outline of Africa and then invented its interior, with the Mountains of the Moon, great lakes fed by a Medusa's head of rivers with griffins, dragons, and lions sprawled on their banks. Sailors saw only the coasts. They landed for water, fresh food, and a break from the stench of death and disease that permeated their small, slow ships. Everyone who rounded the Cape of Good Hope spoke of its great flat mountain that rose a sheer 1,087 meters above the shore. They wrote about the wild seas foaming at the feet of spiny crags that ran from the back of the Table southwards to the end of the continent. They told of sea wolves, penguins, lions, tigers, and monsters.

Most of all, they spoke about the small, yellow-skinned folk who met them on the beaches of this Cape of Good Hope.[21]

They were small. The earliest mariners called them "savages," "Saldanians," even "Indians," but once the Dutch settled into their fort on the beach, the diaries settled on "Hottentots." Considerable dispute attends on the etymology of the name, especially since it became synonymous with savagery and degradation for centuries thereafter. Some speculate that the word arose because they chanted in this cadence, "aten taten" or "Hot, hot, hotten, totten." They called themselves "Khoikhoi" and "Khoikhoin," in the Namaqua dialect of the southwestern Cape, and "Kwena" or "Kwekwena," in the Cape dialect, both freely translated as "men," or "men of men." Their hair curled in tight peppercorns, glowing from a liberal application of sheep's fat. Some raced on board and anointed themselves with the soot and fat from squalid ships' galleys. A rank stench followed them around, but they seemed not to care, for the wealthier the individual, the richer his smell. They wore skins and beads; dried intestines rattled around their wrists, waists, and ankles. In the eyes of travelers, they were at once beachcombers foraging on the shores, mendicants begging for metal, food, drink, and tobacco, and traders possessed of fat-tailed sheep, hump-backed cattle, honey, herbs, fresh water, and women.[22]

The sailors screwed them every which way, lust vying with curiosity since everyone knew that their females' private parts were elongated and that this was a certain sign of savage, uncontrollable lasciviousness. Sailors paid a mere stuiver to look, and doubled it for the opportunity to touch. And why not? Months at sea bred a heightened sense of mortality, watching one's mates sicken, vomit, purge, and die. The unceremonious slide into the sea accompanied by a mumbled prayer—"One, two, three in God's name"—might have been moving at first, but it probably palled pretty quickly as death became commonplace. Mortality statistics fluctuated widely from year to year, depending on plagues and shipwrecks. Then too, a macabre process of natural selection weeded out the more susceptible component before it could board a homebound ship, so that the death rate was always higher on outbound ships. All in all, between one in seven, and one in ten who shipped out to the East died on the outward voyage, and only one in three who ever set sail eventually returned to Europe. Personal accounts speak louder than figures, and the dazed survivors of these hazards must have vowed to seize the day, should they ever live to see that day at all. Seamen spent their time hauling ropes

Fig. 5. The landing of Jan van Riebeeck at the Cape of Good Hope, 1652, by Charles Davidson Bell, ca. 1850 (Cape Archives Depot, M108)

with hands split and encrusted with icy saltwater and eating the same meals three times a day, flour squirming with weevils, sour wine, hard biscuit, all chewed with teeth rocking precariously in scurvy-swollen gums. Cockroaches skittered over the deck and rats grew bolder each day. Deep in the dark holds, foul with vomit and excrement, men rocked in their closely-slung hammocks, drifting off despite the groans and stenches, to dream of the Cape with its strange women and their hot and savage lusts.[23]

The Dutch landed at this Cape of Good Hope in April 1652. With them came pigs, dogs, maybe geese; seeds and seedlings, hoes, forks and shovels; guns, shot, beads, pipes, plates, mugs, parchments, pens and ink. Later they brought a few horses. Wealthy men brought wives and dowries, cedar-lined chests packed with linen, goblets and plates for their tables, fine sheets for their beds. Jan van Riebeeck, the first commander of the Cape, was not exactly delighted with his posting, but then he was hardly in a position to dictate terms to his masters in Amsterdam. He had had a little problem with illicit private trade that the Company decided to overlook, should he succeed in this enterprise. It was his best and only shot at a prize posting at the Company's headquarters at Batavia, Java. At the Cape, Van Riebeeck kept a diary. It told how they dug the foundations of a fort, of the wooden pipe that channeled the stream from the mountain into a reservoir near the jetty. It told of wind, sun, and rain and of the decor used in the Fort Good Hope, where the skin of a lion, pierced to death by an iron pig, or porcupine, hung in the entry chamber.[24]

Most of all, the diary told of the Hottentots.

The Dutch at the Cape outpost, were under orders from the Company board of directors, or the Heren XVII, and much of their routine was regulated out of the larger colonial center in Batavia. The garrison at the Cape were under strict instructions to do no more than run a refreshment station, trading for meat from the local pastoralists and cultivating fruit and vegetables for themselves. They were to deal fairly and kindly with the indigenes and to avoid confrontation at all costs. Slaves might be imported from Africa and Asia, but the Khoikhoi were never to be enslaved or molested. This was the official policy, but both sides knew that it would never really work, because the competition knew no bounds. The Khoikhoi regarded sheep and cattle as more than living meat and flowing milk. They were capital, marks of status, and the main component in a man's access to women, power, and advancement. Therefore, although native herds multiplied faster than Dutch ones, they could never provide enough meat to fill all the demands of the new settlers unless their Khoikhoi owners sold all the stock they had. The Dutch already had fertile land to grow their crops, but unless the Khoikhoi provided all the meat they wanted, the colonists would also need more land to graze their own stock.[25]

Since both sides knew the score, hostilities were bound to erupt. The Khoikhoi were no fools. They smiled when given brandy, beads, and tobacco, but their bright black eyes slid constantly to the knives and guns. They quibbled over the weight of copper trade beads while longing for iron daggers. They developed a taste for the bang from a lungful of black Brazilian tobacco, but truly lusted after the bang of a musket in their own hands. They built no fences, defining their borders according to natural features like hills, hummocks, trees, and rocks, but they knew exactly what a Dutch fence of wild almond meant when they saw it. They cared nothing for the Lord's Day, for prayers, christenings, and burials, but they enjoyed a good scourging and a hanging as much as the next man. They counted the months by the moon, but they knew a holiday when they saw one, and always tried to schedule cattle theft on Sundays. They were banned from owning firearms, but they inferred as smartly as any harquebusier that gunpowder will not fire when it is wet. The natives massed on cold, wet days, hurling spears and invective at the invader who fumbled impotently in the rain.[26]

All to no avail. For every burned farmhouse and slaughtered white hunter, the Khoikhoi paid in men, women, children, and in stock. Again and again, hump-backed oxen and fat-tailed sheep were led from their thorn-ringed kraals to the ever-expanding stockades of the enemy. Pleading their case, in 1660 the natives pointed out that Dutch fences kept them from their former cattle range and their winter foraging ground, where the women were accustomed to harvest bulbs, roots, tortoises and berries against this lean period.

The Hollanders sat in the dim hall of their fort. They tapped their pointed leather shoe tips impatiently against the stone-flagged floor.

Then they uttered judgment: "Too bad," said the Dutch. "All's fair in love and war."[27]

It was not, however, a matter of fairness but of inevitability. From the mid-seventeenth century on, Europe held the whip hand in the colonial stakes. They were masters of politics and power. The Council of Seventeen who ran the Dutch East India Company decreed that although the Hottentots were not to be enslaved, they could work for wages. As trading partners they would earn beads and trinkets, whilst as subjects of the Company they would earn the lash, the scourge, and the rope for infractions such as murder, rape, arson, and theft. They could legally cross the Great Divide from Savagery to Humanity through familiarity with the customs of their masters—that is, through living in European houses, learning to speak Dutch, and then through conversion and baptism. But once Humanity was conferred, they became subject to the more subtle laws of the United Netherlands, to the punishments accorded for crimes against God as well as the State. Retribution came swift and harsh to these back-sliding converts, and none felt it as poignantly as the underclass within the underclass, the Khoikhoi women.

Take, for example, Eva. "Eva" was not her given name, but "Krotoa," yet "Eva" she was to the first commander, Jan van Riebeeck and his wife, Maria. She enters the record shortly after the Dutch first settled at the Cape as a well-connected local girl who was the niece and confidant of several Khoikhoi leaders. She learned Dutch, was baptized a Christian, and acted as the company's interpreter. As their intermediary, she traveled between the fort of the Dutch and the kraals of her relatives, carrying the word of God and the commander in one direction and the word of Oedessoa and Autshumao in the other. On such occasions she cast aside her Dutch clothes and donned the skins and beads of her own people. Her transformations generated a trail of resentment wherever she went. Both sides felt betrayed. The Khoikhoi saw how she manipulated their political aspirations, and the Dutch deplored her repeated switch from demure house-interpreter into savage Hottentot. "Lady into fox," they must have thought, though with none of the tenderness that laces David Garnett's Edwardian parable. They did not mince words, calling Eva "a lewd vixen" for "throwing aside her clean and neat clothing and using old stinking animal skins, like other filthy female Hottentoos."[28]

But Eva continued to straddle both worlds and Company sailors as well. After bearing two children by unnamed Europeans, she married the Danish surgeon Pieter van Meerhoff. The bride was twenty-one years old, the groom, twenty-seven. This, the first "mixed" marriage at the Cape, was accorded all the respect that her baptism deserved. The commander threw a feast and handed over fifty rixdollars to Eva. Van Meerhoff was appointed superintendent of Robben Island, and the newlyweds sailed twelve kilometers across the bay to their new posting. The small, flat island was separated from the mainland by treacherous seas. It was a useful place to house malcontents and felons who quarried stone and gathered shells under the watchful eye of the local garrison. Its only romantic moment came late in its history, being the army base where Harry Oppenheimer, the crown prince of the Anglo-American De Beers Corporation met his wife, Bridget. It would later cease to be known for the seals, or *robben,* that disported there and become infamous as the Alcatraz of political prisoners, known only as "The Island." But around 1664 it was Van Meerhoff's posting and Eva's home.

Robben Island was no honeymoon haven. Eva began to drink heavily. Van Meerhoff, clearly no slave to uxoriousness, was posted abroad on a slaving expedition, only to be slaughtered on a beach in Madagascar. He left a wife of four years, three children, and a legacy of despair. In 1669, whilst Eva was housed in the old pottery works near the fort, she began to crack. Her venery grew loud and violent. She abandoned Van Meerhoff's children, who, sniveling with fear, appeared naked and destitute at the fort, reporting that their mother had sold everything to go and live with some Hottentots on the beach. She burst into the fort and cursed the commander at his own table. It was too much. The fiscal went in search, and found her drunk and defiant, a small pipe clenched in her teeth. The children were entrusted to a deacon of the church, and Eva was banished to Robben Island. She died there five years later, a dog returned to her vomit, so they said. They also noted that only death could quench the fire of her lust, proving that nature, however sternly muzzled, will always come out in the end.[29]

To this sanctimoniousness born of conquest, one asks, "Whose nature?" And well might one ask. They said she was a whore, a wench, a piece of work. That she betrayed the world of civilized people and the institution of marriage. That she abandoned her children and reverted to her savage nature, proving that it was better to import women, orphans, destitutes, even whores, from Holland, rather to consort in the sanctity of marriage with savages. Yet clearly Eva was a child of wit and cleverness. She spoke a little Portuguese, and she learned guttural Dutch when none of those with whom she spoke could twist their tongues round a single Khoikhoi click. Darting from fort to kraal, she took on their manners and their hopes. She curtseyed to the Lady, lace cap bobbing on her tight-curled head, and spread her legs for the Gentleman, shaking her small head in bewilderment when they spat on her swelling belly. Somewhere along the line she grew to know the commander for what he was: She cursed him at his own table. Interpreter, mediator, bridge between two worlds, matron, mother of European children, she was all of these, yet in the end she was nothing but a woman, and a Hottentot one at that.

Then there was Sara. In 1671, Sara, a twenty-four-year-old free Hottentot female at the Cape of Good Hope hanged herself in the sheep house of a considerably freer burgher of the company. The documents note that the diagnosis of strangulation with her own gown band was confirmed by a dissection, but they do not speculate about the reasons for her suicide. Instead, the Court of Justice concerned itself with the more metaphysical question of whether Sara was a savage or not. These were the relevant facts: She had lived from childhood in company lodgings where she earned wages, she attended Divine services, spoke Portuguese, practiced concubinage with Europeans, and all in all enjoyed the protection and privileges of the Dutch mode of life. For these reasons, she was not a savage any more but a member of Dutch society. As such, she had transgressed their laws and defiled their property by virtue of her diabolically inspired suicide. Punishment and purification were needed. The Roman Law of the United Netherlands decreed that Sara's property (such as it was) must be confiscated to pay the costs of justice and that her dead body be removed, dragged along the streets to the gallows, and hanged on a gibbet as carrion for the fowls. This was done. Several weeks later the gibbet fell down. Clearly, Sara's dues had not, as yet, been paid in full, so the gallows were duly raised up again and the remains suspended once again to the satisfaction of justice.[30]

In 1714, long after Eva and Sara were gone, François Valentyn, a minister of religion, visited the Cape for the fourth time. He was struck by the very great inconvenience caused to the burghers by the sudden drop in the number of Hottentots available for housework and farm labor. Ships' laundry had brought the plague to the Cape the previous year. Shortly after the first pox erupted in the slave lodge, an Apocalypse ensued. Hottentots fleeing inland dropped pustulate in their tracks. Their bodies lined the roads and the air was heavy with their curses on the Dutch. Today some say these reports are overdrawn; others see a similar pattern in America, the Pacific Islands, and Australia, where new pathogens flared brightly on an unexposed front. Some Khoikhoi who survived trekked off to new and distant lands far from the Company's stone castle at the Cape. Others become serfs, working as stockmen, riders, cooks, and charwomen on Dutch holdings. Their role was encoded in the Dutch practice of electing Hottentot "captains," who carried a copper-knobbed *rotting,* or stick of office. Four such elevated men, listed in 1714, were Scipio Africanus, brother and heir of the late Hasdrubal; Hannibal, likewise, of Jason; Hercules, of Hartloop; and finally Kouga, son and heir of the late Kouga Sr. The names tell it all: Scipio Africanus, Hannibal, Hasdrubal, Jason, and Hercules are classical names similar to those bestowed on slaves worldwide. Kouga is a Khoikhoi name. But Hartloop is pure Dutch. Used as a command, it means "Run" or "Run away."[31]

Many Khoikhoi did indeed run away. They trekked so far inland that by the 1720s few remained within an eighty km radius of the Cape. But wherever they were, they were no longer the lords of the range they had been when the fleet first sailed into Table Bay. They became servants on their former holdings, farm workers on their former grazing grounds. They were allowed to keep a few sheep in with the larger herds of their masters. Some were paid partly in liquor, receiving a mandatory tot at the week's end, but somehow or other they got sufficient in between to engender a constant round of violence and stupor. And always there was sufficient time out for lust, when the master crossed the Great Divide between his hovel and theirs to create what we call today the "Cape

Fig. 6. Hottentots, observed and drawn by Charles Davidson Bell, ca. 1850, contrast markedly with his idealized vision of them in fig. 5 greeting Van Riebeeck. (Kennedy 1975, B224)

Colored" people. It was a long-standing tradition going back well before Eva's time whose outcome today reveals Eva less as a victim than as an original survivor and a winner in the existential stakes. For whatever she did in venery, she did for material gain. Her children did not all die in obscurity, snuffled out by the cold Cape rains. Two were raised in Mauritius. One married a farmer and returned to the Cape, packaged safely under the lace bonnet and petticoats of a Stellenbosch *huisvrouw*.[32]

For in the long run, breeding, unlike love, conquers all. Some scholars, trying to account for the disappearance of folk like the Khoikhoi as an ethnic entity, conclude that they "literally acculturated themselves out of existence" by becoming something else. Such bald declarations evade the difficulty of declaring that cultural extinction has taken place, because group identification depends as least as much on the choices that people are forced to make as on what they imagine themselves to be. In South Africa, where privilege and phenotype always went hand-in-hand, pragmatism won out in that anyone who could "pass for white" saw good reason to do so. But politics and ethnic labels notwithstanding, the Khoikhoi survived and triumphed, either as part of the broader population of "Coloreds," or as part of the "Whites," who held them in their thrall.[33]

If we know all this from the documents, what more can we hope to discover from the archaeology? In truth, although the documents tell a great deal, they are only a skeleton on which we construct all the rest. Eva—her looks, her dowry, her demure curtsey, and her curses—first emerge from the curlicued script on a laminated piece of Company parchment, but her emotions and her sorrow spring from a deeper sense of common purpose with all women such as she. Turning now from documents to potsherds, what more might we infer from the broken neck of a stone bottle or the tip of a bone spear?

Let's see.

4

Chronicle of a Dig

I became an archaeologist because I wanted to drive around in a big
Landrover, smoking, cursing, and finding treasure. During my fieldwork
in Australia and South Africa, I managed to do all of these things, but as
with all archaeological work, more time was spent washing, counting,
and grouping the finds than getting them out of the ground. In the
course of trying to understand the residues of prehistoric people, I spent
many years studying the lives of hunters and gatherers who survived
colonial contact to interact with travelers, colonists, and anthropologists.
Networks of colonial exchange created striking parallels in the histories
of both these lands. They were explored by the same ships when Dutch,
French, and English trading vessels circled the globe from Europe to the
East. They were governed by the same colonial rulers, whose names are
memorialized in streets, villages, and towns in modern South Africa and
Australia. As for the native peoples, their role in this new global economy
was to receive elements of European material culture on the one hand,
and, on the other, to endure similar patterns of conquest and subjugation
that echoed down into modern times in mutual exchanges of contempt
and bitterness.

I returned to the Cape of Good Hope in 1983 to try to study the
archaeological evidence of interactions between the Dutch colonists and
the indigenous folk, here, at the tip of Africa. Once the Dutch set up
their refreshment station, there were many places where the soldiers of
the Company met and traded with the Khoikhoi. The most famous of
these was their original headquarters on the beach at Table Bay, the Fort
de Goede Hoop, an earthen-walled structure built by the original settlers
and occupied from 1652 to 1674. It had four wings and a central court,
and the walls tended to dissolve and collapse in heavy rain. The fort

originally stood on the beach, but in the course of consequent land recla-
mation, the shore was extended out into the bay; today its ruins lie under
the Grand Parade, in the middle of the Golden Acre, the prime real
estate of central Cape Town. Across the Parade, stands the five-bastioned,
stone-walled, moated castle, which superseded the fort and served as a
military center from 1674 until the present day.

The archaeology of both buildings has much to say about their original scale and identity. A layer of yellow clay marks the lining of the ditch
that once surrounded the fort. A layer of sprayed concrete covers the two
white lions that flanked the castle gates. When the fort ditches were
excavated, colonial residues appeared, ceramics, glass, and pipes, marking
the European presence at the Cape. When the lions were cleaned up,
Oriental terracottas emerged beneath the concrete—a male and female—their couchant bodies swirled by elegant tails. European and Oriental ceramics speak to the Eastern trade, and English ones proclaim the
conquest of the Cape by the British at the turn of the eighteenth century.
Vast piles of bones reflect the soldiers' meals, and beads, intermingled
with an occasional native artifact, speak softly to interactions with indigenous folk.[1]

Decoding the residues in these complex and long-lived structures is a
long and arduous process because three centuries of reconstruction have
blurred many of the original depositions. Simpler, more intelligible patterns, appear in more isolated sites, where a short-term occupation was
sealed by the sterile overlay of abandonment and neglect. Where early
contact at the Cape is concerned, such sites may be found in distant
farms or in a series of outposts strung across the advancing frontier. Here,
soldiers and farmers consolidated the alien presence through trade, farming, and a strong fist, if need be. These strategically placed stations kept
an eye on things. They included trading posts, provisioning stations,
cattle posts, forestry huts, and fishing posts. Some were made of earth,
and after abandonment their walls were washed away, sinking down to
the levels of the surrounding ground. Others, set in desirable spots, were
later bulldozed away to make room for shopping malls. Isolated stone
outposts crumbled and fell, but often the outline of their walls remained
standing. One such outpost was the ship's provisioning post, situated
about 100 kilometers northwest of Cape Town, on the shores of the
lagoon that debouches into Saldanha Bay (figs. 7, 8).[2]

I began searching for the Saldanha Bay outpost in 1983. Its exact
location was blurred with rumor and confusion, but all agreed that it

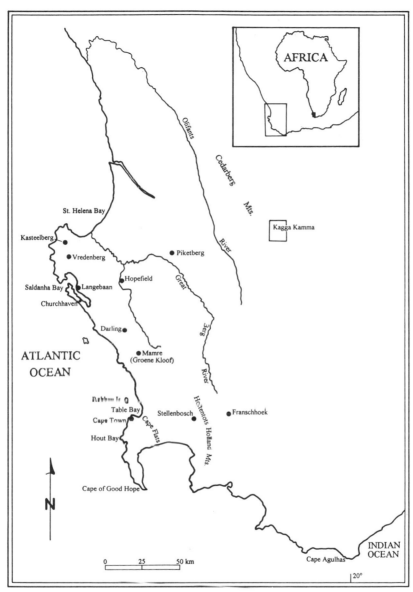

Fig. 7. The southwest Cape, showing the region around Saldanha Bay

stood on the Churchhaven Peninsula, the arm of land that forms the western cradle of the bay. A few early archival references noted an outpost on the eastern shore of the peninsula, on an inlet of Langebaan Lagoon, called Kraal Bay. Eric Axelson, the renowned historian who found the old Portuguese stone crosses on the African coast, asserted that the post still stood. Architects who visited the region went even further and identified as the old post a stone shed standing adjacent to the Oudepost homestead three kilometers north of Kraal Bay. According to them, this was not only the original Company post but also the earliest standing structure in South Africa.[3]

Clearly it was time to see for myself.

I borrowed a tiny car and drove to the Churchhaven Peninsula. The land on which the stone building stood was owned by a powerful private group called the Oudepost Syndicate, whose agent, Bowen Botha, agreed to meet me at the gate at 11 A.M. I headed north on the West Coast Highway, a flat ribbon flowing across the sandveld between the mountains and the sea. Following instructions, I turned left at the 84 km post, onto a dirt road leading to the peninsula. It was hot and dusty. Sweeps of blinding, white dune protruded through the gray veld. Pink statice flowers patched the scrub. An ostrich loped along the road, a solitary striped springbuck watched from afar. Spotted guinea fowl bustled along the road, flapping frantically, to try to elevate their plump bodies as the car approached. The road twisted and rose. Far ahead the peninsula lay spread out like a giant tongue, bounded by Atlantic ocean rollers on the west, and the blue-green lagoon on the east. The swampy, pale head of the lagoon grew darker, as it merged into Saldanha Bay. The track sloped down to skirt the lagoon. Whitewashed cottages with bulbous chimneys stood clustered in small hamlets along the roadside. I rumbled across a cattle grid, turned right to the gate, and drew up in a swirl of gravel.

The air was hot, broken by the screech of insects. In the distance a dust cloud shimmered, grew, and a truck drew up. Mr. Botha got out, pushing his detachable sunglasses back as he approached. He looked ferocious. Huge eyebrows festooned the rims of his glasses, and tufts of hair sprouted from the base of his throat. He smiled genially, unlocked the gate, and gestured vaguely toward the sea.

"I'll just leave you then."

I drove carefully down the hill, past the wide sweep of Kraal Bay and along a narrow gravel track cut into the steep mountainside that sloped precipitously down into the lagoon. Ahead lay the old post house, bounded by the so-called oldest fort in the country. A bright green patch marked practically the only perennial spring on the peninsula. The post house was a plain, single-storied affair. A central door stood flanked by small windows, with no gables or stoop to soften the essentially ugly facade. A large rectangular stone-walled kraal stood off to one side, and on the other, the small, problematic shed. It did not look like a fort at all. There was a large chimney on one side. Two doors faced the bay in front, and two small slits looked up the steep slope out back. All round, the ground was covered with thorns and burrs, and fragments of glass and china winked in the hot sun. I collected a fragment of Oriental porcelain, a broken clay pipe, and a bottle top.

Suddenly a truck drew up. The driver stared out with pale blue eyes. He stuck out his hand.

"Pietie Haumann," he offered, "head of the syndicate."

His voice was deep and guttural.

"Aangename kennis Meneer," I replied in Afrikaans. "Glad to meet you."

We shook hands.

He glanced over my small pickings, then looked again more carefully. He had seen many such fragments on the beach beyond his house. Would I care to look?

We drove back along the gravel and turned down a short, sandy track leading to the shore. Two summer homes stood in the dunes overlooking a dense tangle of bushes that ran down to the shore. I followed Haumann down the path to the sea. He stopped and kicked at a line of stone marking the ruins of old walls. The outline of a long building ran back into the scrub. Haumann smiled.

"It's a pirates' den."

"Pirates?"

Haumann shrugged. It seemed a reporter had told him this tale. He walked toward the shore of Kraal Bay and stopped.

"That's the old Hottentot kraal."

A large circle of messily placed stones lay between the rocky shore and the dunes. I wandered around, scuffing in the sand. Mounds signaled where dune mole rats had come up for air. Fragmented bones and an occasional pipe stem dotted the freshly upturned sand.

Haumann shook his head.

"Missus won't find much left here." he ventured in guttural Afrikaans.

"We've been digging around for years. The kids have found so many pipes, and my wife . . ."

He trailed off.

"Your wife?"

"Well, she found the gold button."

I stared, greedily.

"You can't see it. It's at our farm, way over there."

He waved toward the distant mountains.

I drove home through the pink sunset.

By the time I returned to the United States, I knew that there was an archaeological presence on the Churchhaven Peninsula, but I didn't know whether the architects had correctly pegged the squat shed as the earliest fort or whether Haumann's pirate nest and kraal were for real. I was a prehistoric archaeologist. I had read some archival sources, but I had never dug a historic site, nor had I handled colonial artifacts outside a country antique store. I could recognize walls if they were standing, and I could trace them if their outline remained clear, but more subtle indications might well escape my notice.

It was time to learn. I read, looked at pictures, stared at artifacts in books and in museums, and began to trace the history of settlement in this region. The pirate story turned out to have been written by a reporter who could not remember where she ever heard the word *pirate!* In point of fact, during the 1690s, pirates featured several times in dispatches to and from the Saldanha Bay post. The infamous Captain Kidd was based in Madagascar for some time, and his influence was suspected in the arrival of an English brigantine at the Cape. But the main pirate tale began in 1693, when the *Amy* sailed in to Saldanha Bay flying English flags but looking suspiciously as though she had seen some hostile action. The Cape governor impounded the ship and sent her crew to Holland for trial, but the charges failed to hold, and the captain ended up suing the Company for his losses. Six years later, pirates returned to Saldanha Bay, where the *Amy* happened to be anchored. Some suspected that one of them was the same captain, but before any of this could be proved the pirates stripped the ship, and made off.[4]

An outpost of the VOC had functioned on the shore of the lagoon, but its precise location was unclear. Despite many visitors, swashbuckling or otherwise, not a single picture of the outpost could be found. However, there was a large collection of old maps in the Cape Archives. The

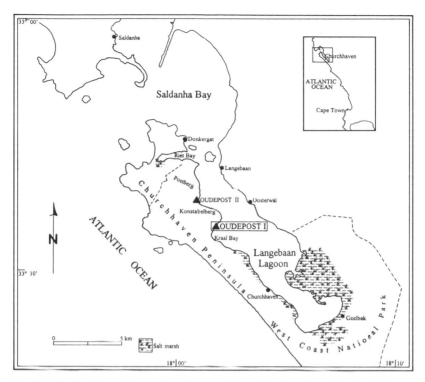

Fig. 8. Saldanha Bay and Langebaan Lagoon, Cape, showing the archaeological sites of Oudepost I and Oudepost II

earliest charts were drawn by a Dutch surveyor sent to inspect the area shortly after the first settlement in Table Bay. He documented the bights and eddies in Saldanha Bay and the watering places dotted along the shores of the Churchhaven Peninsula. The disadvantages of the place emerged even at this early stage, for although this was the one of the largest anchorages on the African coast, it was eminently unsuitable for settlement because there was almost no fresh water. No river debouched into its depths, no lakes dotted its shore. Saltpans glazed the head of the lagoon, but only an occasional soak ringed with green proclaimed where fresh water seeped reluctantly through the sand.

Despite its aridity, cartographic interest was renewed in 1666, when the French announced their intention to annex the bay. The Dutch repelled them, and did it again later the next year, but finally, in April 1669, instructions came from Holland to stop pussyfooting around with would-be claimants and establish an outpost proclaiming the Dutch possession of Saldanha Bay. This was the site on Kraal Bay, which we later named "Oudepost I." It appears as a VOC post on some maps, but from about 1710 on, a conflation of events occurred, and thenceforth it was mistakenly called a "French fort" and then an "abandoned French fort." This post was abandoned for better water around 1732, when a new one was set up at the present homestead, whose shed we labeled "Oudepost II." But mapmakers, being less alert, took a while to get their facts straight and it was not until around the latter part of the eighteenth century that both "Oude Post" and "Nieuwe Post" appeared on their maps (see fig. 9).[5]

It was clearly time to leave the archives and look more closely on the ground. In June 1984 I returned to the Churchhaven Peninsula for another look. By now I had a co-investigator. Cedric Poggenpoel, chief technical officer in the Department of Archaeology at the University of Cape Town, was reputed to be one of the best excavators in the business. He had dug on almost every prehistoric site in the Cape, to say nothing of Iron Age ones further north, but his experience of colonial sites was limited to a few rescue operations, concerning burials in and around Cape Town. Our expenses were covered by a personal grant from the Mauerberger Foundation Fund in Cape Town. The donors generally funded medical research, but were willing to subsidize my work, due to the singular fact that its late founder was my Great-uncle Morris.[6]

Since we had not yet managed to decode the meaning of the two posts on the archival maps, we decided to start work at the "earliest fort," the small shed at Oudepost II. Cedric gridded the ground and began troweling out the soil in a series of small, five-cm-square units, as if he were excavating a rich prehistoric cave. Nothing appeared. He continued scraping, filling buckets, and passing them out to the rest of the team who sieved the earth and sorted the finds. I stood in line, trying to bolster the spirits of our small team whose attention was dulled by the lack of any artifacts in the deposit. Cedric dug on. About seventy cm below the surface, he uncovered a plastic bottle, wrapped in a newspaper.

The date read 1974.

I decided to switch from trowels to shovels. Cedric scowled. A day later, I brought out the pick axe.

"No!" he said. "Absolutely not!"

We glared at each other. In the distance a truck roared and approached. It drew up, and Oom Pietie Haumann emerged, smiling. I took a chance:

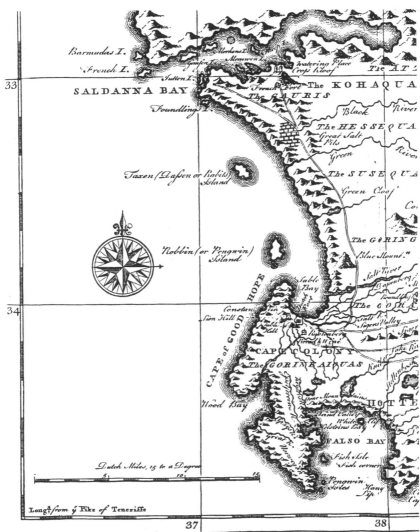

Fig. 9. Detail of an early eighteenth-century map of the Cape, misrepresenting the VOC outpost at Saldanha Bay as a French fort. Note the track from the Dutch fort at Table Bay. (after Kolben 1731, 2, facing 1)

"When did Meneer grade the ground here?"

He thought for a moment, scratched his head and counted.

"About ten years ago, I flattened some of it out, and piled some earth up."

Cedric looked cross.

Fig. 10. The rocky spur on which the outpost of the VOC stands, at Oudepost I, Cape. This bird's-eye view is taken from Konstabelberg, looking southeast, toward the head of Langebaan Lagoon at Geelbek.

Haumann smiled. He put his hand in his pocket and held it out like a conjurer. I recognized a fragment of salt-glazed stoneware, a pipe stem, a glass chunk, and a sherd of Oriental porcelain.

"Where are they from?"

Haumann smiled broadly.

"The pirates' den."

I whirled around. Yelling for the team, I began to throw our equipment into the truck.

"We're off!"

Even Cedric looked relieved.

The pirates' den still seemed unpromising. It stood on a small, rocky spur bounded on the south by the great sweep of Kraal Bay and by the lagoon on the north. Behind it rose the granite walls of Konstabelberg, Constable Mountain. The gray, shriveled scrub of summer had flourished in the winter rains, and impenetrable bushes ran right down to the water's edge. Occasional dune mole rat burrows had brought many buried objects to the surface. We hacked at the bushes around the ruins to clear space for trial excavations. Then we laid a baseline, running about north to south, and pegged out some test pits. We shoveled the sand into sieves and shook them to expose the damp, ocher-colored bones of fish, small mammals, and tortoises, white tubes of old pipe stems, fragments of glass, porcelain, stoneware, reddish earthenware, and rusty bits of iron. The deeper we dug, the more we found. Butterscotch gun flints, pipe bowls, purple, red, and orange glass beads, all lay alongside flat ostrich eggshell beads, coarse, black sherds, and a few stone tools. The colonial artifacts were consistent with the historical records that noted the presence of a post here between 1669 and 1732. They all seemed to be of seventeenth- and early eighteenth-century age, with no later English ceramics, like pearl and creamwares, no Victorian tea cups, no coke bottles, and no newspapers. The indigenous artifacts looked like those found in Later Stone Age sites. The association of these objects was consistent with documents that noted repeated interactions between colonial soldiers and Khoikhoi people at the Company post.

In short, things fitted.

Cedric and I began to nod at each other over the sieves. We grinned. Suddenly the roar of an outboard motor broke the quiet air. A small boat piloted by a lanky boy pulled up onto the beach in front of our dig. A jolly-looking woman got out, dressed in jeans, boots, and a yellow oilskin.

"Well, well!" she said.

I ignored Cedric's hostile stare.

"We're archaeologists, from U.C.T.," I ventured.

"Gawd!" The accent was pure London. "That's the department where all those middle-aged woman pretend to be interested in digging in order to get laid?"

Cedric gasped.

I held her gaze.

"Want to join us?"

She grinned, stuck out her hand.

"I'm Jane."

Much later we realized that the project would never have gotten off the ground without this encounter. Jane Klose was a member of the Oudepost Syndicate, the group of forty-nine shareholders who held title to the land on which the outpost stood. A British dentist, trained at Guy's Hospital, she had grown tired excavating other people's teeth. Even the drama of extractions had become commonplace. She was looking for something else to do. The syndicate treasured their privacy and had no desire to host a large party of workers for months on end on what they

Fig. 11. J. M. Coetzee watches Jane Klose sorting residues. Oudepost I, Cape, 1986.

regarded as their very private preserve. They were already beleaguered by the South African army who had sliced off part of their original holding at the northern tip of the peninsula. Lately, new demands had begun to pour in from the National Parks Board, who wanted to turn the entire region into a nature reserve. Our revelation that an outpost of the Dutch East India Company lay in their front yard drew polite gasps, followed by deep, regretful sighs. It took months of Jane's diplomacy, persistence, and perfect idiomatic Afrikaans to seal the agreement that gave us permission to dig.[7]

It took no time at all for us to make her a full-fledged member of the team.

Although we code-named the site "Oudepost I," to distinguish it from the shed at "Oudepost II," we always referred to it as "Oudepost." By the end of the 1984 season we had cleared two stone structures there.

One was a large rectangular building with a front door set at the narrow end facing the sea. Since archival documents spoke of the Company's lodge at this post, we christened the building accordingly. The other structure was a rough, circular ring of rocks resting, in part, on the bedrock of the beach itself. Following Haumann's advice, we called this the "kraal." We sank numbers of test pits in and around both structures, to see whether their contents confirmed their names. They did not. The kraal was not full of compacted dung, and colonial artifacts and food remains scattered throughout suggested that it had been used in the same way as the lodge. Then, moving to the area between the two structures, a test pit struck a cluster of three iron spikes. Cedric scraped away carefully, then reached for his brushes to remove the rusty stains where the iron had swollen and crumbled away.

He looked quizzical.

The spikes stood upright in the sand, marking a point from which two faint stains radiated out at right angles. Cedric brushed gently, to reveal the corner of a box.

"I think . . ."

He trailed off.

"What?"

"A coffin."

He stood up and stretched.

I looked doubtful.

Cedric squatted back in the trench and went on scraping. The sieves showed only small flakes of rust. Suddenly the trowel slid, squeaking along a smooth surface. Cedric dug a little deeper. A shaft of dark brown bone appeared. He brushed and followed its flare to expose the head of a human tibia, topped with a small kneecap.

I grew silent.

Cedric took a deep breath.

"I think we have a gabled coffin here."

I eyed him skeptically. Gabled coffins are pitched roofed boxes that look for all the world like long, windowless sheds. They appear in medieval woodcuts and as stone sarcophagi, but up till that time, no indisputable wooden gabled coffin had ever been excavated. "Indisputable" is a bit strong here, because there was strong circumstantial evidence for gabled coffins having been used in a series of early seventeenth-century burials at Martin's Hundred in Virginia, where Ivor Noël Hume discovered a row of large nails lying at approximately equal intervals down the midlines of several skeletons. The pattern seemed to suggest that these people were buried in gabled coffins that had since rotted and disappeared completely, leaving the spikes that once secured the gable, to drop down onto the bones below. For over a decade Noël Hume had searched high and low for archaeological confirmation that such coffins were made at that time, but he never found an excavated, complete coffin.[8]

Although Oudepost was occupied at the right time, we had no particular reason whatsoever to expect such a coffin at Oudepost. Cedric remained adamant. The previous night he dreamed that he saw a gabled coffin buried in the dunes. Cedric believed strongly in portents and signs, but there was no time to argue the matter out then. Our field season was running out. We were both due back at our regular jobs. So we covered the spikes and bones with plastic, piled sand into the hole, and tamped it down until we returned the following year.

Up till then we had been relying on a rough sketch map to situate our test pits. On the last day of the 1984 season, we made a site map. Trailing around the kraal with ranging poles and tapes, we stumbled over bushes and loose rocks. A biting wind whipped across the lagoon and forced us to bellow coordinates back and forth. Suddenly Cedric stopped short. He peered down into the pile of rocks, and began to hurl fallen ones aside.

"Look!"

I dropped the tape and raced across.

Deep in the darkness, I caught a glimpse of two blocks, set an angle to each other.

We stared at each other.

"It's not a kraal," I gasped, "it's the bastion of a fort!"

Three consecutive seasons of intensive excavation began in 1985. The work was still funded in part by the Mauerberger Fund, but the main cost was covered by the National Science Foundation, which funded my proposal entitled "The archaeology of indigenous interactions at the Cape, South Africa," with a subvention of about $110,000, to be spent over a period of the next three years. This sum was negligible compared to the kind of support commanded by the natural sciences, but it seemed a fortune for historical archaeology. What was more, it expanded to three times its original value just as the first field season began. The grant was originally priced out when the rand stood on par with the dollar, but in the course of that year an economic boycott began, and South Africa's economic situation changed. Overseas companies disinvested their holdings and the once-stable rand plummeted. Within a short time it plunged to an unprecedented one-third of its former worth. In the time lapse before inflation to set in in response to this catastrophe, prices of food and equipment remained stable. As a result, we were loaded. We could afford to pay good wages, eat fine food, and buy all the equipment we need to work speedily, efficiently, and in the greatest comfort imaginable.

We started digging in 1985, cautiously removing the earth in a series of five or ten cm spits over single square meter units. Broken bones, pipes, dishes, and bottles lay all over the site, in and outside the structures, backed up against the walls and doors, and even, on occasion, washed up on the beach. Clearly, the occupants had not dug rubbish pits, but instead, they threw, or broadcast, their garbage all over the site and into the sea. People made fires and cooked food on the sandy floor of the lodge then trampled the waste underfoot or threw it out the door. Even the paved rooms of the fort were covered with a layer of garbage. We dug, sieved, and sorted until our time ran out and then decided to wind up with the burial, whose edge we had nicked in 1984.

We exposed a wide area above the coffin and discovered the edge of an irregular pit that was dug for the grave. Scraping down further within the pit, we came upon the outlines of the lid of a straight-sided coffin, lying about seventy cm below the ground. The wood had long since rotted, leaving a pale brown stain in the sand. Large iron spikes, their heads exploded into rusty rosettes, marked the corners and sides of the coffin. There were triple spikes at each corner, single ones along the sides, and five horizontal ones, lying at even intervals down the midpoint of the lid. These had once held the pitch of the roof, and they plainly confirmed that this was a gabled coffin, the first of its sort to be excavated at all, let alone in Africa. Cedric bisected the coffin down its long axis, leaving the nails in place. He brushed away the sand, using the puffer that was normally reserved for cleaning the cameras, and exposed the damp, dark-orange bones of half of an extended adult skeleton. We photographed the find, drew every nail in place, and removed the other half of the coffin to reveal the entire burial (see fig. 12).

What we had was a coffin buried in a grave dug about one meter into the white sand. The occupant lay with his head tilted forward, looking as though he had slid backwards when the coffin was lowered into the ground. After an expert scrutinized the remains, we realized that he was an adult male who died when he was between forty-five and sixty years old. Predominantly Caucasoid cranial features suggest that he was probably of European origin. His front teeth were very worn, due to the

Fig. 12. Excavated coffin with the skeleton partially exposed. The outline of the
coffin is marked by rows of nails, and the edge of irregular pit in which it was laid
appears as a faint stain in the sand. Five nails lying horizontally along the midline of
the coffin once supported its gabled roof. Oudepost I, Cape, 1985. Scale in 20-cm
increments.

singular fact that most of his back ones had fallen out. He stood around
169.3 cm tall, and the bony attachments on his arms and shoulders betrayed a once-active life. This did not characterize his later years, however. The pronounced neck tilt was not due to his burial but to the fact
that his cervical vertebrae were wracked with arthritis. In addition, he
had a marked curvature, or scoliosis, of the chest region. He walked

slowly, one shoulder held higher than the other, and as arthritis increased with age, he suffered pain with every step he took.

He probably looked like a hunchback.[9]

But who was he, and when did he die?

No precise date could be inferred for the burial, though the presence of colonial artifacts in the fill of the pit implies that the grave was dug and filled after the post was established. There were no identifying objects on the body, no signs of clothing like buttons or buckles. He wore no rings, and carried no weapons with him to the grave. The archives never mention a crippled soldier at the post: indeed, most of the garrison were young, active men, who were expected to perform a wide variety of energetic tasks. Dispatches are full of ships calling in at the post with a load of sick and dying men, but none makes any mention of a hump-backed captain dying in the bay. It is therefore impossible to say whether he reached Oudepost by land or sea, whether he was alive or dead when he arrived, and, given that the post was occasionally left unmanned, whether it was functioning as such when the grave was dug! And yet for all the unknowns, I call him "Captain," because the circumstances of his burial suggest high status. His coffin might have been made at Oudepost from planks, such as were imported to build the post, or it might have come in on a ship, but given the overall rarity of coffins on ships and the fact that most interments, anywhere, were generally accorded little more than a shroud, it is clear that our man was of sufficient importance to be singled out for a special burial.[10]

Today a photograph of his coffin stands in the new museum at Carter's Grove, in Williamsburg, Virginia. Perhaps one day someone will reconcile his snarled neck and bent frame with a traveler's account and tell us who he was.[11]

After the 1985 season, Cedric and I met in Berkeley to discuss our future excavation tactics with Jim Deetz. Deetz was said to be one of the most informed and "laid back" people in the business. Both of his characteristics contrasted so strongly with mine that we stood to benefit greatly from his advice. We had clearly found the VOC outpost. It had at least two stone structures, and both were associated with a mix of colonial and indigenous artifacts, pointing to the interaction of indigenous and colonial people at the post. Archival sources said that Oudepost was occupied by a garrison of four to ten men for about sixty years, from 1669 to 1732, with a gap of about twelve years following a massacre in 1673. Our problem was to establish an archaeological sequence at the site. There was no point in using radiometric dating, because although the site was full of datable charcoal, we were dealing with a time range of only fifty years, and the standard deviation of a radiocarbon date would outstrip the period of occupation. Where stratigraphic linkages were concerned, it was difficult to relate deposits in the two buildings because they were not connected by traceable levels. Although the site must have been stratified at some point—as for example, when a soldier kicked over the traces of a fire and covered charcoal with white sand or when people threw the each day's garbage out of the lodge door to accumulate a layered heap—natural agents had long since blurred these horizons. Wind still blew the loose sand around, deflating artifacts down into the soil, and rain washed away traces of charcoal and ash. Most of all, if the present was any guide to the past, dune mole rats had burrowed incessantly through the damp sand, tunneling through floors and churning artifacts up, down, and sideways through the site.[12]

These problems might have tempted us to treat the entire site as a single unit that accumulated over sixty years, were it not for one crucial element. Buried in amongst the ruins of Oudepost were very large numbers of broken Dutch clay pipes, whose shapes and sizes might afford an excellent indicator of their age. First, they might provide a relative date of occupation of different parts of the site. Second, assuming that they had once lain in perfect stratigraphic position, with the oldest pipes at the bottom and the youngest at the top, their present position might reveal exactly how much postdepositional disturbance had taken place since they were originally dropped in the sand. But given the range of variation generated in pipe production, no individual fragment could be dated indisputably, and consequently we needed large samples from numerous parts of the site. To retrieve them, we needed to excavate large areas, and process the finds quickly.

Deetz put it bluntly. "Dig the sucker out!"

We needed no further urging. We stopped excavating in small squares and exposed large areas. Instead of shaking the finds through small sieves and sorting slowly through the clotted earth, we adapted a prototype that Jim had used on one of his digs. We built a high-efficiency wet sieve to operate with sea water. We bought a small pump and installed it at the water's edge. A suction hose ran into the sea and another funneled a spray of water into the large standing sieve. The operation was not without difficulties. We lugged the pump up and down the beach in accord with the tides, but our concentration was dulled by its incessant roar. Occasionally the rising tide drowned the machine. Cursing, we waded out to retrieve it from the icy sea, only to find that its delicate mechanism had become clogged up with salt, seaweed, and sand. Time and again we cleaned it out, muzzled the water pipes with nylon panty hose, cloaked the entire thing in plastic sheeting, only to hear it cough and falter again an hour later. Adding injury to insult, was the occasional hibernating scorpion, that became incorporated in the residues. Maddened by the cold spray, the insects struck back, and shrieks of pain drowned the roar of the pump as victims ran from the sieves to douse their burning hands in the sea.

But these were mere pinpricks. By the end of the second, 1986, season, we had exposed two structures completely. The lodge was a narrow, rectangular two-roomed building with one door set in the narrow end facing the sea, the other on the side of the small back room. The fort was a rough, asymmetrical affair, with several paved enclaves that made up two rectangular rooms and a semicircular emplacement overlooking the sea. Bones, shells, and artifacts lay in and around both buildings. Huge quantities of clay pipes lay in a heap in the fort, strewn at odd angles as though they had all been dumped at one go. Standing on this heap, and watching the high tide wash against the wall, it was clear that a great deal of garbage must have ended up in the sea. Occasional water-worn fragments of glass and ceramics washed up on the beach, but although we dug many holes in the wet sand at the water's edge, we never found a rich dump there.

The third, and final season began in June 1987. Now that we had exposed both structures and recovered a large collection of pipes, ceramics, and bones, we could relax and focus our attention on some more specific concerns. We dug about forty test pits, each a square meter in area, to try to assess the extent of the colonial debris and hence the area of the site. We excavated a promising-looking rise just beyond the north wall of the fort and discovered a curtain wall with a small boxlike structure set just beyond. We labeled the small structure "GCL" in honor of Paul Simon's "Graceland," which played endlessly on our scratchy tape recorder, without realizing that this was the name of Elvis Presley's home. Our GCL remained problematic. Its walls were a single course thick with a neat outer appearance that belied its haphazard interior, crammed with large lumps of decomposed sandstone. Although its walls

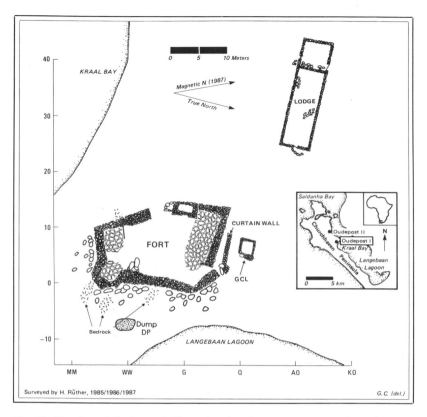

Fig. 13. Site plan of Oudepost I, Cape, showing three structures, set above the beach

resembled those of the other buildings, GCL contained little debris, either inside or out, suggesting that it was never inhabited, per se. It was apparently not a privy, since it contained hardly any refuse at all, and its unprotected location on the beach ruled out the idea that it might have been used to store powder or some such valuable commodity. It might have been a platform, with a flagpost jammed into the loose sandstone blocks.

By the end of the last season, we had excavated about 17 percent of the estimated 2,500 square meters of the site. Ruins of three stone buildings stood clearly exposed alongside boxes and boxes of neatly labeled finds. All digs start with a ruined wall, a suspicious-looking rise, a dark cave, and end up with a deep, neatly cut hole or a series of exposed walls.

What distinguishes one from another is the details, the decisions, the mistakes, and the insights, even the personal issues that journals don't want to publish. This is the essence of research.

A site is like a lover. Early on, you fool around, testing, probing, seeing other sites, but eventually you either dig it or you don't. If you do, it costs money, it takes time. There is a bond between you, and it's yours for the duration. You map it, chart its depths. You forgive the barren regions, and revel in the rich ones.

Of course, it's never yours, not even if you buy the land. When you leave, someone else can come in and dig it again. They don't even have to ask. But whilst you're digging it, every day you walk down the path and swagger in pride and sheer pleasure of possession.

After the first season the excitement fades a little and things become familiar. You no longer drool over a fine cup, or a glistening bead. You reel off the Dutch stamp on a pipe with hardly a second glance. Because now you realize that the site is not the simple thing you first took it to be. It has been changed through time by wind, rain, and burrowing. It is getting to look its age. For time alters every site, muting its original, virginal depositional pattern. Time confers a taphonomic history on every level, every feature, every artifact. In the honeymoon days, everyone dreams that their site is perfect, but later a certain sense of reality reveals it for what it really is—a puzzle, a palimpsest, changed and altered by known and unknown factors.

Now comes the real test. Can you hack it out to the end, decode the message, recreate what it was before time blurred the edges? Some feel the site has betrayed them; they break and bolt. Others publish fast before the true nature of the site is exposed by someone else. The best stay the distance. They don't terminate. They are at one with the site because its problems and inconsistencies are what confer character and challenge on the whole affair. They disentangle its confusion, smooth out its ruts, and expose its original integrity.

And, finally, when all the digging is over, there remain the last rites. There are rules and laws, and most agree that there is a moral obligation to protect, but some fill in the holes, some shore up the sides, and others simply walk away and leave the deposit to collapse. The site may be described in full, or briefly, or even not at all. The finds may be packed in velvet, highlighted in a museum or gallery, or they may be boxed and lost.

It all depends.
It's up to you.

Oudepost was different from other sites I had dug, because right from
the start I felt that it was mine. This possessiveness grew as the dig pro-
gressed, in part because instead of working with a work force of colleagues and students, our team was, in most respects, family. There were
Cedric's brothers, Freddie, Charles, and Gary, all taking time off from
slow seasons in the building, engineering, and fishing trades. There were
our children too. Between us we forged memories that went far beyond
the routine of a dig. The day Freddie Poggenpoel leaped vertically into
the air when he trod on a hibernating puffadder, one of the most deadly
snakes in the world. The game my son Reuben played with Gary Poggenpoel, putting a lizard and a scorpion into a bucket together to see
what would happen when you beat the side. The day "something" happened in the bucket, and Reuben brought a limp corpse round to where
we were digging, shaking his head, with a bewildered expression on his
face. I chased him over the trenches and down the beach, brandishing a
pickaxe handle and swearing vengeance on the life of the lizard. The day
the pump was swept out to sea, and no one dared tell Cedric who had
spent the previous night cleaning it out completely. The day Tom Klose
found an Allen key and got the pump working again. The day Jane excavated the only intact clay pipe among the 7,000 broken fragments, and
rushed over to Cedric, who scowled, and said he knew it was there all
along. The day I cursed a small yellow bird for chirping. The day my
daughter, Nina, learned to light the spirit lamps without dropping the
matches and then smiled so widely at a neighbor's dog that he ran off
howling at the sight of her new, shining, braces.

And the nights. Jane lived in her thatched cottage up the peninsula,
but the rest of us rented her other house in the little hamlet of Churchhaven. It was a tiny, two-bedroomed affair crammed with bunks. Dinner
done, everything was moved aside to make way for a miniature billiard
table. Beer caps snapped, the air filled with smoke, and laughter punctuated the soft click of billiard counters and dominoes. The Poggenpoels
spoke "Kaaps," a dialect said to be the original Cape Creole. It sounded
much like Afrikaans, but since that tongue was widely regarded as "the
language of the oppressor," we referred to the Poggenpoel patois as
"Kaaps." Cedric told of many things, how to dig a cave, how to plan an
Iron Age village, and how to race pigeons. Best of all were his shark

stories. His father owned a small fleet of fishing boats that were moored in a small harbor across the peninsula from Cape Town. From the stoop of their house above the harbor, the Poggenpoels guided the boats, watched the tides, and on occasion tracked sharks. Cedric told of Submarine, the greatest of all the Great Whites, whose barnacled back had swamped several boats, but who still cruised the waters of False Bay.[13]

The children shuddered and curled up tight in their beds at night, dreaming of the Great White's teeth. Outside the Southern Cross shone brilliantly in the black sky, and the Milky Way lay swathed across the dunes.

We became friends, all of us, though in the mid-1980s, it was still uncommon to find people like us, listed as belonging to different ethnic denominations, openly sharing living quarters. Tensions engendered for centuries, and encoded for decades, sometimes peeked through the fabric of friendship, as on the day that Reuben and Jane stood sorting mechanically at one of the trays. Reuben held up a large lead musket ball and declaimed in a Cockney accent: "Ere it is. The last ball, bowled in the last over, of the last cricket match between the Khoikhoi and the Dutch. Score at close of play: Dutch one, Khoikhoi zero."

Cedric's voice rose mockingly over the sea wind: "Listen boy," he called, "the match isn't over yet!"

For all its memories, Oudepost was never even remotely mine. I held a National Monuments Council excavation permit that was valid for three years, but actual access was controlled by the Oudepost Syndicate, who owned the land. The area was barred to the public except during the peak of the wildflower season, when for about six weeks visitors could cruise around on specially demarcated roads to see the carpeted veld and the exotic herds of zebras, buck, and eland.

I was lucky to be there at all.

So why do I say "mine"?

Familiarity, I guess, mixed with a sense of intellectual proprietorship. I walked the site, scrabbled in its sands, I sniffed it out in the archives, and I mapped it in the surveyors office. Documents relating to the Saldanha Bay outpost spanned the decades that it was occupied, as well as the later years, when it fell into disrepair and was mythologized as an abandoned French fort. They included the daily diary kept in the castle at the Cape, letters sent by the post holder and ships' personnel to the Cape, as well as those sent to the post, supply lists, resolutions of the

Fig. 14. Cedric Poggenpoel excavating an iron shovel at Oudepost I, Cape, 1986

Political Council, and rulings of the Court of Justice. The Company soldiers of the pen kept prodigious records of commodities bought and sold, and the archives at The Hague still house the list of provisions sent to set up this very outpost in 1669:

> *For trade:* 203 pounds of tobacco (36 pounds of Virginia, 167 pounds of Brasilian tobacco), 3 gross tobacco pipes, 140 pounds of copper (50 pounds sheets; 90 pounds wire), 4 *massen* sorted beads
>
> *Equipage:* 1 sloop, 4 oars, 1 drag, 1 drag rope, 2 rope for cable yarn, 2 lines
>
> *Bethillis (cloth) to make flags:* 1 red, 1 white, 1 blue
>
> *For cooking:* 7 copper kettles; tinware: 4 saucers, 6 plates, 2 cups, 1 salt cellar, 1 mustard pot
>
> *For the construction of a house:* 12 one-inch beams from the Cape, 8 poles of 16 feet long each, 8 pieces of 8–18 feet long, 42 rafters, 200 round slats,

180 wall-stakes, 36 pounds of flat lead to nail the Company's arms to the poles, 66 pounds of nails, 2 shovels, 2 spades, 4 bundles of rattan to cover (the roof)

For arms: 100 pounds of gunpowder, 100 pounds of lead to mold bullets, 6 bullet molds

For food: 960 pounds rice, 69 *mengel* Spanish wine, 36 *mengel* brandy, 225 *mengel* or 1/2 bushel arrack, 960 pounds of hardbread, 288 pounds of bacon, 192 pounds of meat, 24 *mengel* olive oil, 24 *mengel* vinegar, 30 pounds of butter, 70 pounds of sugar

For horse fodder: 2 bushels barley, 6 bushels oats[14]

For all the specificity of this list, we could find actual no plans for the construction of the outpost itself. Records say a small garrison of four to ten men threw up a fort when they first took possession of the bay. Later they note that men were housed in a thatched lodge. These Company soldiers were drawn into service from the United Provinces, Germany, the Baltic ports, and Scandinavia. They included George Frederick Wreede of Brunswick, who compiled the first Hottentot vocabulary; Hans Jürgen Kling of Hamburg, known on occasion as "the gallant"; and Carl Hendrick of Hartmansdorff. Their job was to maintain a presence at Saldanha Bay, to provision passing ships who could not make the Cape in their long voyage to and from the Indies, and to trade as peaceably and effectively as possible with the resident Khoikhoi pastoralists for fresh meat, sheep, and cattle. Men hunted, rode horses, smoked, drank, and squabbled. Documents attest that the soldiers of the Company and the indigenous Khoikhoi met repeatedly, face to face, right here at the outpost, but the texture of their interaction is thin. We have no diary of a day in the life at the post and no memoir of early days at Oudepost. The best we have are lists of supplies and letters, and it is from these that we construct the flavor of the colonial enterprise and its effect on the indigenous people.[15]

There can be no question that relations changed over time. In the early days, back in 1670, when the French were still threatening to take the bay, the Khoikhoi sided with the Dutch by offering to hide the Company stock in their kraals with their own beasts. A mere two years later, affability soured when Gonnema, the Cochoqua chief, fell into disfavor for his occasional unwillingness to trade stock, for threatening some Dutch hunters who trekked up to the Berg River to shoot hippo, and, in short, for failing to show the proper respect for those who would dispossess him. The following year, the chips were down. In 1673 a rumor reached the Cape, that a party of Dutchmen, out to shoot big game, had once again been surrounded by the hostile Khoikhoi. Punitive forces set out from the fort to teach the natives a lesson, but no sooner had their wagons trundled off than they were overtaken by runners with the news that the garrison at Saldanha Bay had been attacked, men slaughtered, and the place laid bare. The punitive expedition was now extorted to exact vengeance: they were to attack the Gonnema tribes and to kill any male they saw. They returned about two weeks later, leading almost 2,000 head of captured sheep and cattle, to report that no one had been killed because all of the enemy fled at their approach.[16]

Eventually, it was decided that a certain Khoikhoi, Kees, had led the massacre at the post. This should have absolved Gonnema of blame since the accused was not a Cochoqua herder like him but a San, or Guriqua, hunter. This nicety escaped the notice of the colonists, and although his complicity was never actually proved, from that point on Gonnema became the *erffvijand,* or hereditary enemy, of the Honorable Company. Sarcasm attends on the accounts of his movements thenceforth. Whatever the truth of the matter, the reader must surely view with growing disquiet, if not outright disbelief, the notion that punitive expeditions against the Cochoqua were seldom, if ever, attended by violence and death. As for Saldanha Bay, the Company played it safe. They abandoned the outpost until 1685, when they deemed it safe to return, and they continued to interact with local Khoikhoi people there until the post was shifted three km up the coast to better water in 1732. Throughout this time, former Khoikhoi landowners served as Company help, herding sheep, carrying messages, and hunting runaway slaves, shifting from hegemony into those patterns of servitude and obsequiousness that would later crystallize into the hated strictures of apartheid.[17]

Bearing these records in mind, we tried to interpret the archaeological evidence from the excavated site. The settlement consisted of several ruined structures built on the beach sand of a small rocky promontory, between the high-water mark and a point about forty meters inland. We defined three main structures. The lodge, named for its designation in the archival records, was a rectangular building facing the beach. The fort, or redoubt, was an irregular-shaped structure with a series of small enclaves, one of which stood so close to the sea that it was periodically percolated by the high tide. Finally, GCL was a small structure separated from the north wall of the fort by a curtain wall. All three were made from the local undressed granite rocks such as currently litter the shore-line, making it likely that the small sandy beach in front of the lodge was in fact created by clearing building materials off its former rocky stretch (see fig. 13).[18]

The lodge stood about thirty meters from the water's edge, its front door set in the narrow end, facing the sea. It was built by digging long trenches 0.7 m wide, which were then filled with rocks to serve as foot-ings for the walls. The structure measured about 19.85 by 5.65 meters, dimensions that translate into more simple vernacular readings of about 62 by 18 Rhineland feet. But the makers made an error laying out the walls, and as a result they produced a building without a single right angle in the entire affair! Likewise, though most of the walls stood on footings, short stretches were missing, and parts of the walls stood di-rectly on the sand. The walls were generally 0.54 meters thick, built as a double tier, with occasional slabs laid across the entire width for added strength. It had two rooms, the larger open to the sea in front and the smaller rear room through a door in its north wall. There were no paved surfaces or other evidence of floors inside, but fragments of shell plaster sticking to the joint between the footings and the wall suggested that the walls were once covered with plaster. No chimneys were found, but heaps of charcoal reveal that fires were lit directly on the sand up against the walls. In the back room several well-placed rocks and iron bars showed where a rough grid once supported a kettle or pot.

The fort, its curtain wall, and parts of GCL, rested directly on sand or on the bedrock of the rocky beach. The fort walls and the curtain wall were generally between 1.4 and two meters thick and consisted for the most part of two outer walls filled in with broken rocks. Paved surfaces were found in three parts of the fort, with granite and sandstone slabs interspersed with an occasional yellow brick. Crude though these floors were, they were not laid haphazardly. The floor in the northern side of the fort was laid from the walls inwards, whereas the southwest one grew from a few central stones, outwards. Fragments of shell plaster clinging to the cracks suggest that it might originally have covered the entire floor. Finally, GCL lay just beyond the curtain wall. It measured 3.55 by 2.85 meters, with walls 0.50 to 0.75 meters thick. Two walls rested directly on the sand; the others lay partly on the sand and partly on a dense secondary fill of charcoal, rubble, and broken bricks. The origin of this fill is unknown, but if it was generated on this site, its stratigraphic posi-tion suggests that GCL was not the first structure built here.

Fig. 15. View of the rough stone fort, at Oudepost I, Cape, looking southeast, over Langebaan Lagoon.

Architectural similarities suggest that all the buildings were part of a single settlement. Provision lists specify that beams, slats, rafters, and rattan were sent to build the station, but since we found no postholes to suggest the presence of upright roof supports, it seems that the roofs rested directly on the low walls. Fragments of shell plaster imprinted with reeds imply that they were thatched. Then too, various lines of evidence suggest that this settlement was built after the colonists had been living here long enough to accumulate some garbage. The floor in the northeast section of the fort was set in sand stuffed with broken pipes and bones, and two walls of GCL rested, in part, on a fill of charcoal and broken bricks that must have been generated in the ruins of a previous structure. An earlier foundation lay alongside the dividing wall of the lodge, running under the outer walls of the back room. Finally, the footings at the entrance of the lodge were packed with ash and garbage that accumulated while the men built the lodge (see fig 16).

In and around the structures lay broken bits of glass, stoneware, earthenware, porcelain, iron, and tin. Two large rusty locks and some broken pintles suggest doors or hinged windows. Activity areas were evident in the predominance of gun flints, shot, and metalware in the fort, as opposed to more broken glass and earthenware in the lodge. The recon-

Fig. 16. View of the lodge, at Oudepost I, Cape, looking east across the lagoon.
The remains of an earlier structure may be seen as a line of large rocks in the back
room, running parallel to the dividing wall and under the side walls at both ends.
Scale in 20-cm increments.

structed squalor says that this was not a Dutch home of the sort
immortalized in genre paintings but, rather, a rough frontier settlement
occupied by lads working off their contract to the Dutch East India
Company. They trampled their garbage underfoot or broadcast it all over
the place, rather than placing it into pits, as was customary in colonial
sites of the later eighteenth century. Soldiers melted lead and poured it
into bullet molds, dropping blots of molten metal and lead pulls in the
sand. They wrote on slates with stone pencils as similar to those found
in wrecks of the VOC ships dated from 1629 and 1656 as they are to
modern ones, used in Holland today. They cut patches out of tin sheets
and riveted them with nails to mend their rusted kettles. Behind them
they left masses of snarled, metal cutouts, as an archaeological signature
of distant frontier outpost, where broken pots and pans were conserved
rather than dumped. The men stewed fish in kettles, tossing out a mass
of cleanly defleshed bones and scales when they were done. They butchered their meat with hatchets and knives and grilled it over embers,
throwing away the charred bones with their tell-tale cut-marks. Their
hearths sat directly on the sand floor of the lodge, and the men probably

coughed and hawked inside, as the smoke percolated slowly through the damp, thatched roof.[19]

Historical sources told us that we were dealing with a discontinuous occupation spread over some sixty years, but we needed a stratigraphic time frame to draw the archaeology closer to the documents. Since there were no direct stratigraphic links between the buildings, we carefully examined the artifacts to see if they would help us infer a sequence. Beads and coins, though promising, were rare, so we turned to ceramics. Here too the Oudepost collections were small when compared to those found in other colonial sites, especially in old privies, where hundreds of broken vessels might be recovered from a single pit, as opposed to a total of 280 vessels from the entire Oudepost dig!

Nevertheless, using what we had, we began with the earthenwares. Plates, small tripod dishes, porringers, colanders, and bowls were decorated with dull green, yellow, rust, and red tin glazes. Although these seemed potentially definitive of time and space, they were not. Similar wares were made since medieval times in Europe and without microscopic analyses of sherds and clay sources, we could not even distinguish imported vessels from those which were made at the kilns that operated at the Cape since 1665.

Turning next to stonewares, the jars and bottles, which probably held wine, liquor, vinegar, and medicines, were certainly not made at the Cape, but any expectation that these, or other vessels like them, might be tightly seriated according to the stamps on the necks and bottles had been dashed some years earlier when a shipment of stoneware bottles, or bellarmines, excavated from the 1629 wreck of the East India Company ship *Batavia,* was found to include every style formerly thought to form a succession over several centuries![20]

This left Oriental porcelain. Despite its predominance at Oudepost, where it made up almost 50 percent of the sherds and over 70 percent of the minimum number of vessels present, porcelain never appears on the supply lists to the post. This is probably because the tea bowls, dishes, bowls, and plates at Oudepost did not come overland from the Cape but, rather, from ships sailing home from the East, who called in here for supplies. Incongruous though it may be to imagine soldiers on a rough frontier outpost sipping from a porcelain teabowl, one must recall that for all its rarity in Europe, coarse South Chinese provincial wares were so common in Asia that they probably occupied the same role on a homeward voyage as did earthenware and tin vessels on the outbound run. Records attest that Company men were entitled to export a certain amount as private trade, but contraband far exceeded the allowance, so that the weight of these shipments was, on occasion, enough to sink a homebound ship! Porcelain draws its name from the white cowrie shell called *porcella,* or little pig. Its deep, drowning blue set on a white sheen and the sweep of the bowl up from the small, neat, foot to the prim everted lip excite the prospective seriator. For all their elegant features, the best way to date porcelain is in reference to dated cargoes from shipwrecks. But unfortunately there are, at present, too few such wrecks to provide appropriate fine-tuned comparisons with the Oudepost material, so that its porcelains cannot provide a key to the relative age of different parts of the site.[21]

So we turned to the key to such chronological conundrums, namely, the clay tobacco pipes. Briefly, after tobacco was introduced to Europe from America and the West Indies, smoking became fashionable, and pipe-making guilds sprang up in England and Holland in the late sixteenth century. The earliest pipes were short stemmed, with small, squat bowls to hold small amounts of this valuable product. As shipments of tobacco proliferated, pipe stems grew longer, terminating in large bowls, for a more leisurely, cooler smoke. Unfortunately these very general stylistic trends do not serve as a tight dating device. Turning from form to decoration, makers stamped their names and coded dates of manufacture on the bowl, stem, or heel, but these signs usually provide a relatively long time range that brackets the duration of the factory, rather than specifying the year, or decade, of manufacture of the pipe. If this were all the information encoded in clay pipes, they would be no different from other artifacts, such as porcelain bowls, stamped with the mark of a Chinese dynasty, and glass bottles that were fashionable for a sixty-year span. But clay pipes carry a potent and subtle time code in the diameter of the bore that runs the length of the stem, from the bowl to the mouthpiece.

Over forty years ago, "Pinky" Harrington observed of colonial sites in Virginia that the older the site, the larger the holes in the broken clay pipe stems that littered the ground. Since stem bores grew smaller as a direct function of time, the average diameter of a set provides both a relative and an absolute age, to a decade or so, for assemblages of pipes. Most subsequent conclusions about stem-bore chronology were established using English pipes, and since the Oudepost yielded about 7,000 fragments of clay pipes, almost all of which were made in Gouda, Holland, the question was whether the Dutch pipe stem bores had shrunk over time like the English ones. It turned out to be so, possibly because pipemakers interacted across the Channel, even to the point of shipping clays from England to France.

Jim Deetz and I started to analyze the pipes while the dig was still in progress. He set up a table at the University of Cape Town and stuck graded drill bits into the stems of thousands of pipes. He lined up a series of nine styrofoam cups and labeled each one according to the diameter of the stem bores. A tenth cup was filled with their modern equivalent, namely, the butts of his filter-tipped cigarettes. We then persuaded two successive statisticians to explore the nuances of stem-bore distribution in different parts of the site. They concluded that although we could use the pipes to show the relative age of different parts of the site, using stem bores to calculate the mean age of a site was intrinsically doomed unless pipes there were deposited in a constant, unbroken rate over time.

Typologists expanded on the limits of heel-stamp dating. I traveled to Leiden in the winter of 1988 to consult Don Duco, the world's expert on Dutch clay pipes. We were especially concerned about a small collection of fragments stamped with the arms of the city of Delft that lay at the very bottom of the deposits in the lodge, in close association with hearths there. According to Duco's published list of heel marks, these pipes were made in a very narrow time range, between 1744 and 1749, a date which threw our entire site into confusion, if, as we believed, Oudepost I was occupied from 1669 to 1732. Duco's scholarship and passion for pipes had led me to expect an old man with nicotine-stained fingers. The youthful scholar in his unheated Georgian museum threw me off guard. We sat at a polished table and pored over the Oudepost pipes. Duco was in shirt sleeves, I huddled in my coat. I trembled, in part from the cold, and partly from apprehension, as I drew the "Wapen van Delft gekrooned" specimens from their plastic bags.

Duco took a quick look. He seemed unmoved.

"Oh, forget it," he drawled. "I must have got the date wrong!"

"Wrong?"

"Sure," he snapped. "The old lists are often full of errors."

I turned to more immediate concerns.

"Tell me," I said, "are you warm in here?"

Duco looked puzzled.

"Oh no," he replied "if I were warm, I would take off my shirt."

The published report on pipe analysis confirmed and supported the documentary sources which said that whole site was occupied from the late seventeenth century to about 1730. It also showed that despite the ravages of wind, water, and burrowing moles, a succession still survived, with the lower levels having more, older, large-bored pipes than the upper ones. It revealed that the lodge and fort were occupied around the same time, in contrast to the small square structure, GCL, which was the latest building on the site. It told us nothing about the age of the burial, however, because the fill there was too shallow and mixed to lend itself to dating.[22]

Now we could try to reconstruct what happened at Oudepost and what the behavior and events signaled by the artifacts meant in the larger framework of Dutch-Khoikhoi existence.

Historical archaeology seeks to tighten the embrace of archaeology and history beyond the confines of each discipline by relating objects first to context and then to behavior. The actual evidence under review is often so tenuous that the enterprise resounds with disputes and disagreement. Interpretations at Oudepost are no exception as may be seen in the following controversies over the archaeological evidence for Dutch-Khoikhoi interaction at this site and the impact of the Dutch settlers and soldiers on the land.

Archaeological interactions between colonists and Khoikhoi at Oudepost are inferred primarily from the association of patently indigenous artifacts with colonial rubbish. Stone tools, coarse-tempered pottery, bone points, a tortoiseshell bowl, and ostrich eggshell beads lie cheek-by-jowl with colonial hoes, bottles, and porcelains. They cluster in and around the buildings, suggesting that the post was in use when the debris was dropped. Simple though these observations may appear, they merit deeper scrutiny because Later Stone Age people probably lived in this region for more than 35,000 years, raising the question whether the association of artifacts signals interactions at the post or merely reflects an accidental intermixture of colonial and indigenous refuse.

We argue that it denotes interaction and, moreover, that the indigenous material represents the material signature of contact people. For starters, this particular little beach was not viable real estate until about 2,000 years ago, when the slightly raised sea level fell to its present position and exposed the sandy land on which the post was erected. But if geology rules out 33,000 years of Stone Age presence, we still need to prove that the indigenous artifacts excavated at Oudepost are a mere 300 years old. Some prehistoric archaeologists were disturbed by the fact that the chipped stone tools at Oudepost are different from those found at the only well attested Cape Khoikhoi camp at Kasteelberg, some forty km away. They argued that the Oudepost association is fortuitous, that the outpost stands on the site of an earlier herder encampment, similar to those on the coast nearby, and that the indigenous artifacts were churned upwards by wind, rain, and moles, to end up in apparent association with the colonial garbage. When confronted with a total absence of any underlying indigenous deposits, or for that matter any typically indigenous debris, such as a dense shell midden, coupled with the presence of patently undisturbed Stone Age artifacts—including an ostrich eggshell necklace buried against the lodge and a typical Khoikhoi bone spear point stuck deep into the fort wall (see fig. 17)—they retract momentarily. Regrouping, they argue that the concentration of indigenous debris around the Dutch buildings does not signify interaction but rather, separation, in that the Khoikhoi must have occupied the ruins when the Dutch were gone, either in the twelve years immediately after the massacre of 1673 or later, after the post was abandoned in 1732.[23]

The passion of published exchanges on these matters hints that what we might be seeing here are different rules of evidence in prehistoric, as opposed to historical, archaeology. Colonial artifacts are seldom found in prehistoric caves, kraals, and rock shelters because after Europeans drove hunters and herders off their traditional territories, these sites fell into a different ambit. They accumulated only the odd glass flake, bead, or pipe when used peripatetically by Khoikhoi shepherds out pasturing their new employers' sheep. In contrast, colonial expansion drew indigenous people into new towns, farms, and trading posts where they became transformed from herder-landowners into an underclass within the new colonial society. Their imprimature now changed, as, for example, when traditional arrows and spear points were chipped from superior materials like glass and porcelain. The archaeological implications of artifacts such as these are neatly expressed in Tasmania, where an excavator needed to prove that natives reoccupied a colonial stock camp *after* it was destroyed by fire. Flaked tools made of glass and gun flints, coupled with traditional bone points fashioned from introduced dog and horse bones, proved his case, pointing as they do to Aboriginal scavenging for their raw materials in an abandoned colonial midden. A more subtle expression of indigenous presence, which is often more difficult to read, is the signature of this underclass in inferior ceramics, cheap cuts of meat, bottles of cheap liquor, and reused pipes.[24]

Fig. 17. An indigenous bone point, stuck in the stone wall, in the southwest corner of the fort at Oudepost I, Cape. Scale in 20-cm increments.

Where evidence of contact at Oudepost is concerned, although indigenous tools lie in direct and on occasion patently undisturbed association with colonial ones, there are no scrapers fashioned from glass and porcelain, no iron spear points, no bones butchered with stone tools, nor any points made of the bones of colonial imports, like pigs and horses. The only cultural swop that we have found is a small collection of chipped stone tools made from local silcrete with tell-tale iron stains lodged in their crevices that seem to be gun flints or strike-a-lights. Since the Khoikhoi seldom, if ever, had guns, we infer that these objects were made by the garrison when their normal, imported flint ones ran short. But if the colonists were so inventive, why not the Khoikhoi? Surely they perceived the advantages of iron and glass over stone? If they had no chance to try it while the garrison was emplaced, they certainly would have had all the time in the world, had they camped for any length of time in the ruins. But there are no porcelain or glass scrapers and no iron spear heads in the Oudepost collections. Thus lacking all such indications, the demand of purists that each and every stone tool at Oudepost be shown to represent an actual artifact dropped by a particular Khoikhoi person at a documented instant in time simply cannot be fulfilled.[25]

The second issue concerns the interpretation of the archaeological food remains. Oudepost I was littered with mammal, fish, reptile, and bird bones, some burned in cooking fires, others bearing the marks of butchery with iron hatchets and knives similar to those found on the site. There are many ways to estimate the relative importance of different animals, but a favored tactic is to count MNI (Minimum Numbers of Individuals) present by grouping all the bones that could possibly have come from one creature. Analysis of the large excavated collection reveals that soldiers ate three times as many wild as domesticated mammals, as well as large numbers of tortoises, fish, and game birds.[26]

This pattern of hunting is consistent with the records on some frontier stations but utterly at odds with the majority of dispatches regarding Oudepost I. Frontier farmers tended to save their stock for the market, and consequently they hunted and gathered wild food all the time. The cull was monitored in principle, if not in practice, by a series of proclamations and rules, duly noted in the Game Books. The garrison at Saldanha Bay, who had to provision ships, bought and traded meat on the hoof from nearby Khoikhoi herders, from colonial farmers, and from Company stock posts all year round, but the archaeology suggests that they did not rely on this to any great extent, where their own needs were concerned. This discrepancy prompted a closer look at the primary records. The Company Meat Books—great sheets of parchment housed today in the Royal Archives at The Hague—record shipments of butchered meat made to various outposts. The quarterly rations for the troops were dispatched according to a weight formula per man, but between 1725 and 1732 we find that significantly less meat was sent to Oudepost as compared with other posts. This suggests one of two things: either the passage of stock here was so effective that the men did not need any more meat or else the garrison at Saldanha Bay hunted so efficiently, that they had no need of the Company's provisioning.[27]

The predominance of wild foods at Oudepost is therefore not surprising, but it does carry ominous implications where the local Khoikhoi people were concerned. They were herders who hunted and foraged for food year round, especially in those seasons when pastures were sparse and the stock grew thin. They slaughtered their stock when they could afford to do so, and they relied on wild foods to buffet their losses in hard times. The colonial stock trade probably seemed feasible to them at first, but as its demands escalated and as their stock was confiscated for infractions, Khoikhoi herders lost more animals than they were accustomed to cull. Analysis of the Oudepost sheep bones confirms the documentary evidence that sheep were consumed all year round, and, as such, it contrasts with the situation found on many indigenous sites of the past 2,000 years, where sheep were consumed only at specified times of the year, when the flock was largest. After the famous conversation of 1660, when native chiefs begged for access to forage on land they had lost in what the Company regarded as a just war, the Khoikhoi came to realize that from then on the land and its yield were no longer the province of the spear, bow, and poisoned arrow but of the gun and the horse. The residues at Oudepost afford chilling confirmation in a comparison of the minimum number of game birds there, as opposed to those commonly found in food debris on precontact Khoikhoi sites in the same region. Prehistoric sites generally yield around ten species, some of which were probably "wash-ups"—exhausted or dead birds thrown up on the shore. In striking contrast, the Oudepost series, boasts forty-two different species of birds, a startling tribute to the gun and bird shot.[28]

The bottom line, then, is that the Oudepost bones illustrate in detailed material terms one aspect of the colonial grab of native resources in this newly invaded land. Extrapolating beyond this post to the long chain of other posts and farms along the frontier, we may envisage in very specific terms, how the new settlers cut a broad swathe through the wild food base, swamping the old Khoikhoi pattern of a small persistent cull with a sudden vigorous onslaught.

This is a very satisfying conclusion because it refocuses the bland archival record into a tighter, simpler vision.

The only problem, where Oudepost is concerned, is that it is wrong.

Three years after digging ended, in the winter of 1990, Jane and I wandered down to the site again to check what the sea might have washed up during some particularly high tides. We noticed a large bone, glinting in the mud of a shallow rock pool. Scraping off the sand, we pulled, and watched in astonishment, as a huge bone sighed reluctantly out of the mud, revealing a dense mass of other bones below. We crouched down at the pool, digging with bare hands before the tide returned. The dark ocher fragments were waterlogged and heavy, and some showed scars where they had been smashed by repeated blows from iron hatchets. Sandwiched alongside were bits of porcelain, glass, clay pipes, a gun flint, and a coin, a few bits of Khoikhoi pottery, and stone tools. Jane and I stared at each other. We began laughing wildly as the tide crept in and covered the pool. We stuck a pole in the mud to mark the spot, and returned on the following two days to retrieve the rest.

The contents of the rock pool, which we unceremoniously labeled "DP," for "Dump" (fig. 13), were jammed into an area of about four square meters, down to a depth of about thirty cm. The accumulation seemed to be the lowermost level of a large heap of colonial garbage that was dumped into the sea. It fell onto the rocky platform, where most of it was washed away, leaving only the bottom-most stuff wedged between the rocks. Comparison of its 61 pipe stems, with the other 7,000 from the site suggests that the event took place around the end of the seventeenth century. A single coin, dated 1658, does not dispute this claim, nor do the associated fragments of porcelain, earthenware, glass, and iron. One particular piece of porcelain was originally part of a Kang Xi Chinese bowl, whose other fragments lay scattered around the fort. Its translucent white body sported bright cerulean designs of the eight horses of the emperor Mu Wang outside and pine trees inside, all utterly characteristic of bowls made in the second half of the seventeenth century.[29]

But although the dump contained the same mix of colonial and indigenous artifacts as we found in the land-based collections, its 1,700 bones looked quite unlike those found in the rest of the site. The dump contained the partial remains of twenty-one mammals, including a hippo, a probable hartebeest, five cows, six sheep, three seals, a pig, a few buck, and a rabbit. These were represented by numerous large bones, that contrasted with the many small ones in the land-based collections. In addition, while wild mammals outnumbered domesticates three to one on land, there were twice as many domesticated as wild mammals in the dump.

The most obvious question is whether the colonists habitually dumped the different parts of different animals on land and in the sea. To answer this, we need to rule out postdepositional winnowing by asking whether the dump once contained the remains of many smaller animals, which were subsequently washed away, leaving mainly large ones behind.

An analysis of body parts of cows and sheep suggests that this was not the case. The sheep are represented largely by twenty-eight small teeth, and had whole sheep been dumped there, the teeth should have been winnowed away every bit as easily as the rest. The cows, on the other hand, are represented by five solitary teeth and a mass of postcranial bones. Had whole cows' skeletons been dumped, the resilient heads and jaws should have withstood the tidal effects better than they did. In other words, winnowing notwithstanding, it seems that where this episode was concerned, sheep heads, and cow bodies were dumped in the sea.

The next question is whether people dumped different butchered residues on land and in the sea. The dump contains proportionally more large bones, and twice as many domesticates—cows, sheep, and pigs — as were found on land. Assuming that this dump was representative of the garbage that the soldiers customarily threw into the sea, then clearly the garrison butchered many farm animals at one time, threw most of the big, beef bones in the sea, and scuffed the smaller pork and mutton elements underfoot.

But since it is clear that the garrison also ate a lot of wild animals, we need to ask when periodic butchering of large numbers of domesticated animals cropped up? Historical records note the arrival of ships all year round, crammed with sick and starving men who demanded fresh water, meat, and herbs from the Saldanha Bay post. The corporal was repeatedly instructed to attend to these demands at once, buying or bartering stock from local herders, nearby farmers, and from the Company abattoir at the outpost of Groene Kloof (modern Mamre), fifty km away. The garrison was ordered to butcher very carefully, saving heads, plucks, and other offal. These provisioning episodes must have generated large piles of bones, guts, and hides. Excavations show that they did not dump rubbish in pits, nor could they rely on carnivores to clean up the mess, for according to the rare incidence of gnaw marks, it seems that there were few dogs or wild animals scavenging around the site. The only way to avoid accumulating fly-blown heaps all around their living quarters was to gather it up, or load it in a wheelbarrow, walk a few steps down to the beach or across to the fort wall, and tip the lot into the sea, leaving the tides to do the rest.[30]

Assuming that the episode, whose debris ended up in our little dump, was only one of many such moments of disposal, it opens a window on the taphonomy, or postdepositional history, of the residues at Oudepost I. If butchered remains of cows and sheep were selectively removed and dumped in the sea, then clearly the excavated collection does not tell the entire story of what people hunted, butchered, and consumed at Oudepost. The land-based remains give a misleading impression that the colonists depended heavily on smaller wild animals, hunting and fishing in the former ranges of the pastoral foragers. At the same time, the remains fail fully to reveal the dependence of the colonists on domesticated stock. But does this realization, when extrapolated to other posts and settlements, diminish the degree to which the Dutch colonists invaded the food base of the indigenous people? Had the indigenous Khoikhoi been purely hunter-gatherers, we might have had to back-track pretty smartly from our original conclusions. But the Khoikhoi were pastoralists, and as such they were locked into a demanding trade in stock. Consequently, the large numbers of butchered sheep and cows that must have been consigned to the waves point every bit as strongly to colonial inroads into the indigenous food base as do the residues of wild animals scattered around the site. For although many of the sheep at Oudepost were brought there from colonial farms and outposts, they were mixed breeds, the outcome of persistent cross-breeding of a small imported pool with a larger indigenous one obtained through trade and capture. As for the cows, cattle were not imported in any quantities until the late eighteenth century, so that all the cow bones may be traced to an ultimate indigenous source. In other words, whether we argue that the animals bones from Oudepost reflect the way the Dutch invaded the wild food *or* the domesticated food base of the Khoikhoi, the process of colonial conquest and domination still emerges strongly from these findings.[31]

Saved by the bell, one might say, and rightly so. The archaeological arguments end up looking rather like the evidence from which they emanated in the first place—scattered facts chewed over, broken down, boxed up, and finally, trotted out for view. Excavated finds from Oudepost rendered written accounts of contact with the indigenous Khoikhoi into tangible form, conferring texture on the words. They confirmed interactions in the associations of Chinese porcelain and flaked stone tools, of iron hoes and bone points. They epitomized trade relations in the association of cattle and sheep bones with broken wine bottles, tobacco pipes, and trade beads. The plan of the outpost and its list of residues revealed where soldiers lived, what they ate, and how they passed the time. It also told us about material objects whose passage to

South Africa is not in the records, including the gabled coffin, certain porcelains, and some European vessel forms.

But what, might one ask, did it tell us about the past that we didn't know before? This frames the question wrongly. The issue is not what new facts were revealed but rather what new emphases were stressed. In the early stages of the dig, each locale seemed to yield a different set of finds, and every bone, sherd, and pipe seemed unique. Then, a few weeks later, everything seemed the same, and each time a bucket was tipped into the sieve, we waited in bored expectation of the same types of beads, gun flints, bones, and stones. But once analysis began, variations emerged anew. Some locales were older than others, some were richer, and some were characterized by large numbers of a particular class of artifact. Patterns of site use and behavior crystallized, and realizations crowded in that here were not only markers of time and place but also icons of taste, trade, class, and phenotype. The artifacts emerged in a different light with rolls of lead, shot, gun flints, and bones, denoting conquest, loss, and death, and broken bottles and pipes signifying narcotics that increased the natives' willingness to pass their land over into these new hands. And finally, beads—black glass octagons, pink raspberry prunted balls, gold disks, olive green seeds with a red core, and copper tubes—emerged as the currency of this exchange.[32]

The bead trade had its own momentum, buffeted by the same storms of supply and demand that dominate all currencies. But there is a deep inequality encoded in beads that exposes the colonial enterprise for what it really was. To explain this better, we need to return to the archival records that itemize the number of animals that passed in trade, war, theft, and reparation between the Dutch and the Khoikhoi. It is said that all historians enjoy one climactic "cliometric moment" when the fruits of monumental delving are condensed into a single table. Richard Elphick's moment is his table showing the 50,000-odd head of sheep and cattle that the Dutch traded or took as booty from native people between 1662 and 1713. He uses it to illustrate the scale of Khoikhoi losses and goes on to argue that the main reason that they became powerless was not simply because they lost their stock but because in Khoikhoi society, stock was owned by families and individuals. Thus losses, once incurred, could not be recouped by help and succor from a wider lineage group. Before the Dutch arrived, hard times might have forced a family from hunting into foraging and servitude, but a good rain or a good raid could

equally well catapult a loser back into herding. In contrast to this, Khoikhoi who lost their stock to colonists, having no extended family to help
them out, went into bondage and stayed there.[33]

Elphick sees things differently from an archaeologist, whose documents of clay, glass, and stone, leave little room to mince around discussing the inherent limits of social organization. Instead, archaeologists
who count butchery marks on Khoikhoi cow bones and classify fish,
buck, and forty-two species of edible fowl wonder exactly what commodity the Khoikhoi got in exchange other than a stiff drink and a good
smoke? One answer is beads. The Dutch traded in glass and copper
beads, weighing them out by the *mas* (about 38 gm). If their supply lists
are any indicator of market expertise, then the Dutch were clearly at
home in this currency. They specified red beads for cattle and listed other
strings with intense specificity, to produce a rainbow of images, in light
blue, orange, milk-white, blue glistening like crystal, violet, striped crystal, yellow, green speckled with yellow, blue speckled with white, and
crystal with white stripes. But whereas the well-versed colonist might
use beads to buy his way *into* the indigenous base of women, stock, or
land, even the most canny native dealer, could not use them to buy his
way *out,* because beads were not a two-way currency. The Khoikhoi,
who wanted to fight for their *erf*—their heritage—needed land, power,
guns, and iron. These could hardly be bought at all, and certainly not
with beads. In sum then, the pretty baubles lying in the Oudepost sand
encode how the Dutch barred the Khoikhoi from entering the trade
network as equal partners by keeping natives on the bead standard while
colonists grew rich on land and stock bought for beads and sold for hard
cash, gold, and silver guaranteed in banks worldwide (fig. 18).[34]

The Oudepost dig, like any other research project, started off clear
and bright and gradually became convoluted, contradictory, and complex. The deeper we dug, the more we choked on the artifacts of conquest and the bones of subjugation. But for all the ominous messages of
beads and pipes, there is a sweeter side to material things, one that breeds
a gentler view. At Oudepost, such a vision is construed from two ostrich
eggs excavated on the site, one bored with a single hole, the other, carved
with visions of an empire that extended far beyond this trivial rocky spur.

The bored egg is identical to those used to hold water by traditional
hunters and herders to this day. It was excavated in the sand just beyond
the lodge. Perfectly intact, stained dark from the soil, it lay there, as
though in wait for later retrieval. The carved one came to us in frag-

Fig. 18. Exchanges of beads for fish at the Cape of Good Hope in the early eighteenth century (Kolben 1727, 2, facing 117; Cape Archives Depot, M143)

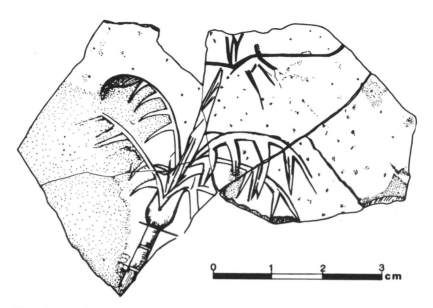

Fig. 19. Ostrich eggshell, carved with leaves and brachts of a tropical palm, Oude-post I, Cape

ments, washed out of the fort wall by the sea. It is decorated with a tree, not a pine or oak, such as may have grown in Europe or even by then at the Cape, but with a composite of tropical leaves, bracts, and trunk of palm trees, cycads, and tree ferns, such as flourish in low latitudes on the African and Indian coasts and the islands of Southeast Asia.[35]

Both eggs evoke visions of their makers. A small Khoikhoi woman crests the dunes along the bay as the dawn mist rises from the sea. She squats in the sand, pulls two sticks from her bag, and makes a small fire. Warming her hands at the blaze for a moment, she reaches into the bag and removes an ostrich egg. She stands it carefully in the hot sand, then taps the top until it cracks, and, taking a pointed stick, chews it, and pushes the frayed end into the egg. She twirls the yolk until it curdles, sending forth a fragrant steam that announces that the meal is ready. Eating done, she scuffs the fire out and walks delicately to the water's edge to rinse the egg. Then she sets off toward the watering place. The fountain is muddy, but she digs into the sand until it pools and clears and, bending carefully, so as not to dislodge any of the beads around her forehead, she fills the egg, plugging its hole with a twist of grass.

Water slaps around as the egg bobs in her skin bag. It bumps up against a parcel of honey that she hopes to exchange for three glass beads. Later, as the day cools, she squats near the wall of the lodge and, lifting the egg, drinks deeply. She uses the last of the water to wash the soldiers' musk from her legs. She smiles at the thought of the sparkling beads tied carefully into a corner of her kaross, scoops a hollow in the sand, and carefully buries the empty egg, to wait there until she returns next week.

The soldier is tired. Inside he is still glowing a little, yet his legs ache as he sits on the fort wall watching the sea come in. Humming tunelessly, he turns to the egg that he and his mates ate last night. He reaches for the dagger that he keeps tucked into his belt, and begins to carve, imitating as he does the Danish sailor he once met, who decorated a walrus tooth, scoring the cream surface with lines and curves. A tree emerges under his blade. It looks like those he saw in Macassar last year. He wonders when he will smell the cardamom again, whether he will ever again taste a clove, and he smiles, remembering the veiled women, who seemed to tinkle as they minced past.

A sudden wave splashes against his leg. He starts. The egg smashes on the rocks below. Cursing, he turns back to the lodge. The woman is running toward some herders who have appeared over the hill. She calls out their names, skimming across the dunes like a curlew as she hastens home.

5

Chronicle of an Outpost

The scholarly discourse of the Cape renders the indigenous Khoikhoi, or Hottentots, people whose response to colonial invasion was blunted by two crucial failures. First, they failed to grasp the full implication of the initial Dutch presence, and second, everything they did in response to the colonists was undermined by their decentralized social system. Although they mounted a counter-offensive again and again and although they managed to win some skirmishes, these two failures meant that they would, and in fact, did, lose every war.

In this context let us read briefly the strategies of one Gonnema, a Cochoqua chief at the Cape of Good Hope around the third quarter of the seventeenth century. He knew how to outflank the enemy, how to retreat rather than risk stock losses, and how to attack with spears on rainy days when the Dutch guns would not fire. What he did not know was that all this was trivial. Gonnema did not realize that unless he destroyed the invader, the world as he knew it, was for all purposes, ended. He saw the Dutch as temporary sojourners who would eventually whistle up their men, dogs, geese, sheep, and cattle, and leave. What he completely failed to realize was that when the first iron shovel cut the maiden ditch of the first fort, the proverbial chips were down, and for the Khoikhoi, the party that seemed to be beginning was in reality well and truly over. Gonnema never realized he was playing deep outfield in a game that needed eyeball-to-eyeball confrontation. For in order to survive, he had to slaughter the Dutch. He had to tear apart their ribs, devour them, and spit out their bones to bleach and fracture on the hard clay. In short, he had to behave like the savage he was supposed to be. For his failure to grasp this salient point, he paid with his earthly possessions, his power, and eventually his cultural identity.

True, he had not much choice, yet nevertheless, in this particular respect he stands indicted not so much for a savage as for a fool.

Historians classify Gonnema's failure of realization as a crucial moment, a turning point that altered forever the course of events. Here at the Cape, their tale of "if only's" and "what if's" is encapsulated in a chronicle of the domino effect, where natives living closest to the Dutch yielded first and most dramatically, while those farthest away gave in last. Confrontation, assault, and capitulation differed from place to place, but in the end it was the Dutch who created the events and the currency of conquest, promising goods valued at thousands of reals of eight and rendering actual payment in a single exchange of tobacco, brandy, bread, and beads. They posited every welcoming chief as a friend and every resister an enemy. Gonnema was writ as a betrayer, a man who welcomed the invader at first, only to turn against him later. Latterly, history has been kinder to him. Revisionists view Gonnema as a victim rather than aggressor, not because they have new facts or documents, but out of a more fashionable sense of history that tries to imagine the feelings of the silent and illiterate natives and bequeaths to them words that cast a skeptical eye on everything reported by the invader.[1]

And so, when all is said and done, no one knows what Gonnema ever thought or what actually happened.

Proclamation of the Year 1672

1672 April 19. Agreement entered into between the Commissioner Arnout van Overbeek with the Council at the Cabo de Boa Esperance, on the part of the general chartered Dutch East India Company, on the one part; and the Hottentoo Prince Manckhagou, alias Schacher, hereditary sovereign of the land of the Cabo de Boa Esperance, on the other part.

First; the said Prince Schacher promises . . . to sell, cede and deliver . . . to the said Company, the whole district of the Cabo de Boa Esperance, beginning from the Lion hill, and extending along the coast of Table bay, with the Hout and Saldanha bays inclusive . . . with this understanding, however, that he and his kraals and herds of cattle may come, freely and without molestation, near to the outermost farms of the said district, and where neither the Company nor the freemen depasture their cattle. . . .

The Honorable Company promise, on the other part, to give and present to the said Prince Schacher, for this surrender and sale of the whole Cape district . . . once and for all, a sum of four thousand reals of 8, in sundry goods and articles of merchandize . . . the Company shall assist and protect him, and . . . he shall once a year . . . deliver as tribute to his protectors, the Company, some presents of cattle, receiving, in return, an entertainment at the expense of the Company.[2]

Chronicle of the Year 1673

January 8 (Sunday)—*Arrival of the new ship* Hellevoetsluys. *Left Holland on the 5th July with 229 men, had [?] deaths, brought 50 sick. . . . In the Bay of Sera Leones she had been attacked by two English vessels . . . but she had repulsed them in such a manner that they were obliged to leave that refreshment station. . . .*

January 10 (Tuesday)—*The soldiers of the* Hellevoetsluys *were landed today— in a very poor state, and, for the most part, insignificant-looking and undrilled fellows. . . .*

January 11 (Wednesday)—*During the past night the house of a burgher, distant half an hour from the Fort, and situated in the country, was, with the stable, sheep-shed, and 480 cross-bred sheep that were in the latter, completely burnt down. The housewife, who had endeavored to save some, remained behind too long in the burning house, and was so hurt with the flames that she died this day.*

January 16 (Monday)—*To our great consternation this afternoon there was found on the roof of the carpenter's shed near the Fort a burning piece of wood, no doubt purposely thrown on it by some God-forgotten rascal in order to cause a fire. Thank God, it was discovered in time.*

January 20 (Friday)—*The house of a farmer about an hour's distance from this was completely destroyed by fire, with all the grain which had been stored in it. The cattle and sheep, however, were saved. Origin of the fire still a mystery.*

January 23 (Monday)—*Two Hottentoos, having pretended that they knew how the most recent fire was caused, accused a certain free servant, who, being summoned to the Fort and strictly examined, declared himself wholly innocent, and would not confess anything to his prejudice. He was accordingly provisionally set at liberty, and another freeman, at present a day labourer, examined, in consequence of the information of the Hottentoos. Being confronted with his accusers, who professed to know him, they vacillated so, that no dependence could be placed on their evidence, hence as nothing could be discovered prejudicial to the two freemen, they were discharged until something further was discovered.*

January 25 (Wednesday)—Pieter Ziegfried, late resident at Saldanha Bay, arrives overland with some sheep bartered by him there. . . . at the present time there (are three) there, among them being Corporal Dirck van der Herengraaff, to whom he had properly transferred the Company's effects.

February 10 (Friday)—The Hellevoetsluys *leaves for Batavia.*[3]

Testimony of Jan Nielse, Soldier of the Company, at the Fort of the Cape of Good Hope, August 11, 1673

Strange to say it so plainly, but I have hated the Company since first I answered the drums of the East India recruiter on the wharf at Amsterdam almost a year ago. There is no mystery here: I being the third son of a Swedish merchant in the herring trade, there was no capital, business, or training for me, at home. So, like other foreigners from Sweden and Germany, I sought work with the Dutchmen sailing abroad. But since I remained in the employ of the Company despite my hatred, then I must explain why I deserted. I was young, hopeful, foolish, no doubt, in my eagerness to see the world. I wanted to stand at the mast and feel the spray, hear the lookout shout for land, swagger ashore, and fill my senses with perfumes, silks, and jewels, with smooth skins, and dark eyes. Instead, I rotted on the ship.

We cleared Goeree, outside Rotterdam, bound for Batavia, in early July of 1672. The *Hellevoetsluys* was no more a ship of death than any other. All around me were men who had been seduced into the service of the Company by promises of making a fortune in a distant land, or less gullible ones, who had been sold into service by struggling parents, unable to feed their own children any longer. Many were weak and sick even before we sailed, and no sooner were we at sea, than some began to die. As I stood at the rail I felt a lad at my side slump over. He sank to the deck. I watched curiously, wondering if he were drunk, or perhaps overcome at seeing his gray, flat, Fatherland sink from view. But suddenly my feet were swamped in a hot rush of vomit from his mouth. He gasped, struggling for breath, and he died. I felt dizzy and sick. I shouted for help. At nightfall, when we were on the open sea, we slid his body overboard. Of course he was dying when he boarded, but one wonders how he walked on at all? The surgeon ordered the ship to be cleaned, and sprinkled with vinegar to prevent further losses.

Its sour stench percolated every fiber, but the sickness continued.

Clearly vinegar does not cure the flux.

We called briefly at the western coast of Africa, at the Sera Leones. Here black men are sold on the wharf. I am told that slavers reap a hearty profit, even though their cargo is more than halved by death before ever they reach their destinations on the sugar fields of the Caribbean. I called to one brute, standing with bowed head: "Man, look up!"

But he did not move. His eyes stayed riveted to the shackles that bound his ankles with chains to others. Now this surprised me at first, but of late, I have thought they made him into a beast, a beast such as accepts what no man could contemplate.

In the bay stood two English vessels, which challenged us for the cargo of silver we were taking to the Indies. Our Captain ordered us to man the guns, and we fired repeatedly at the English warship, whilst keeping our eyes sharp for the merchantman that harassed our rear. Four of our men were killed in the skirmish, but the Captain ordered us to stand fast. The English ships hove to and left, the more I feel because our cargo was not worth the slaves that they were loading from the wharf.

Then, after sailing westward almost to the shores of South America we turned to catch the winds for the Cape. But the air was still, and we lay becalmed in the doldrums. Men died as much of the heat as of the food. There was hard biscuit three times daily with beans in the evening. Salt pork was a rare treat, as was the spirit that burned into our gullets, reminding us that there was warmth and pleasure to be found elsewhere. But even as the men sickened and fell, there was no question but that common sailors were sicker than the officers. Their gums swelled, their teeth fell out, their bowels ran with the bloody flux. They died in their hammocks, or curled up like dogs in piles of rags in the dark recesses of the hold. For the officers dined in style, with wine and meat or so it was said. They appeared each morning, rested and well, commanding us to clear the holds and bury the dead so that the day's work might continue with a lessened load. Some walked the decks with a sponge soaked in vinegar held delicately to their noses. I laughed at the sight, because vinegar has no effect below decks. But then, I wondered, why were they well?

I pointed this out to the men. "Do you see how well they are whilst we die?" "Fuck 'em," one replied, hauling on the rope to the mizzen mast. I am not put off by sailors' talk, and I repeated my questions to others. A warning was issued to me to stop this sedition, but I ignored it. I waited for the outcome which was not long in coming. A dying sailor asked for wine, and I bribed the officer's servant for a glass. He, in turn, betrayed me to his master. A dozen lashes were decreed the next day. At first I gasped, but then I held the screams back until my throat swelled. I cast my eyes up into the sky. Then I roared, timing it, so that the crack of the lash covered my sounds, timing myself, like a woman in labor.

They threw salt water into the gashes. The officer rubbed it well into my flesh.

Now let me say that although this sounds harsh, my punishment was in no way unusual on ships such as these. Men were beaten for much less. But I cared not for others. I burned with resentment. In the hold that night, I heard an older man tell of the riches of the continent, of the gold and jewels, the Mountains of the Moon, the treasures of the king of Monomotapa. I knew then that I wanted fortune, not service. So clear was this realization, and so intoxicating, that I laughed out loud. Nor was it long before I found others who felt likewise. Wouter Larois of Gorcum, Dauwe Janszoon of Beeq, and others too, all men greedy for gain and who can blame them? Crude, filthy, and unread they were, but we were all linked by a common purpose. We gathered three more with us and planned our defection. I dreamed of treasure in the heart of Africa and when we anchored in the roads beneath the Table, I knew that it would be mine for the taking.

The *Hellevoetsluys* docked at the jetty where a wooden pipe poured fresh water off the slopes of the Table Mountain into a cistern. Our spirits rose after so many weeks at sea. Men carried the officers to the shore on their backs, waist-deep in water. We were a shabby crew as we mustered on the beach that first day, and then, strangely, as if in repetition of the day we left Goeree, it happened again. A man fell senseless, right there on the sand, bloody flux spurting through his clothes. None of us moved to help him until an officer bellowed the word, and even then, it was only when he ordered out four by name, that the man was carried to the hospital.

The sick man died before nightfall, but that is by the way.

I was preoccupied, planning our escape. The Captain should have mustered the men daily, but he was erratic. Consequently, fugitives could count on a day's grace before before a search party set out to find them. The *Hellevoetsluys* planned to stay one month at the Cape before leaving for the East, and although it was tempting to wait until the last moment to flee, her Captain and crew were so weak and dispirited from the voyage that they seemed unlikely to mount a spirited pursuit of fugitives at any time.

Then too, it was high summer. A hot wind blew daily over the Table Mountain, hissing through the dry trees to the beach. Crouched there, my face stinging from the blasting sand, a plan came to my mind. Recall if you will that this was a town of thatched houses whose susceptibilities I knew only too well, having been raised in such a cottage outside Stockholm. So for three nights I set a diversionary trail of fires. The first was at a farmhouse standing well beyond the fort. I walked the distance after the sun had set. It grew dark. The moon rose, hot and glowing. I drew my flint stone from my pouch and lit some straws beside the barn. I threw them into the hay. The housewife rushed out at the first plumes of smoke, flapping her apron as if to fan her hot, red face. She gasped, hands slapping her face, and then, amazingly, she rushed inside, back into an inferno. I fled. The wind was high and the fire crackled behind me, and through my panting gasps I heard frantic bleating overlain with a higher shriek that put wings on my pounding heels. Five days later I repeated this act, but this time, with no marked success. The brand fell off the roof, and into the yard of a carpenter's workshop, where he was standing. He doused it in the rain barrel immediately and rushed to the fence to find the perpetrator, but I was well hidden. I then waited another four days, before a successful burn on a more distant farm.

By now the talk of fire was on everyone's lips. Company servants worship property, and slaver for ownership. Nothing afflicts them more than the loss of capital, whether it be a house, a barn, stock, even a wife. So as to maintain a high degree of watchfulness, I instructed my five companions to raise the question of arson as often as they dared in taverns around the wharf. Anxiety rode so high that extra watches were posted every night, sleeping it off in the hot, windy daylight hours. So, having set the hounds after the false hare, we prepared to travel by day. We left the settlement separately to avoid drawing attention and met up again across the bay, on a long white beach from whose vantage point we had a magnificent prospect of the mountain, and of Robben Island, where felons, the likes of what we had now become, worked in chains. We stumbled across the dunes and through the low scrub that lined the beach. By day we slept in the bushes, creeping out at night to harvest oysters from the rocks and to drink brack water from holes that we dug in the sand. Continuing thus, we passed three nights and then struck inland, heading north.

A singular realization informed all my thoughts, and it was this: we could not survive this continent alone. Sailors who knew the Cape had little to say about its people, other than those that loitered about the wharf. On landing I saw some Hottentoos sleeping against sacks on the jetty, begging, even working on the new castle ramparts. For the most part they wore small aprons, and skins across their shoulders. A woman with a tiny lace cap on her woolly head swayed along. Stockings made of dried intestines rattled on her legs as she walked. Her body was utterly bare but for a small apron of shells and beads. My fellow sailors spoke disparagingly of these folk. Lazy people, said one, with strange knots of hair. Fast runners, good hunters, but rank with the sheep's fat that shone on their skins. Another sailor claimed to know some words of their strange tongue, and amused us with a series of sharp clicks and low grunts. Like every sailor I had heard that their women had privates with unusually long lips, and, that for the payment of a stuiver, one might look. "If the stench does not kill you," replied one crass lad, whose own rankness was hardly able to be missed, even in the bowels of the *Hellevoet-sluys*.

This was all I knew of the people of this land.

After fully five days stumbling in the heat, we drank at the clear brown pools of the Great Mountain River that the Dutch call "Berg." Stumbling on its round white rocks, we reached the farther shore. The air was filled with a metallic shrill. Dozens of red locusts clustered in the dry grass, their incandescent wings whirring at our approach. We slapped them aside, but one caught in my hair, and I tore at the jagged legs before stamping it on the ground in a fury of distaste. One of my men laughed. "Eat it," he said, "there's nothing else man." I shook my head and shuddered at the faint oily stench of the insect, even though I knew that our supplies of biscuit and arrack were all but gone. I still carried a twist of tobacco and some pipes, as well as a sack of beads as a mark of friendship for the natives, but we saw no one. We did, however, notice faint traces of smoke, which we followed, only to discover their camps, one after another, recently deserted with the hearths still smouldering. We slept at one that night and woke at dawn to find five men of the Hottentoos squatting on the edge of our group, watching us quietly through slitted eyes.

They made to us to follow them, and thus we came to the kraal, beyond a rise, of King Gonnema of the "Goenjemans," as the Hollanders said, he being the leader of these savages and king presumptive of all the Hottentots living under the new hegemony of Jan Compagnie.

The king was a large, dark man. His skin glowed with grease, his oily curls seemed ablaze in the morning sun. He wore a breechclout of cloth and the skin of a tiger across his shoulders. He greeted us, seated on a rock. Between his legs stood a copper stave, a *rotting,* on whose head was carved the sign of the Company to show that they had invested him with power on their behalf. About his waist, a garland of dried intestines, with seeds rattling within; around his neck, chains of copper beads interspersed with ones of red glass. A spear lay at his feet; he shuffled his toes repeatedly down its length, as if to remind us that it was there at all times. He stared fixedly at us, snapping questions to his interpreters who translated into broken Dutch.

Where were we from? What did we want? Where were we headed?

I replied with the utmost courtesy that we were former servants of the Company now fleeing from a harsh master, that we wanted to live with friends, and that we might be of help to such friends in our management of the Company. Of treasure, gold and riches, I said not one word, and it was just as well, for the discourse that I held with him that day, and indeed, the many others we enjoyed until the day he made me leave, revealed an aspect of the savage that I could not have imagined.

What I was seeing was a statesman dressed in animal guts, contemplating the politics of his time. For it was not that Gonnema fully grasped the situation, nor that he knew how to handle it, nor indeed that he could see a way out of the onslaught that faced his people. Gonnema was struggling with the forces that would pull him to a new world. Nothing in his life had prepared him for the Dutch onslaught. And yet he engaged in the discourse, he puzzled over the matter, every bit as assiduously as did Gustavus Adolphus during the Thirty Years' War, or Philip of Spain when dealing with the accursed Netherlanders.

Fig. 20. Hottentots tearing animal entrails at the Cape, ca. 1660. The chief seems to hold a staff of office in his right hand. (Dapper 1676, 271; Kennedy 1975, D141)

For as Gonnema saw it, his people, the Cochoqua, now faced loss of land, power, with the promise of worse to come. Repeated entreaties to the Masters at the fort brought no relief, no changes, only a stubborn reiteration that all the land from the fort to the Great Berg River had been ceded by a miserable peninsular chief and was now officially Company land. Although war had been waged earlier, its outcome was inconclusive. Gonnema needed violence to prevent traders and settlers moving deeper into his land. Direct warfare was out of the question: how could the Cochoqua fight muskets and bullets with spears and arrows? The Dutch were wise to their tactic of luring them out in wet weather, when the muskets would not fire, and they now remained indoors when it rained, whatever the provocation at such times. The only weapon left to the herders was their refusal to barter. But once the Hollanders moved inland, with stock of their own, the situation changed. Now direct trade was done only to supplement the herds of the invaders. Khoikhoi rights of movement were restricted, and they could bring no further pressure on the Dutch. Under no circumstances would the Dutch barter knives or arms, and although such things could be obtained from freemen, only the most inferior were ever actually traded.

It was full summer. Gonnema's tribe lived in small groups now, camping close to pools of water in the river, not daring to risk the lives of their stock on the hot and waterless plains. They spoke longingly of the cooler months spent in large encampments near the coast where they feasted on sheep, seals, and oysters. In the early hours, women dug on the sandy flats, excavating roots and bulbs which they roasted at night. The men hunted in the hills, bringing meat and tortoises home in their skin bags. They were infinitely patient, squatting for hours in the shade until a deer came to graze, then crawling toward the quarry, inch by inch, until a sudden spear brought it down. Occasionally we were treated to honey, and on days when the yield from the veld was poor, Gonnema ordered a sheep killed. The cool nights fell slowly, but the breeze revitalized the company, who rose with the moon and sang to a *ghorra,* a twanging bow that sounded like a Jew's harp, and that broke the dark with a sweetness I had not heard since I left my mother's hearth.

Day after day I puzzled over Gonnema's dilemma. I listened with a growing sense of amazement. For here was a man besieged by a hydra. A war of attrition on one frontier might damage one head but the rest would still thrive. All year long, ships anchored in the lee of the Table Mountain to off-load a seemingly endless supply of goods and men. I turned my gaze back to Gonnema. He sat staring ahead as though rethinking his position, a corpulent man, decorated in guts and beads. He noticed my stare, turned, and smiled. I warmed to the gesture, to the kindness. I realized then that God works in strange ways, and that I, Jan Nielse, was sent here to advise this ignorant savage; that I, versed in the Gallic Wars and the Nibelung legends, might avenge myself on the Company through the education of this strange man.

My companions showed no such interest. Even as I listened to Gonnema, they lay in the shade of a thorn tree, sharing our last flask of arrack with two women, one of whom lolled openly against the britches of the man. I noticed that she slapped his hand, more in jest than anger as he tried to lift her apron, whilst the others goaded him with lewd jeers: doubtless they too had heard the wonder of the Hottentot privates. I was torn between a reprimand and a sense that this might be as good a way as any to cement our stay here, for after all, we had no reason to travel farther north, we had no maps, nor did we carry supplies for a long journey. Then one day, squatting on a rocky outcrop at sunset, arms hugging my knees, I watched a locust excavate a hole in the dry sand, and saw with some revulsion, as the black and yellow segments of the abdomen contracted in a series of waves, to evacuate a froth of eggs into the nest, and I thought how by tactical advantage the savages might squeeze the Company out of their fastness at the tip of this continent. I recalled the master of my school, how he drew out the wings and pha-lanxes Caesar's armies to explain the way in which the pincers snapped shut upon the enemy, not in heat, but in thoughtful deliberation.

And then it came to me, that if Gonnema were to make immediate and powerful alliances with his hitherto hereditary enemies, together they might destroy their common enemy. It was no easy matter. First Gonnema had to be persuaded to confer and compromise with the Sous-quas, the Obiquas, and all those others of whose savagery I had by now heard so much, and secondly, they in turn had to be persuaded that the benefits of the Company were worthless, in comparison with the impor-tance of their freedom. But what means freedom? I heard the voice of my schoolmaster, and saw his smile. What is freedom to those for whom life is brief, to those who live under the whim of a chief who metes out justice with no counsel, deliberation, or explanation? For often in those months I saw Gonnema listen, but desultorily, to a dispute, and with a wave, a gesture of his thumb, condemn one or other of the disputants to death by stoning or by strangulation. The speed was such that barely had the words of the parties ceased, than the sound of choking and the stench of spasmed bowels was on the air.

But had Gonnema played his game of cat and mouse in his head too long? After all, the Dutch had been emplaced for twenty years, and he had not dislodged them yet, nor could he establish ascendancy over all his people. Sitting with a pipe of their *dacha* (for my tobacco was long since gone), and speaking with careful deliberation, he determined (at my urging) to retract the enmity he still held with his brothers the Souswas, and with the Goringhaiqua chiefs. These were the despicable Dackkgy, called Cuijper, and Schacher, known to Gonnema as Osing-khimma, or Manckhagou, whom the Dutch dignified with the title "Prince" when he sold them the land from the Cape to Saldanha Bay for a pittance. Gonnema's contempt for these men was great, but he knew what he must do. Moreover, he now saw that the retractions had to be made in a manner that would allow them to save face, by declaring hostilities at first, and then yielding to their demands in a new alliance. Then, together we planned to draw the fire of the Dutch by challenging the right of some of their men to hunt, uninvited, in our land.

Chronicle of the Year 1673, cont.

February 20 (Monday)— . . . *the chief Gounema, assisted by the Cape and Saldanha Hottentoos, . . . declared war against (the Soeswaas) and their allies, the Oebiequas. . . .*

March 14 (Tuesday)—*The war was still being carried on by the respective tribes, and Gounema had carried off the whole kraal, as well as the cattle of Captain Claas.*

March 15 (Wednesday)— . . . *one of the Gounema Hottentoos carrying a musket . . . fired very skillfully on the Soeswas . . . the Hottentoos had obtained it, with some powder and lead, from one of our burghers in exchange for a fine fat ox, which had been killed and put in a barrel (salted down) at once.*

March 20 (Monday)— . . . *Some Hottentoos from inland have brought the news that an eternal peace had been established between Gounema and the Soeswas.*[4]

The Testimony of Jan Nielse, cont.

The false war and the ensuing peace were done. It was winter and we were camped atop a large hill overlooking the plain that stretched to the sea, waiting for the seals that would wash ashore later. Now that we had plenty of water the company was large. We lived in many huts, with the sheep and cattle free to roam in the rich pastures close to the camp. Many pipes were smoked at night. Music thrummed into the darkness, whilst legs encircled with dried animal guts clicked in dance. I began to wish I had been born into these people, that I were a child in one of the huts, that I were Gonnema's child, (why deny it?), playing in the sun, and nestling up to my mother at night. I slept dreamlessly, waking each dawn to wonder what hunting we might attend, whether to dig for roots with the women or to teach the children a game of dice with knuckle-bone counters.

How the gods must have laughed at my hopes.

I awoke to the sound of running feet outside the hut. It was dark, but birds were already crowing in the cold, false dawn. I heard a stifled shriek, then silence. Grabbing my trousers I stumbled out. Dark shapes hurtled in the mist. Feet pounded. I began to tremble. My arms were grabbed from behind, I was shoved back into the hut my men shared. I blinked in the dark. A shape lay against the mat wall, a boy, his legs in disarray. Dark smears glistened between his knees. My men, all five, lay half inside, pinioned by Hottentots.

"Jan," one gasped "tell them it was with consent!"

My head was reeled. "Consent?" I screamed. My gorge rose, sour vomit welled in the back of my throat. The men pointed to Hendrik Pieterszoon of Deventer, a man whose pale face trembled as he drooled. "You dog!" I shrieked, beside myself. Their cries rose from all quarters, howls of Dutch overridden by sharp, high clicks. Over all howled the wail of the child's father, one Couca, whom my men called Kees.

He threw himself over the child, shuddering.

Gonnema strode into the hut. He spat upon the floor. His men pointed to Hendrik and I drew in my breath, expecting to hear him convene the Council. Instead, Gonnema leaped on the perpetrator. Teeth clenched, he raised his copper-headed cane of office and struck the felon in the belly. Vomit gushed upon the sand. Gonnema whirled the cane again and smashed into the head. Bone and matter spurted from the blow. Kees leaped from his child, eyes streaming, and made to snatch the cane from Gonnema's hand. The other Hottentots gasped at this impropriety. Gonnema kicked Kees to the floor, and held him captive there. Kees beat the sand with his fists. Then rolling over he began to claw crazily into the vomit and the bloody mess, thrusting it by handfuls into his mouth.

My belly trembled, my piss spurted. Whirling about, Gonnema pointed to me and my men.

"Go!" he shrieked. He pointed to the sea. "Go to your people, or to the dogs!"

Crouched in the bushes, we watched Gonnema and his people prepare to leave in one direction, Kees and his, in another. The huts were dismantled and loaded on the oxen, all except the one with the dead child, which remained as a sentinel over the body. The parties grew smaller, and finally faded from view. We had nothing, other than my knife. "Fuck 'em," said one of the men. Tears stung my eyes as I sat, turned to stone. The stench of blood, vomit, and piss hung over us all. I rose stiffly, and like a puppet unfurled my legs and walked into the gathering dusk after Gonnema. Behind me rose entreaties, then curses.

Dawn broke, and I saw Gonnema's fires about a mile ahead. I lived as a dog, on the outskirts of the camp, moving when they did, scavenging for scraps, in fierce competitions with the dogs and the hyenas that howled near the midden all night. They surely knew I was there, and I was certain that once Gonnema had adjudged that I was alone, he would send for me again. I would live with them, as one of them, if only I had the patience to wait. I watched the daily round, nostalgic beyond expression as familiar scenes unraveled: the women bringing water from the pools, a man returning from the hunt, a deer slung on his shoulder. Children yelped nearby as they discovered a nest of eggs. I hummed snatches of their chants, I whispered to myself that he would send for me. "Papa . . ." I murmured "Papa," I sang. "Papa!" I howled, "Call me!"

But there came no word. Not that day, nor any other.

Then one day five men appeared from the south. Although dusk was falling, I recognized Kees among them. They walked swiftly, being with neither women nor stock, and were greeted with high cries. I crept closer and listened. Words came to me, of Hollanders, of hunters, and of sea cows. Slinking back into the filth of hyena droppings, I saw a small party led by Kees leaving camp again. Suddenly, I had had enough of waiting, enough of cowering. I loped off after them, my stride lengthening as we traveled. Southwards we hiked, toward the great Bay of Saldanha. I followed Kees, his brother, two women, and a herd of sheep. They made no move to stop me, and I kept my distance, pausing only on occasion to scoop a tortoise off the sand. Beyond niceties, I twisted the tiny legs off and sucked the salty flesh, and with this hard-cased packet of food clutched to my chest, I slunk across the veld, the doppelgänger pariah dog. A lightness covered my vision and informed my limbs: I giggled at the adventure, waved to the Southern Cross, white and clean in the black sky. When it rained at night, I curled under a bush, clutching myself tight, until morning when I rose to run again.

Three days later, we reached the western shore of the bay. Across the gray sea rose the mountain wall. At its foot, rose a wisp of smoke from the outpost of the soldiers of the Honorable Dutch East India Company.

Chronicle of the Year 1673, cont.

June 18 (Sunday)—*The person in charge at Saldanha Bay sent us, under the guard of some Hottentoos and two Dutch soldiers, four of the soldiers lately deserted. They had been captured . . . in St. Helena Bay, [and] . . . sent overland to Saldanha Bay. We also received 53 sheep bartered here [and a letter from the Corporal in charge of the post, Dirk van der Heerengraaff].*

June 21 (Wednesday)—*The four recaptured deserters having been examined, threw the blame on one of their comrades, a Swede by birth, not yet captured. They accused him of having persuaded them to desert, but this merits little belief and does not excuse the crime.*

June 29 (Thursday)—*Some Hottentoos of Gounema's tribe reported . . . that Gounema had surrounded somewhere . . . eight of our burghers, with two wagons and eight oxen, who, without permission, had gone up to shoot some large game for the needs of their families. His object was to cut them off from all supplies, except what they had with them, that they might perish in consequence, but as this rumour seems to be rather untruthful, it was accepted as false.*

July 10 (Monday)—*One of the deserting soldiers, named Jan the Swede, was this day captured, and acknowledged that he was the chief instigator of the desertion, having urged his other comrades to run away.*

July 11 (Tuesday)— *. . . it was decided to send out an immense expedition under the ensign Jeronijmus Cruse, strengthened with 36 strong soldiers and a similar number of burghers, who are to depart to-morrow evening for the kraals of Gounema, with orders to repay with similar measures those retaining our burghers there with violence, and liberate the latter from the barbarians . . . and . . . to take such revenge as will be a memorable warning to them no longer to offend the Netherlanders. . . .*

July 14 (Friday)— *. . . we heard of the frightful massacre committed by Gounema's tribes under the pretence of being anxious to barter sheep to Corporal Dirck van der Heerengraaff, another soldier and two freemen. Not only did they miserably beat them dead, but they also afterwards carried off the Company's effects. . . . We also command you . . . at once to attack the Gounema tribes, and annihilate them root and branch, sparing no male.*

July 24 (Monday)—Unexpected news received from Ensign Cruse. . . . He had found the kraals of the Gounemas, and having killed some, had obtained a large quantity of cattle as booty.[5]

Testimony of Jan Nielse, cont.

But let me not omit anything in this account, not yet. I followed Kees in a wide arc along the lagoon to the Company's Post. We crossed beaches and waded through reed swamps. Water birds rose in clouds at out approach, scattering as Kees cracked his whip to keep his small flock of sheep on the move. Pink storks glided in a rosy cloud over the water at our approach. I forget, are they a sign of good luck or of ill? Does it matter now?

The outpost lay quiet, shrouded in mist and smoke. A smell of stewing fish reached my nostrils, and saliva ran down my beard. Nostalgia seized me for home, for my farmhouse, thatched too and tiny at the lee of the water. For the storks nested in the church, for my mother. What kind of sentimentality was this from a dog? I watched Kees encamp in the shade of some stunted trees, then I scuttled up the mountain slopes, ascending the rock wall on all fours, until I found a cave. Its floor was strewn with bones, and the owner announced himself shortly, when a porcupine rattled in, then turned to race out, down the slope.

From my vantage point I could see the Hottentots making a kraal of bushes on the flats below, and I watched Kees walk to the outpost. The corporal came out of the lodge:

"Hey man," he called. "Come in and smoke a pipe!"

Clearly Kees was here to trade, and clearly these men were on familiar terms. I closed my eyes, and imagined the mouthful of arrack burning my throat, and the hot pleasure as the smoke slammed deep into my chest. I wanted to sit with the men, to sing a shanty. I wanted to lie about the black women I had seen in the Sera Leones. I wanted my own kind; I hated my own kind. I wanted to talk, I wanted to sleep. What did it matter what I wanted? Voices drifted up to me in the rising north wind. Curled in the cave, sucking my thumb, I fell asleep.

The day rose gray and wet. A cold wind funneled up the bay, splattering the ground in spiteful drops. The grass lay flattened under its heavy burden of rain. Salt wind tasted fresh on my tongue. Kees's camp was silent; a few melancholy sheep cropped the bushes. I waited for the sun, knowing that when it broke through, a rock rabbit, what the Nether-landers call "dassie," would warm itself in the open. The wind suddenly veered, the sun broke through, and, as if by virtue of my will, a dassie appeared outside my cave. Squirming on my belly, I wriggled closer. The creature turned its small furry face, nose twitching, toward my sound. I stayed absolutely still, exactly as I had watched the Hottentots do so many times. I crept forward again, then stretched, reached hard, and grabbed the beast. It writhed frantically in my fist, squealing in terror. I paid no heed until its companions, responding to the cries, appeared. Then, fast and hot, I shoved the Judas goat into my waistband, sprang, stamped, and snatched, until I had my feast ready and waiting.

Shuddering with anticipation, I bit into the first throat, sucking the sweet blood, tears of pleasure mingling with the snot that ran freely into my beard.

I drank, I licked, I reveled.

A shriek broke the air. Below, at the post, figures raced and fell on the sand.

Screams sliced the wind.

Down on the beach, running figures. Dutchmen raced from their pursuers. Kees and his brother, kierries aloft in one hand, spears in the other, loped in pursuit.

"God preserve us!" screamed one.

"Make loose!" cried another.

Two Dutchmen broke and ran for the water, heading for a small boat bobbing offshore. Its occupant waved frantically to hurry up. One turned for an instant, and cried, "Dirk, Dirkie," the other flailed toward the boat. Kees stabbed a huddled form, again and again, then raised his head and shouted to the boat, a curse on the soldiers and the Company.

The wind picked up, the mist returned, and a shower splattered through the sun.

The escapees hauled themselves over the side of the boat, then turned and made for the open sea. The Hottentoos ran into the lodge, and out the other end, shrieking as they went. They scrabbled through the shelters at the corners of the redoubt. They spread a large blanket on the sand and filled it with plunder. They tipped stone flasks to their mouths and drank deeply. Clouds of smoke billowed from the post. Flames crackled. The sun sank, the day faded. I heard their laughter over the fire, but presently it too ended. At dawn the post lay silent, smouldering in the mist.

Kees and his people were gone.

When the sun was high, I picked my way down the slope and walked into the post. The roofs still smoked. A saddle lay against the outer wall of the back room. Broken bottles and jars littered the place. A mess of boiled fish, tipped from the kettle, lay pooled in the sand. Near the water's edge were two bodies, face down in the sand, flies gathering where the kierries had struck. I ignored them and wandered into the post. The corporal and a soldier lay sprawled on the ground. Broken glass lay scattered on the paved floors, and flies buzzed madly on the midden against the sea wall. A scorpion sunned itself on a rock. Gulls picked over a sack of rice scattered on the sand.

The stench of death and of blood rose to my nostrils, caked as they were with my last meal. I, former soldier of the Company, of Stockholm, Sweden, latterly advisor to the King Gonnema, Doppelgänger to one Kees, and Watcher at the Massacre, I, Jan Nielse, stood dully on the beach as a sullen sun disappeared behind the gathering clouds. The months rushed together, ships' biscuits, fires in the hot wind, the plucking of the *ghorra* on the night air, the dark hut, Dirk, Dirkie? I turned slowly, and trudged away, back along the beach wondering if I would ever turn north again. Gonnema had thrown me out, and the land was cold and remote. In the distance, snow gleamed on the high mountains, promising a more bitter winter than I imagined here. The water birds were silent, only my heavy tread marked the passing of time as I lowered my head and walked away from the Company post.

The soldiers found me two days later.

Signed at the Fort of Good Hope this day, Thursday, July 27, in the Year 1673. Jan Nielse.

Chronicle of the Year 1673, cont.

August 11 (Friday)—Court of Justice held to try various delinquents, among then the soldiers who had lately deserted. . . . One of the deserters, named Jan Nielse, of Stockholm, who had already during the voyage hither on the Hellevoet- sluys *attempted to commit various thefts on board that vessel, with the intention of escaping on his arrival at the Cape, and on his arrival here had persuaded five soldiers to desert with him, one of whom is still missing, was sentenced to be hanged, and his comrades to be scourged and to view the execution with nooses round their necks. It is a melancholy thing that such rigorous punishments have to* be applied here, and that people are not deterred from crime by examples meted out to others.

August 12 (Saturday)—At the usual hour the sentences were carried out with good order. A northerly breeze afforded a pleasant day's weather for it.

August 20 (Sunday)—After service, two of the Hottentoo captains who had been summoned by us, viz.: Cuijper and Schacher, arrived with a large company, bringing with them as prisoners four of the Chief Gounema's tribe, whom they had discovered and attacked near their kraals. They mentioned that from the moment of their capture the prisoners were, after their manner, doomed men, and might at once have been killed, but in order to show their good feelings toward the Company, . . . They had accordingly spared the lives of the four prisoners in order to deliver them for trial to us, and after that to proceed in the presence of everyone to follow their custom.

Thereupon the prisoners were examined by the Governor in the presence of some members of the Council, regarding the massacre of our burghers and the Company's servants. Two of them were by confrontations proved to have immediately murdered one of the freemen and one of the soldiers, whilst the other two had been participators in this nefarious work. They were accordingly delivered to the Hottentoo Chiefs Cuijper and Schacher, with their confession, in order to treat them as their own prisoners in their usual manner, as they deemed fit. Hardly had this permission been uttered when all the Hottentoos, to the number of more than one hundred, collected together and . . . began to shriek out, "Kill the dogs! kill them!" . . . At the same time every one provided himself with a heavy club, and awaited the delivery of the condemned with impatience, who being at last brought outside the gate and delivered to them, were welcomed and greeted in such a manner with sticks, that the one after the other fell to the ground and slipped the ghost. After they had sufficiently cooled their courage by beating and treading on the dead bodies, the latter were buried in the sea.

This tragedy having been ended, and the sun in the meanwhile having set, a dram of arrack and some tobacco was given to the Hottentoos who had helped in carrying out this scene, and all were dismissed.[6]

Gonnema's Discourse on the Savage, ca. 1674

(Gonnema, Gounema, a.k.a. Goenjeman: Custom demands that I describe him in terms of his color, scent, shape, clothes, weapons, his sheep and cattle, his ox, and the way he dips his head to the brother of his dead mother. This I reject, for nowhere is it mandatory to describe the ethnographer. One thing only I do concede, and that is that he sits with knees apart, a copper staff of office between his legs. Smeared with ash and fat, a little sweaty from the heat of the day and the effort of recall, Gonnema renders the Dutch.)

Their land: They come from beyond the mountains they call Hottentots Holland. They speak of Holland as a land of cows and water, and of their master, Jan Compagnie, who sends commands on skins, with marks that speak as words. They travel in ships, great creaking pots that heave and buck, where the men catch the winds in cloth and rope, hauling, spitting, cursing, heaving the beast this way and that. We have not gone aboard a ship since some of our men were taken away against their will, but the man Jan, who lived with us these last moons, Jan says that within the ship the stench is great, especially below, in the dark belly where men sleep in hanging bags and piss and shit in the corner. He drew a picture of this ship in the sand. Men hang like grubs in a cocoon, bloody wastes spurting through the net. When these sick men die, they are thrown into the sea, weighted with a rock, but often the cocoon remains behind, carrying with it the body wastes of the dead man. They do not burn it, but leave it for the next man. No wonder the spirits of their dead never rest.

Their stock: They trade for profit alone. We act as middlemen, robbing our kinsmen for their profit. True, we hate our kinsmen, but what is that to the savage? They want cattle but they will settle for sheep. They fatten the beasts, then kill them as the ships appear in sight. They want land and grass, space, and beach. They do not share: their kraals are barricaded day and night, our pastures they call theirs, are fenced with thorns.

Their families: They have no women to speak of, and such as do come off the boats, die soon thereafter. I have to tell the tale of Gomma. He worked in the house of a Dutch woman and saw strange things. Her feet, white and swollen in the water every night, her hair, straight and long, like the tail of a mole that swims the stream. Her breasts pocked with sweat, swaddled in the cloths that bound her close, day or night, hot or cold. She squatted in the yard behind a fence. He went to see what she had left, and seeing him, she shrieked. The men whipped him till his back ran blood. We think they worship body wastes. They have no herbs and know no poultices. They stink of the meat and also of the skins they wear. Greens they stuff into their jaws. They fuck like worms, or so our women say. Lying above or alongside, they tear and thrust, because they do not know that taken from behind, a woman can be moved so that the man controls each moment at will. In sexual heat they pant and shout and snot runs down their face. It drips upon the woman, pinned as she must be below. She cannot move or turn, serving only as a poultice for their sneeze. They have no gods.

Clothing: Their skin is pasty and covered with sores. Consequently they cover it from view with cloths. The men wear breechclouts with leggings, but the women wear long aprons front and back, that drag in the dust and prevent their running away should their men approach. They do not use fat and herbs upon their skin, or in their hair, and consequently they stink. For this reason, our people sense their approach from a distance, and would run away, were it not for the arrack and tobacco.

Weapons: They have no spears or bows. Their fire sticks are large and powerful. They explode, slamming the shoulder, they smoke, and they kill. They will not trade them to us, because they fear that with our numbers, we would kill them all. We have managed to obtain some muskets from them, but the price is very high, and the powder is hard to find. One thing we know, however, is this: unless the powder is dry, the gun will not fire. So on rainy days, they cannot fight, and we have learned to fight them then, when their guns cannot fire. They have knives that cut and skin with great ease, but these we have to steal, because they guard them closely and will not trade even an ox for a knife.

War. Their wars are not like ours. We face each other with spears, we slice into a man's belly and sometimes, we use their women after blood has run. The savages live behind a stone fastness at the Cape and we have seldom been able to draw them out. Jan Sweed advised us on this matter when he and his men lived at our kraal. He explained tactics of diversion, of harassing the flanks of the enemy to keep them off balance. These I understood, and planned to use. We were outflanking the Dutch at the Berg River, taunting their hunters to draw the men out of their fort, when Kees slaughtered the men at the post. Kees's act drew too great a retribution. I knew that we had lost everything, all chance of a surprise move. We fled to save our lives, but we lost many cows, many sheep, and many men, all dead and gone.

Justice: They drink arrack and they shout. They fight with knives. Once I saw two men call upon a third to strap their left hands together tight, with the inner wrists facing. Then they made to kill each other, each with a knife in his right hand. The first slash opened the face of one so that his nose hung down, and the bone gleamed. Spewing blood, he cut the throat of the other with an underhand sweep. Another time we watched them spread a man upon the ground, tying each limb to a thong attached to one of four horses. They whipped the beasts, and goaded them, pricking them with knives. One horse reared, and then the others shrieked and bolted, all four in a different direction. The bound man stiffened for an instant as the thongs drew tight, then he screamed high and loud, as his limbs were torn apart. My brother once squatted near such a man, to hear the first limb crack its joint and rip loose. All this is not a simple as it sounds. The horses are not oxen. They have to learn to run all at once or else the man is dragged not torn. His shoulders pop first, then the hips. The dust hides the blood. The head is placed on a pole, so that flies burrow in the eyes. We saw a man tied to a cross, his back wet and bloody. People watched. The whipper bent over, panting as if he had run a race. Arms on his knees, head hung, he turned and smiled.

The Commander pressed coins into his hands.

When I saw that whipper's smile I understood that these men, living for the most part without their women, enjoy watching pain. This is not to say that I do not: well I know the way my heart races seeing a spear enter the belly of a felon, feeling the beat transfer into my groin as the spear is twisted to expose his guts. And the excitement watching the victim clutch his ropy organs that fall against his buckling legs.

And knowing this of them, I realized I could now deflect the force of their retribution. After an incident with their hunters, and after Kees killed their men at the post, and after the Dutch stole our cattle, it became clear that there would be no parley, I sent four men to our secret allies Dackkgy, known as Cuijper, and Osingkhimma, called Schacher, for sacrifice at the fort. We told the Hollanders that these four were guilty of the murder, and liable now for whatever vengeance these savages, our masters, might care to exact. The Commander said the Hottentots are as nothing. They do not work, they run away. They are all as one, one as all. I do not understand what this talk means, but I knew that if we did not give them men, their raids and killing would never end. At any event, I sent the four as prisoners to the Master of the fort. Stunned animals they were, sent lowing into the stockade. The whites of their rolled eyes looked like the full moon when the hare lopes in the night. They fixed their gaze upward, waiting for the slash at their throat. Fearful lest they lose courage and deny their guilt, or that one of their kin renege on his part of the bargain, we tore the men to pieces ourselves. We gouged their faces, stamped their bellies to a pulp. There is nothing in this to surprise the Hollanders; they see it every day. But without so much noise. We are masters of the chant. We chanted, choking on the dust. Of course, the scraps could not be mounted on a pole. We left them in the dust and the Dutchmen threw them into the sea later. Soldiers rewarded our men with arrack and with a handful of beads.

I think our chants enchant the Hollanders. They watch and they shake their heads, and once they asked why we stamp and what are the words that we repeat with such intensity? That day we had sung the praises of the men we were stamping, and the names of their sons who would be ours to cherish from now on. But we told the Hollanders we chanted "Kill them; kill the dogs!" The fools who cannot speak our language, these fools smiled. But after all, what do they care about our ways? The curers, the travel of the soul propelled by rhythms, such things are not within the mind of barbarians. They drink, they chew tobacco, and when they smoke our *dagga*, they either sleep or kill. They cannot float free, nor travel. Such is their shallowness; what more can I say?[7]

Chronicle of the Year 1676

October 27 (Tuesday)— . . . these hostile Goenema Hottentoos . . . cannot, in spite of all practicable measures attempted, be brought in a friendly manner to a condition of rest and peace with us, so necessary for the cattle trade, and through too long a forbearance toward that unworthy brood, without gaining anything, the illustrious reputation of the Company and respect for it are in the meanwhile only made to suffer . . . in consequence . . . it was decided for these and other reasons, once more to send an expedition against them. . . .

*November 1 (Sunday)—Memorandum for the Hon. Captain Dirk Jansz.
Smient, Commander of the Company's forces, and Chief of this Expedition . . .
It is unnecessary to mention why you are sent out against our enemies, the Chief
Goenema and his adherents. . . . You shall carefully attend to the following:—*

*In the first place and especially, we urge you to take proper care of our Nether-
landers. . . . call upon the name of God every morning and evening. . . . The
manner of treating the enemy you are well acquainted with; that is endeavouring
more to destroy the males, and excepting the women and children, rather than to
seize a portion of their cattle for our satisfaction. . . . you will act together as brave
men, and courageously endeavour to avenge the blood of our murdered countrymen.
You have been abundantly supplied with provisions and ammunition, and we now
wish you all a happy and successful journey. (Signed) Your good friend, Joan Bax,
Named Van Herenthals. In the Fort the Good Hope, the 1st of November, 1676.*[8]

Journal Kept by the Expedition to the Rebellious Gounema Africans

*November 11 . . . as there seemed no chance of overtaking the enemy, we consid-
ered in Council that Captain Kees, also an adherent of Gounema, and guilty of
the murders committed on our countrymen, was at present encamped at Saldanha
Bay with his people, and . . . that Lieutenant Cruse with 24 men should be
despatched thither in order (if possible) to surprise him.*

*November 15 . . . all had turned out fruitless; nor could any one point out any
other way to reach the enemy, and hence it was unanimously decided . . . not to
waste any further time in searching for the enemy, but to march back to the Cape
as quickly as possible.*

*November 19 God be praised for all His mercy. [Signed]
DIRCQ JANSZ: SMIENT, J. CRUSE, and HERMAN GRISNIGT.*[9]

Chronicle of an Expedition of the Governor Simon van der Stel to the Land of the Hottentots, 1685

Anno 1685, on Saturday, August 25th, in the morning at 10 o'clock, in
the name of the Lord, Amen, we marched out of Fort Good Hope to
the Copper Mountains, with our baggage, our strength being 57 white
men, and one prince of Macassar, with his servant, and also three black

servants of the Honorable Commander. In addition, one carriage with six horses, eight asses, fourteen riding horses, two field pieces, eight carts, seven wagons, one loaded with a boat, two hundred and eighty-nine draught or pack oxen, and, to take us to the Elephant's River, six burghers with their own wagons, each yoked with eight oxen.

We traveled onward through the country and came to a valley which the Honorable Commander named St. Martin's Valley, walled on both sides by high mountains. An elephant came toward us and the Honorable Commander ordered the trumpet blown and the drum beaten. We named the place Elephant's Valley. Then we traveled to a small mountain called Uijlenbergh because of the many owls there.

Approaching the Hottentot kraals, the Honorable Commander issued an order that none of our people should have carnal intercourse with the Hottentot nation under penalty of being whipped and expelled from the Honorable Company as a rogue. Our reception by the natives varied from one place to another. Some declared that they would attack us whenever we entered their country and take all our cattle. Others departed as soon as our arrival was heralded, either from fear lest their cattle should be taken from them as a punishment for having risen in rebellion against their chief and taken his cattle from him, or because they were unwilling to barter at all. Still others celebrated. We came upon them slaughtering a sheep. They split it and drew the entrails out while it still lived. They ripped off the skin, cracked the ribs, and saved the blood for boiling: nothing wasted but the dung. We saw hunters, thin and frail owing to a great hunger. They eat only bulbs, tortoises, caterpillars, and locusts, which are found here in great numbers. The Honorable Commander made them a present of some brandy, with which they made merry, dancing, singing, and shouting. It was undoubtedly, as they themselves confessed, the first joyful day they had had in all their lives.

We came upon the kraal of Captain Nonce of the Amacquas. He rode a pack-ox and another ox carried his baggage. He offered to trade with sheep but would not barter fairly with his cattle. His son, Joncker, tried to deceive us by showing us the wrong route through the land. The Honorable Commander grew angry. He arrested Joncker and another as well, one Rabi. Now Captain Nonce determined to barter fairly. Five more captains appeared including one Oedesson, who stroked the Honorable Commander on his body repeatedly, pointing again and again to his own heart to indicate the kindness he felt there. The two malcontents recanted now. Joncker was notified that he was not to bear the name of

Fig. 21. Camp of the Hon. Commander Simon van der Stel, in the Copper Mountains, 1685 (Van der Stel 1979, 139–41, Cape Archives Depot, M121)

Captain any more, but would be an ordinary soldier. Rabi presented the Honorable Commander with a cow in gratitude for the withholding of his beating. Then we negotiated with the Amacquas to live in peace to cease from war with each other, to assist them if needed in times of conflict, and to come in freedom and liberty to the Cape of Good Hope to deal with the Honorable Company.

Captain Oedesson offered to guide us to the Copper Mountains.

On the Honorable Commander's birthday, Sunday the 14th of October, the Amacquas gave him a musical entertainment. They stood in a ring, about twenty altogether, dancing, with one hand to their ear and the other firmly holding the reed to their lips. Outside the ring, men and women danced and clapped their hands. All this passing off very decently, considering that they are savages.

Onward, we reached the Copper Mountains. Here we cleared the stones, we laid the charges, we smelted the ore and packed it up to be assayed at the Cape. Then we turned for home. We passed our old camping places, such as one called Touse by the Amacquas Hottentots and Sant River by us. Now, suddenly, the Amacquas captains who were our guides, especially Captain Oedesson, and one Nonce, changed. They would not show us the way. They said that talking made their heads ache, and they remained stayed silent all evening. We made prisoners of them, but still they would not speak. Struggling to find a route without their guidance, the Company men became bewildered and lost, coming at last upon some Hottentots who berated Oedesson for antagonizing the Dutch. These said that if the Honorable Commander did not punish him, they would kill Oedesson themselves, according to his deserts. The Honorable Commander issued a severe reprimand to Oedesson. He watched as Otwa, a loyal Hottentot chief flogged Nonce on his naked body with a stick. But this did not move Oedesson. He threatened to break the necks of the Hollanders and for this, he and the loyal Otwa fought with sticks.

After many days we captured a Sonqua man who told us that the river we had reached was called Touse. This is the same one that we crossed on leaving the Copper Mountains. They said it received its name from buffaloes that were found there which they call Touse. Its proper name will now be Buffels River.

In the morning we traveled on. Now Goenjemans Hottentots approached our party. Their heads were shaved as a sign of mourning. They told the Honorable Commander that old Goenjeman (Gonnema) had died. They asked that his son be appointed chief now. When this was done, they thanked the Honorable Commander.

On Saturday December 26th at noon, the Honorable Commander arrived at the Castle of Good Hope. All of us were in the same condition as when we left on our journey, for which, may God Almighty receive the highest praise. We pray that henceforth blessing and loving kindness may be extended over us and everything from now to Eternity. Amen.

These then are the Namacquas nation: They belong to the Hottentot race and have no fixed abode. According to the season of the year, they go into the mountains and then back to the valleys and the shore, wherever they find the best pasture. The men wear an iron plate on their foreheads. They know how to make these plates and they polish them so smoothly that they shine in the sun. They wear skins, before their pudenda they wear an ivory plate and beads, made cleverly from gum, threaded artistically with copper beads. In their hand they carry the tail of a wildcat stretched on a stick, with which they wipe their faces and particularly their eyes. Their weapons consist of poisoned arrows and assegais. Whoever has the most cattle is held in greatest esteem. Mendacious and deceitful, they eat everything that comes their way down to rats, dogs, cats, caterpillars, locusts, but will never eat of the hare. They drink milk and smear their bodies with butter. They are of a cheerful disposition, and lend their wives freely to one another. The less jealous the husbands, the more lascivious are the women. They seem to fear nothing but thunder and lightning.[10]

The Discourse of One Oedesson, an Amacquas Hottentot, on the Expedition of Van der Stel, Anno Domini 1685, Dated October 1686

After his death, the death, that is, of Chief Gonnema, I, Oedesson, assumed some part of power here. Their wheels cut into our land, leaving lines that stretched to the sky. Each party scrutinized the tracks to follow the path of the previous one. In the cold time, word came to us that yet another expedition was on its way to the Copper Mountains, and that the wagons had already rolled past the sacred stones, along the rivers, slaughtering the elephants for their tusks. Horses, wheeled carts, pack-oxen, and false Men of Men driving with whips, smiling at the masters and then at us. They carried sacks of goods. Beads, pipes, black tobacco, rings, bells, and the fire drink they call "arrack."

They needed our help to find the way, and they needed our meat to live. They said nothing at first of women, though we knew this too would come. Mostly we thought of the arrack and the tobacco, of the heat and lull that follows them, of the dancing and merriment. That arrack erases mind and time, burns out the memory of things past, and empties limbs and mind.

Our women were restless at their coming. Some decorated their bodies with paint, drawing stripes of ash around their eyes to make them shine and stare, as though amazed at what they saw. They hung beads around their necks, on wound them around their arms, and their bellies. They fastened rattles on their legs. The young girls giggled and covered their faces; being unaware of sexual acts as yet, they contemplated what gifts might come their way. Women are as cattle: they can be used to strike a bargain, or in exchanges.

When the wagons came the Dutchmen passed out the gifts, the largest to the chief, and smaller ones thereafter down the line. Some stared at the women, and one drew stealthily aside, and with gestures and words asked boldly for their favors. The chief nodded, then pointed to my youngest daughter.

She was a shy and foolish child, who until then, had shown no blood, nor had she known a man. But she had sweetness in her gaze, and I was fond of her. The man who asked for her was red. His thick legs encased in hide, a knife dangled at his waist. His mouth was loose; he was a man who dribbled. I watched, for it was not my role to deny, watched as the two were led into a hut, then I turned away and walked some distance from the kraal. It was only later, when her shriek rent the air that I leaped up and ran. In the dark hut, sun speckling through the mats, she lay, legs sprawled apart. Blood gushed between her legs. The man was gone. He was nowhere to be seen. The caravan was moving on it seemed. I could not reach her, because the women were there, but it was clear to me that he had used his knife to gain a swifter entry. I bellowed, but the others held me back. I struggled; they beat my head with sticks. I fell. Toward evening the child grew quiet. Her wound was packed with grass and with a poultice of herbs, but still the blood trickled to the dust in which she lay. On the second day she grew hot, her lips split and bled, her eyes grew dull. On the third [day] we buried her beneath a cairn of rocks and moved on. I do not recall the journey to our new place.

I knew I had to kill the man. But the chief forbade this: it would bring death to us as it had to Gonnema's people before us. I demanded that they take me along as a guide. I had seen the way their wagons took the land, the way our people could neither hunt nor gather herbs and roots. My kinsman, Nonce, came too. We led them to the mines, then turned and led them astray. A false man (his mother be accursed) beat Nonce. I fought him later, but did not kill him then for I was still trying to lead them into a trap. But they were cunning, and after they had reprimanded us, Nonce and I, they led us out behind a rise and beat us with the ends of their fire sticks. When I regained my senses, I heard the buzz of flies at Nonce's mouth. I piled his body with stones to keep it from hyenas.

I have vowed to wipe the seed of these false men from the earth. It will take long, but we have the time. The white men know nothing of these things; they need know nothing, because they hold the power in their flasks of arrack, and in the knives and guns they carry.[11]

Diary of the Landdrost Johannes Starrenburg Kept during His Journey to the Gonnemaas, Grigriquaas, Namacqua Hottentots, etc. (1705)

Tuesday, October 20: In the afternoon we were informed, that the Gonnema Hottentots . . . had no desire to deal with us, and therefore were gone over the mountains . . . to avoid us; but that one captain, by name Bootsman, *lay with his kraal across the 24 Rivers, whither we made our way, reaching there at sunset. As soon as we had pitched our tent, we greeted this Chief with a dram and a good tabeetje (gift) in the name of the Hon. Company, and told him that we were sent to barter with him in all amity for some work-cattle for the Company. . . . We gave him one or two drams, but to no avail, his reply being that we must first go to the other Gonnemas, and that from what happened there he would know what he ought to do.*

While he had yet another drink I went to look at the cattle . . . which was a lovely herd, except that he had sent all his best oxen away on hearing of our coming.

Wednesday, October 21: [Bootsman] *went from the tent to the kraal, coming soon after with 3 oxen. I continued in the same manner, telling him, that he was mad to imagine that I was come so far with so many men and waggons to barter 3 beasts, and that he could go back to his kraal and I would strike camp and go forward. Finally I got 9 fine oxen and seven wethers, for which I gave 10 bunches of copper beads, 13 pounds of tobacco, some glass beads, and some brandy.*

Monday, October 26: . . . we reached Hannibal's *kraal, where 6 captains were come together, making in all 23 huts.*

They let us see their cattle, which were few in number, and for the most part cows. I asked them how it happened that they had so little cattle, seeing that the Hon. Company had never bartered with them, whereat they informed me: that a certain Freeman, generally called Dronke Gerrit, *was come to their kraal a few years previously, accompanied by some others, and without any parley fired on it from all sides, chased out the Hottentots, set fire to their huts, and took away all their cattle, without their knowing for what reason, since they had never harmed any of the Dutch. By this they lost everything they had, and were compelled to betake themselves to the Dutch living further out, and there steal cattle again, and, if they could get anything, rob their own compatriots; . . . And in addition they are also plagued by raids from a Nation of Hottentots living in the almost impassable mountains beyond the Olifants River. . . . These vex them continually, and they are seldom able to have revenge on them. . . .*

Thus they are compelled to be sparing of what few cattle they still own, and to get food and meat for their wives and children must daily fight against the elephants, and thus seek their sustenance in this way with the uttermost danger of their lives. . . .

And truly I have found in the character, conduct and actions of these folk far more real good-heartedness than among other Hottentots.

Friday, October 30 . . . the Hottentots lying around here have fallen . . . into the most extreme poverty, and are compelled to resort to elephant-hunting, and by this kill or drive away the animals.

Wednesday, November 4: . . . I have realized with regret how the whole country has been spoilt by the recent freedom of bartering, and the atrocities committed by the vagabonds, since when the cattle of one kraal is carried off by the Dutch, they in turn go to rob others, and these again rob their neighbours. . . . so from men who sustained themselves quietly by cattle breeding, living in peace and content-ment, divided under their chiefs and kraals, they have nearly all become Bushmen, hunters and brigands, dispersed everywhere between and in the mountains.[12]

A Child's Chronicle of the Year 1950

The northern road goes to the land of the Little Namaqua, where the Khoikhoi live. Mountains stand dark in the shadow of the setting sun, but on their sunny flanks, great carpets of orange daisies turn heliotropic heads toward the light. Dusk falls suddenly in winter: a dog howls, a woman trudges up the road that leads between the Baas's farm and the worker's huts. The farmer's washing is bundled on her head. Her children wait at home with granny, but her man will go on cleaning out the shed long after dark. They own nothing, no house, no land, only perhaps the clothes upon their backs, and that by kindness of the Baas's wife who passes the family's worn-out goods down the line. Their shack belongs to the Boer, even the patch of pumpkins at the back is his, though he has never asked for one yet.

The world is too big, the stars are too close. Smoke drifts white against the moon. At sunrise, the Namaquas huddle in the pale sun, capturing its rising warmth against their corrugated iron shacks. Gap toothed doors patch the wall with black. A goat bleats on the stony hill, two dogs sprawl and scratch in the yard. There are no matted huts, no oxen, no herds. Place-names have changed too, and everything is something-fontein, and whatever-berg. Wire fences run across the hills and along the tracks, declaring the boundaries of ownership. But crickets still shrill, a hawk still wheels above, and beetles click across the black, polished pebbles that litter the veld.

I was a child when first I came to see these Poisoned Mountains. My father had heard about rock paintings in the Gifberg, and at dusk Meneer van Niekerk, owner of the farm, Snorkfontein, drove us there. We sat in the front of the truck while a Colored woman and her child rode in the back to show the us the path to the cave. We reached the cliffs and gazed

at the faded images, then set about making dinner. The woman gathered
wood. The farmer put chops, sausages, and bread on a makeshift table.
We gathered round, hungry and cold. Faint rustles betrayed the woman
and her child, squatting against the rocks. She would not eat with us,
neither could she and the child draw closer to the fire. I gathered up a
handful of walnuts and almonds, and stealing away, I pressed the food
into their small hands. Reentering the light, I laughed, pretending to be
wandering about for no reason at all. "Look at me," I said. "I'm a Bushman." The adults laughed indulgently. Shivering, I turned to the fire. Its
flames felt cold.[13]

I have tried to show both sides, invader and native, to let each explain
what they were after, as well as letting each reveal the world they thought
they knew. These mimic the written discourses of the day, but lacking
such records of the Khoikhoi, I flounder in their world.

How to resolve this?

Try this: A woman of the Namaqua people. One woman. Small, her
fine skin crinkled round the eyes, buttocks swaying above slim legs. Five
children have grown in her belly and kicked beneath her heart. Five
struggled out, awash in blood and water, as she crouched, head bowed,
behind a hut. One lay blue and lifeless on the ground even as the fluids
pulsed between her legs. Others cried, twisted, and fed at her breast, two
to die in their first year, mewling as birds cry when their necks are
wrongly wrung. One child, robust and cocky, walked at an early age,
running on plump legs to grab at her legs, mount and nurse at will. He
was born bold into this world. He carried a switch to crack against the
trees in imitation of his father's oxhide whip. Curious and solemn too at
times, he would inspect a flower, pulling the petals apart to reveal the
core within, and then dusting his face with the pollen that puffed out
from the stamens.

He senses something sliding on the stones, whips round, and sees a
flash as the snake lashes against his leg. Shrieking, he runs, stumbling in
fear and pain. She rocks him, staring at his leg, her face aflame, and
prickling with anticipated loss, for what grown man, let alone a child,
could survive? She suckles at the punctures, cupping his small head as he
suckles simultaneous at her breast. Shrieks turn to whimpers. His leg is
tight and swollen, and disembodied by its fever and its size, the child's
eyes start to droop. Women crowd around. They make a shade around
the child, shaking their heads like trees in a wind, as the child begins to

shake. She stares ahead, thinking this is but a dream, hoping for the dawn. Dusk falls instead. The air grows cool, and the child, too, grows cold. In the dark she thinks how he would leap into her arms.

(Demographers should note that she had one child left, and indeed, that was her replacement to keep the population stable at its set pace, not one more and not one less. Figures of stability are of no account to her, of course, nor is their message of inevitability of any interest, whatsoever.)

Now this, A European woman at the Cape. Her face and hands are mottled white and puce, blue traceries cover knuckles, bruised from work. Her face is scarred and pitted from the childhood pox contracted in Haarlem when she was six. The farm was cold and wet, the pigs fed all day long on slops thrown out in the mud behind the back wall. At night, the wind roared across the flats, frosting leaves and icing up the ponds and the canals. Here, at the Cape, there is no ice, but the wind howls even louder, and spiteful knives of rain lash in its wake. She came out here to marry a man she never knew, but he died even before her ship stood anchored in the bay. Three weeks now she has waited to hear who will take her in his stead, fearful in her loneliness, yet even more afraid of who it might be. She works in the kitchen of a Cape family, alongside the slave woman who pads, barefoot, on the cold stone floors. She boils cabbage and carrots with mutton fat, skimming the gray foam along the side. She takes a handful of gray rice, wets it, and leaves it to soak in an earthen bowl, for it is said to cook better after it has absorbed some water. She bends to wipe the kitchen floor, and through the gap at the bottom of the door, she hears the wind. She doubles over, eyes screwed shut, wishing only that this were the gale across the fields, whipping around the muddy ice in the pigpen.

(Demographers will note again, that she will marry and will breed. She will die with the second child, her womb foul and swollen from the midwife's filthy hand, that reached in deep to pull the dead child out. But since she is replaced by one, things are stable, are they not?)

In Cape Town, at sunset, the huge mountain loses its detail and becomes a black monolith. Sodium flares light the city at its foot, smaller lights twinkle up the slope. The castle squats where waves once broke. Now a railway station blocks its view of the bay. On the mountain slope, a large tract of prime city land lies bare and empty. This was District Six, the old slave enclave, that bustled with Muslim traders, Colored shopkeepers, and curious tourists. It was bulldozed into oblivion thirty years ago, by a repressive power bent on the ethnic cleansing of their Mother City. People who might have lived there, now jostle at the castle walls, waiting for the gypsy cabs to take them home to their enforced exile out on the Cape Flats. Across the bay, oil refineries spurt fire into the sky. The beach glows pale, its polluted sand strewn with globs of oil, old plastic shoes, and styrofoam cups. Among the refuse, fragments of porcelain washed from the hold of a sunken East Indiaman gleam in the reflected light.

6

Chronicle of a Hamlet

"Khoikhoi? What do you mean, Khoikhoi? Hell man, there's no Hottentots here, you have to go way up there to Namaqualand to see Hottentots. There's a couple of Coloreds here, in those houses on the edge of the kraal, see? But *magtig,* there's no Hotnots here!"

Marta shrugs and turns back into the house. It stands on the very edge of the road leading to Churchhaven. Its thick walls are whitewashed and lumpy. In front, salt marsh runs from the road to the lagoon. Flamingos clump rosily at the water's edge. Egyptian ibis pick their way through the reeds, plucking with curved black beaks at frogs and newts. A pheasant flaps along the muddy verge, and stops. Suddenly he corkscrews, then straightens, like a general, surveying the field. On the stoop wall, a large ginger tomcat watches impassively. Markings endow his face with intense seriousness. He yawns, stretches, and lopes up the dune, into the dense bushes behind the house.

Inside, the house is dark. Doors and woodwork are painted dark green. A tired sofa, with faded brown velvet cushions, faces a low table. Another table and chairs line the opposite wall. Two plastic ladies, adorned from crown to foot in feathers, flank a mirrored bureau. Its top is cluttered with beer mugs, papers, a yellowed nautilus shell, and a tarnished silver trophy. One wall is hung with scenes emblazoned on velvet: Table Mountain, a farmstead, a line of camels, all rendered in a violent luminosity that defies nature. A film star with wavy hair covering one eye smiles seductively from her golden frame. Behind the sofa, hangs a gallery of sepia-tinted relatives. A large portrait has pride of place.

"That's Arthur," says Katrina, pointing to the angelic-looking boy with chrome yellow hair, pink cheeks, and lime green eyes. He has the startled look of one who has been mummified against his will.

151

"Just three days after his twenty-first, he was on the ship sailing for Antarctica. Then, the oil, the cooking oil you know, caught fire, the whole thing exploded." Katrina shakes her head. "Whole blerry ship, just blew up!"

She purses her lips to get the story straight, and continues, holding up four fingers.

"There were four men killed, but three were married with children." She smiles fondly, nodding towards the picture.

"Shame!"

The boy's face glows luminescent in the gloom.

"My baby!"

In 1503 the Portuguese explorer Antonio de Saldanha, rounding the Cape on his way to the East, watered at Table Bay. He climbed the mountain, and, after a dispute with the locals about a cow, took a Khoik-hoi spear in the arm. This bucolically savage incident (if an oxymoron may be permitted), was commemorated by naming the place for him, even though most sailors continued to refer to the bay and its great flat-topped sentinel as the "Cabo de Bonne Esperance." A hundred years later, in 1601, Joris van Spilbergen made it official: although the English continued calling the bay at the Cape of Good Hope "Saldania," where the Dutch were concerned, "Table Bay" lay at the continent's tip, and "Saldanha" referred to its present eponym, that great bay, about 100 kilometers to the north of the Cape of Good Hope, that extended from the Atlantic rollers at its mouth, down into the pouch of a shallow lagoon at its head.[1]

More than a century went by. In 1623, Jón Ólafsson compared the Saldanha Bay to a wide fjord; twenty-five years later, Etienne de Flacourt thought it resembled a great lake. A mere quibble this: perhaps one man spent more time near the mouth, and the other at the head of the lagoon. Clearly though, both men were homesick. But if the scenery evoked nostalgia, such sentimentality never affected Flacourt's reports on the native peoples. He was considerably more impressed with the wildlife than with the resident savages, and the local folk echoed his distaste when the Frenchman offered to take a couple of local boys along with him to smarten them up. As an inducement, he showed the natives two Mada-gascans, who looked very smart indeed in their uniforms and swords. Flacourt's offer was refused. After spending one week there, and presum-

Fig. 22. The natives of "Souldanja" (later "Table") Bay in the early seventeenth century (Herbert 1634:17; Kennedy 1975, H 111C; South African Library, PHA, Table Bay: 1626)

ably speaking no native tongue, De Flacourt described the local people, their color, marriage customs, weapons, beliefs, and testicles.

"Nature's frankest vagabonds," he proclaimed, "[who] never cease from begging."[2]

In 1652 the Dutch East India Company took possession of the Cape as a halfway stop on their voyages to the Indies. Their decision was based on a report by a party of sailors from the *Haarlem,* who were shipwrecked there in 1647. Sixty men built a fort on the beach and stayed for a full year, during which time they noted the fertility of the soil, the abundant water, and the willingness of the local Khoikhoi folk to trade sheep and cattle. The VOC had in mind an isolated supply base, not a full-scale colony. They thought in terms of their headquarters on a spit in the harbor at Deshima in Japan, or perhaps they recalled the splendid isolation that had they created by exterminating the natives of the Banda Islands in order to monopolize the nutmeg trade. Isolation was the keynote of an official assessment by Rykloff van Goens, a former governor of Dutch Ceylon and later grand commissioner of the Dutch East India Company, who recommended that a canal be built across the neck of the peninsula to cut the settlement off from the rest of Africa.[3]

Van Goens was no stranger to Dutch tastes.

"Our men," he once wrote, "cannot be made to avoid drink."[4]

Perhaps he saw sobriety in isolation.

But economic dependence binds far tighter than any device contrived even by God to keep people together, and here at the Cape it engaged Dutchmen and Khoikhoi in an implacable embrace. The Dutch wanted only to operate a factory from which they might trade, but this soon proved unfeasible, and they were forced to take possession of land in order to produce for themselves the food that the Khoikhoi would not trade. For no amount of parlaying or coercion could ensure a steady flow of meat from the Khoikhoi. To the Khoikhoi it seemed that the invaders were insatiable. There were not enough sheep, cows, and oxen in the world to satisfy the demands of Dutch butchers, and even if there were, stock was a Khoikhoi man's capital. They were his token of power, his trump card in that greatest of all games, the stakes to get a wife, to breed, and to multiply. In the end, the colonists and indigenes could not achieve a fair balance. One had to win, the other had to lose. Existentially speaking, the triumph of one meant the eclipse of the other.

Yet despite their misgivings, the Khoikhoi visited the great fort on the beach at Table Bay time and time again (figs. 4, 18). They brought sheep, cows, tusks, skins, and ostrich eggs and traded for beads, trinkets, tobacco, and arrack. The Dutch couldn't get enough meat. They demanded more sheep, more cows. The Khoikhoi demurred. They saw their capital dwindling away, but realized that unless they were willing to impoverish themselves, the Dutch would seize their pastures and raise herds for themselves.

It was an impossible situation. War erupted time and again, and on each occasion the Dutch won more land. European settlement spread north into the sandveld and the dunes of the west coast, up to the head of the lagoon at Geelbek, around the bights of Saldanha Bay, and eventually up deep inland, to the black soils of the Piketberg and the stony wastes of Namaqualand. Guttural growls replaced soft, sharp clicks, and Company men planted the flag and their seed, assuming toponymic hegemony as they renamed every rivulet, waterhole, kopje, and kranz.[5]

But there was more going on here than loss of land and power. There was, shall we say, a certain observable betrayal of phenotypic integrity. Khoikhoi-Dutch breeding was well on the way to producing the so-called mixed-race Colored people of the Cape, to say nothing of its so-called Whites. The old East India Company joke about necessity being the mother of invention and the father of the Eurasian might have rocked the sides of a squalid tavern near the castle, but where the Khoikhoi were concerned, there was something more poignant going on. For them, by and large, there were practically no marriages, no exchanges of goods for breeding rights, nor any acquisitions of significance through casual mating with intruders. Instead, light-skinned children emerged between their women's legs, time and time again, with ginger tufts on their heads, and pallid blue eyes that stared rheumily into the sun.[6]

Many Khoikhoi trekked inland to stay at the kraals of distant kin, but some remained bonded to their lost land, linked every bit as effectively to its pull as they were drawn to the narcotics at the trading posts. Former cattlemen became servants, shepherds, field hands, and builders. They lived in huts within shouting distance of the master's house, holding both hands out for the weekly tot, a mug of wine or spirits, that constituted pay.

Clearly, the Dutch had come to stay, and what was more, they would brook no intruders. So when in 1666 the French under the Marquis de Mondevergue sauntered in to claim Saldanha Bay, their smarmy asides were met with an immediate dispatch of Company men to build a fort at Saldanha, to set up a post to protect their interests, provision passing ships, and trade with the local Khoikhoi people.[7]

Katrina was born more than eighty years ago on a nearby farm. She moved to the cottage on the lagoon, after her first three children were born. Lines crease her small, pointed face, converging all around into a tiny, sunken mouth. Strange black encrustations pepper her cheeks and hairline. She counts her six children off by name. Today only four survive, including her present baby, Marta. They have no visible means of support.

"Isn't it lonely here?"

Marta shakes her head emphatically. "Nee wat skattebol."

She snaps a cigarette from its pack, turns to preen in the mirror. Dull jet-black hair frames a broad smiling face, powdered to a glazed apricot sheen that defies classification.

"No what darling!" she laughs "There's all those policemen in Langebaan, Saldanha . . ."

We are still within an hours' drive of her house.

". . . Hopefield, Darling, Vredenburg . . ."

The distance has grown alarmingly (fig. 7).

"They keep coming over to protect my old Mom here, and end up attacking me!"

Katrina whoops, a lewd screech. Her gums gleam. Marta nods approvingly at her audience, pats her knee, and blows a long stream of smoke to the roof.

The outpost of the Honorable Dutch East India Company was finally built in 1669, on a rocky spur on the western shore of the lagoon (figs. 10, 13). Southward lay the broad sweep of Kraal Bay, powdered with fine, white sand. Soldiers transformed the rocky beach in front of their outpost into a half-moon of sand by removing most of the rocks to build the post itself. They measured out a rectangle and dug narrow foundation trenches in the sand. Above they built a two-roomed lodge, with a low thatched roof. On the rocky spur they set a rough redoubt with thick walls and small paved rooms, thatched for protection against the broiling sun and the winter squalls. The post was manned by a handful of Company men, who hired a few disgruntled Khoikhoi to mind the sheep. Water was scarce, welling up in a reluctant soak behind the lodge, only as long as the men scratched and dug into the sand to keep it clean. Provisions were sent up from the Cape every three months, though passing ships often handed over a flask of arrack, a bowl of rice, and a few pipes.[8]

Dispatches back and forth, to the Cape, detail the quality of daily life: "Clean the fountain, hand over sheep to the ships at the pro-rated amount of one half pound per person per day. Hoe the ground, plant the seeds, give the cabbages to the captain. Harvest the purslain. Give three beads to the Hottentot, and a mug of arrack to his chief. Tell them that you are in charge here. Say he must return. Tell the soldier to go to the abattoir at Groene Kloof, for meat. Insist that he comes back without fail. Take the letters from the ships and send them with the corporal to the castle. Leave immediately. Mend the boat. Cut the reeds. Thatch the house. Please do this immediately. I am displeased with your tardiness. I trust you are well. Do not walk unarmed in the bush. Take all possible care. We are at war with Gonnema, he is our hereditary enemy. The Company is relying on you. You are to come immediately to the Cape. Go back as soon as possible."

The replies: "I have done everything as instructed, but the Hottentot will not return. The fountain is clean. The fountain is dirty. There is no water. When you read what I have written, you will understand that I did no harm. The ships will not pay for the sheep. The boat has a leak. Send gun flints. Send tobacco. The natives want Brazilian tobacco, they will not trade Virginian. Send cloth for flags, send rice. The natives are hostile."[9]

Imagination textures existence a little further. A man calls from the ship that lies at anchor in the bay, his voice carrying over the pale shallows to the beach, where smoke rises from the roof of the lodge, to the sky. The ship creaks: its stench carries to the shore, mingling with the smoke, and with the scent of delicate herbs that grow green and rich on the sandy beach. A shot rings out in the high dunes. The soldier looks up from his fire, salivating as the tortoise broiling on the coals, begins to steam. Two others lean against a rock, smoking, as they toss dice. One whoops, the other frowns. A sheep bleats from the kraal, as the herdsman dozes against the brush wall. Gulls wheel and scream, swooping over the ship to feast upon its offal, then flying back to shore, to strut along the wet sand.

The fountain grew low. In 1732 the post moved to a clear, fresh spring a few kilometers away. Gulls still flocked to the old post, waiting for the men to return. Silence swallowed the spur. The stone walls fell back into the sand. Lizards sunned themselves on the rocks, and scorpions scuttled between the cracks. The fort crumpled into a vague circle and was mistaken for a sheep pen, lending this misnomer to the adjacent Kraal Bay.[10]

Finally, Europe took out time to call in the chips. Holland allied herself with her former foes, France and Spain, against England. In 1781, the British strutted in to this remote but strategically placed Dutch enclave. Warships stood out in the bay, pounding the homebound Indiamen that cowered there for shelter. With each explosion, Commodore George Johnstone, hard and relentless, showed the Dutch what lay in store for the Verenige Oostindische Compagnie. English soldiers marched to the

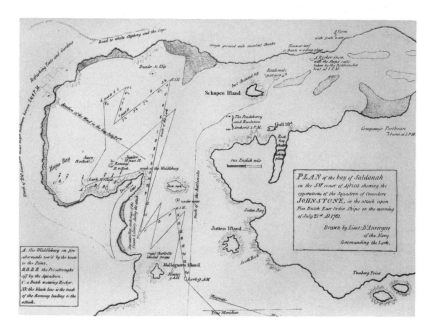

Fig. 23. Map of Saldanha Bay, showing the attack on the Company's ships by Johnstone in 1781. Note the reference to the burning of the Company's posthouse at 1
P.M., in the upper right quadrant. (Cape Archives Depot, M748)

post and found it abandoned and in flames. They marked the discovery
with precision, noting on their map of the engagement: "Company's
Posthouse burnt at 1 P.M." (fig. 23).[11]

By the turn of the century the Company lay in ruins.

"Vergaan Onder Corruptie," said some, as they spelled out the initials
of the VOC, to mean "Collapsed through Corruption."[12]

Company men, living at the Cape, held fast.

"Die Kaap is nog Hollands," they sang. "The Cape stays Dutch."

Farmers watching the eventual loss of the Cape to the British between
1795 and 1814 knew little of the details of the Napoleonic Wars that
convulsed Europe and heralded the first ceding of the Cape to the British
in 1795. Nor of the Treaty of Amiens that gave it back to the newly
formed Batavian Republic in Holland from 1803 to 1806, nor indeed,
of the London Convention of 1814, when the Dutch formally ceded the
Cape back to the Brits. And cared less. But they knew loss of autonomy
when it appeared on their doorstep in the form of British promulgations
about laws and servants and taxes. They also knew about gold and dia-

monds, and they cared greatly for them, especially when these were taken away by outlanders, smart intruders with German accents, Oxford educations, and European connections.

Khaki-clad British soldiers invaded the Transvaal. Perched atop each kopje, ragged-clad Boers watched every move they made. They picked off the rednecks with fearsome skill, firing a single, well-placed, shot, that barely betrayed their position. Then they remounted and retired to the hidden mountain passes, where they bided their time. They brewed coffee and chewed beef jerky, which they called by its Malay name *biltong.* Then they smoked a leisurely pipe. After all, they had all the time in the world.[13]

Some eight years ago, Oom Jakkals, a farmer from across the lagoon, courted Marta. He would drive over at lunchtime. Marta greeted him each time as though it were the first, deep gasps and sighs of gratitude mingling with disbelief as she inspected his offerings of cigarettes, milk, bread, and, on occasion, a cabbage.

"Oom!" she shrilled, "Oomie is too good to us!"

She listened with studied absorption to his troubles on the farm. There were the sheep, the chickens, the workers. The sheep wandered into unsuitable pastures. They coughed, they spat, sometimes they died. Chickens laid furiously, raising hopes of solvency and freedom from the strangling bank bond. Then, suddenly, a mongoose would slither in, and next morning, the night's yield would lie cracked and spoiled in the nest. The bank manager's angry red face would swim into view. Worst of all were the laborers. They grew more distracted as the week went by, waiting for the Friday tot of brandy that now grew to a whole bottle of cheap wine. The weekend passed by in an alcoholic daze.

Oom wrinkled his nose.

"All you ever hear round their huts is fucking and fighting."

Marta patted his arm sympathetically. She wondered how he knew so well what went on in the huts, but she said nothing.

"Sometimes," said Oom Jakkals, "it seems like only a white man knows the meaning of a week's work."

Marta wondered how she would organize the farm. She imagined helping the laborers' wives, holding their children, the *klonkies,* on her lap, and smiling into their eyes.

Then the farmer's wife grew ill. Oom Jakkals drove his pickup truck back and forth to the hospital, in Darling. Marta noticed that his visits to her, though frequent, grew shorter. The doctors were always busy. They turned away from the sick woman, patted the farmer on his shoulder.

"Have courage," they said. "Hou moed!"

Marta listened attentively to the progression of the disease, sighing with pity, as he spoke. She waved, blowing kisses, as his truck roared off. Turning back to the house, she smiled conspiratorially at the two feathered ladies. Her elation shone back from the mirror. Carefully, she altered her expression, cocked her head to one side, composing her face into a moue of sympathy as she dampened down her hopes into a more appropriate sorrow.

She waited.

The wife died. An involuntary whoop burst from Marta's lips as the news crackled over the party line. Her smile grew wider, anticipation welling from the corners of her mouth. She dreamed about welcoming people into the big farmhouse, patting and cosseting them to sit and have coffee.

"And would the Dominee like a piece of cake then? A rusk?"

She bridled with pleasure as the words came to mind.

"Another cup then for the road perhaps?"

But Oom's visits, though they lasted longer, grew ever less frequent. He seldom phoned. He still visited, but never enthusiastically. He checked his watch repeatedly as he took coffee with Katrina in the living room, tapping the crystal as though in disbelief that so little time had elapsed. His eyes darted from the feathered ladies to George. He held his watch to his ear to check if it still worked. He seemed to be waiting for a school bell.

Eventually he stopped coming altogether.

Marta had always listened to the party line. Everyone did, though no one admitted as much. Although few secrets remained, propriety insisted that all gossip be greeted with amazement, hands flying across the mouth of the listener as though to prevent it spreading any farther.

But panic made Marta indiscreet. Frantically she phoned her lover, pitching her voice to a note of gay insouciance to hide the shrill fear beneath. Oom grunted in reply. He would not parry, he would not flirt. He grew more taciturn with every exchange.

Then Marta heard that he had married the widow from the adjoining farm.

Marta trudged up the hill to Churchhaven. From their stoop, the old people watched her come. They smiled and waved, greeting her in a sing-song. She did not nod, nor did she answer. Head down, she walked to the well, where summer water lay dark and brack, and threw herself over the edge.

The folk leaped up.

"Magtig!" cried one.

"Dear God!" breathed another.

Racing to the sound of her wails, they hauled her out. At Darling, the doctor listened to the story, took one look at Marta who was hyperventilating with despair, and called the asylum in Cape Town. Here Marta met many others, pulled from the borderline of oblivion to sanity's edge. Medicated almost to the point of tetany, she 'tsked her sympathy through lips made wooden with tranquilizers.

She waited.

A year went by. The doctors halved the dosage, and seeing a calmness in their patient, stopped medicating Marta altogether. She made plans to return home.

"Poor Marta," as she now became, fell into Katrina's arms: a year is a long time.

Along the western border of the Cape, farmers pressed their wine in the mountains and pastured their sheep on the sandveld. Herds seeking lush winter pasturage trotted along the trail from the Franschhoek Mountains in the east, across the veld to the Churchhaven Peninsula. The new Company's post, or "nieuwe post," built in 1732, was ugly symmetrical house with large stone kraals on one side and a freshet bubbling in front. Neighboring farms had no such spring and they worried constantly about water. Each household collected rainwater from the gutters of their roofs and stored it in a tank alongside the kitchen door. When these tanks ran dry, there was always the well, a deep hole in the sand, that oozed a reluctant pool in its darkness. Practically the only perennial spring was at the post, but in spite of this, the place ceased its official function in 1821, when a residency with a small military attachment was established across the bay at Oostenwal. Farmers continued to use the pastures around the old and new posts, and in 1838 seven owners of five different farms combined their holdings into one single entity named for its most powerful component, "Oude Post" (see fig. 8).[14]

Now eddies swept an American deserter named George Albert Lloyd ashore around 1860, to found the hamlet of Churchhaven. Others came from Norway, St. Helena island, Devon, and France. The men fished, went whaling in Antarctica, and processed whales at Donkergat, the Dark Hole, at the tip of the peninsula. A small school near the church served their needs, and the village shop sold almost anything. Everything else could be foraged in much the same fashion as the Khoikhoi before them. People hunted buck and gathered tortoises in a veld crammed with bulbs, roots, and wild asparagus, called *hotnotskool,* the cabbage of the Khoikhoi. They trawled the lagoon and strung bunches of smoked mullets from the rafters of their dim, low-ceilinged, houses. The small yellow-white fish swayed in the dark. Their pungency mingled with the smell of damp thatch, to produce a scent that was at once both sharp and nauseating.[15]

They nursed each other with bush herbs and poultices, and just as well. The only doctor lived across the bay at Langebaan. On one occasion a Churchhaven woman went into premature labor with twins. It was a cold, blustery day. Squalls whipped down the bay into the lagoon. The husband ran to the beach and rowed over to Langebaan, where he found the doctor dead drunk. Bellowing with rage he carried the physician, bag and all, to the boat. Both men vomited all the way back across the bay, one from fear, the other from acute alcoholic poisoning. Once at the house, the doctor summed up the situation as best he could. He braced his trembling legs against the foot of the bed, plunged both hands between the mothers' legs, and hauled the impacted babies out. They emerged in a fountain of blood. The husband watched in horror, then fled the house. His feet slapped against the sand, drowning out the plaintive entreaties to come back.

He returned a week later. The twins lay in two drawers of the big wooden chest, washed and fed by the other children. The wife lay behind St. Peter's Church, under a fresh mound of sand.

The children gasped. His once jet-black hair had turned completely white!

As for the doctor, he continued to minister to his patients rowing back and forth across the lagoon to certify a new child's arrival, or the end of the road, as the case may be. One thing he always had to certify was the race of his charges. It was no problem, because everyone knew who was who. As a result it came as something of a surprise to find the Grand Inquisitors of the new Nationalist Government bursting through the dunes in the early 1950s, to fulfill the demands of the Population Registration Act and its logical spawn, the Group Areas Act. Their job was to classify every person in the land as White, Colored, Indian, Chinese,

Malay, or, of course, Black. The precise meanings of these terms were never specified because, when you get down to it, everyone knew what they were, and they also knew who everyone around them was too.[16]

There was very little argument.

Today, anthropologists say there is no such thing as race, and geneticists sniff at the very concept. But who can sneer at phenotype when destiny is encoded in skin color?

Perhaps all depends what is meant by destiny.

Take, for example, the Oudepost Dilemma. Around 1920, the last government agent at the post house, found himself torn at the prospect of the monthly visit by the local peddler or *smous*. Most itinerant salesmen were Jewish immigrants from pogrom-wracked villages beyond the pale, but in this particular instance, the *smous* who serviced the post was not Jewish.[17]

More important, according to common knowledge, he was not entirely white.

Everyone, even the maid, knew he was a tiny bit Colored.

So the dilemma was this: how might the family enjoy the company of the *smous* during dinner and simultaneously observe the strict outward rules of behavior that bound every South African community, namely, the obligation to lead separate existences at all times?

The answer came quite suddenly. Two tables were laid in the front parlor. The family sat at the large one, and the *smous* at a small table, right alongside the master of the house. Propriety thus so patently observed, the maid could serve dinner without embarrassment. They listened to the peddler's tales. He told of poor white folk begging on the roadside up and down the country and of farms abandoned by owners who could no longer afford to feed their stock or even to buy grain for the chickens. Then leaning back in his chair, he patted his stomach, and started to tell of a farmer's wife who had hit upon a more carnal solution to her poverty. Mother hustled the children to the kitchen to help the maid. Father leaned forward, eyes aglow. Mother returned. Her expression stifled Father's gasp in midbreath. The *smous* fell silent, as though shot. They all returned to speaking of the weather.

But if issues like the *smous*'s position at table were easy to solve, solutions to the larger questions of racial identity proved more thorny. The need to classify everyone, everywhere, triggered tears, conspiracy, and action. Con men hit the road, promising the palest possible ascription for a price. Bribes were offered, accepted, and often betrayed. At

Churchhaven, a sister who was on the spot, became "white," whilst her absentee brother who was whaling in Antarctica during the Inquisition, returned home to find himself "black."

"Can you believe it?" asked Nannie, pouring tea for her guests. "Can you believe that they say that Kobie there is black?"

She pronounced it "bleck."

Jacobus regarded his sister with confused disbelief. Neither of them had been white when he left for sea.

In 1947 the Oudepost Syndicate was officially founded. Since a group of fifty members would be liable for certain taxes, the syndicate numbered only forty-nine. Many of them had once farmed there, but now they presided over the development of other interests, including a speculative phosphate mine. But the land was too attractive to escape wider attention, and too strategically well placed to stay locked in private hands. In 1983 the Donkergat peninsula became a military base, and a few years later, all the rest of the land was incorporated into the West Coast National Park.[18]

Some years after Marta returned, an Englishman living up the road asked her to mind his cat whilst he went away on holiday. He brought the animal over in his car, a handsome ginger and black striped tom, named Rubbish. Marta and Katrina watched, as the cat turned a baleful eye on them and raced into the dune. They observed its striped face peeking through the bushes, checking the place out, and patiently, they enticed it with scraps and pats. Marta addressed the cat only in English. After all, it was the only language it knew.

Eventually, Rubbish relented. He washed his face in a sunny corner of the yard, and took to sleeping on Marta's bed.

Three months passed. The Englishman returned to reclaim his pet. They drove off. Marta watched the striped face gazing out of the passenger window in what she assumed was sorrow. A dusty cloud spurted under the wheels. Marta sighed. She put a kettle on, and stood squinting at the lagoon, nursing her cup of tea.

Suddenly, she heard a sound, and there it was, returned.

The Englishman panted after the cat.

"Poor puss," he whispered, tucking it back into the car.

Marta noticed with some gratification how Rubbish squirmed in his master's arms.

Rubbish persisted in running back to Marta. The Englishman pursued the escapee time after time. He sat on the stoop drinking coffee with the women, waiting for the solemn orange face to emerge from the scrub. Patiently they watched the cat grooming in the yard, and rolling in the warm sand.

Then the owner pounced. Holding Rubbish by the scruff of its neck he hurled it into the car.

"Bloody hell!" he roared. "You're mine!"

But Rubbish persisted. Marta began to wonder if the wretched cat understood English.

Eventually the owner gave up.

But now that Rubbish was truly hers, he gave Marta no peace. He padded along the road. He yowled at night. Nor did he return each night to sleep on her bed. Strange cats peered out from the bushes, as though reminding him of other more pressing business than Marta's bed.

There could be no question of what he was up to.

After Rubbish had stayed out three successive days, Marta's patience, already worn thin, snapped. She called the clinic in Hopefield and made an appointment with the vet. The shopkeeper drove everyone into town. Marta sat sandwiched between the driver and her mother, holding the cat firmly on her lap, while her legs straddled the gear shift.

Rubbish growled, a low, almost premonitory moan.

Marta held him closer.

"Hush now, it's your own fault."

The shopkeeper watched her covertly. He fumbled as he shifted gears, hands tangling in Marta's skirt. Katrina shot him a glance.

"Pasop!" she hissed, "Watch yourself, man, or you'll end up like Rubbish here."

The driver crashed the gears, face flaming.

Both women laughed, knowingly.

All three were quiet on the way home. Entombed in a narcotic haze, Rubbish snored on Marta's lap.

A few months later Katrina noticed Rubbish playing in the yard with what seemed to be a mole. Yelling for Marta, both women ran after the creature, but it skittered into the scrub. On reflection, they realized that it had run off in a straight line, proving that it was not blind. Furthermore it had no fangs. In short, it could not have been a mole. The mystery was solved a few days later when it returned. It was a small ginger kitten, clearly Rubbish's last by-blow.

They named it "Veldman," to remind them that it had come to them from the bush.

Rubbish died of cancer. Veldman flourished. He slept on the bed. But, like his father, he ran into the bushes. He loped along the road, and he wailed at night. Eventually he took to staying out, night after night. Marta acted with immediate despatch. Off to Hopefield they went, where the vet. operated at once.

As though by divine decree, at that very same moment that Veldman lost his manhood, the region abrogated its autonomy to the bureaucrats at the gates.

The syndicate had stayed outwardly calm when the army sliced off Donkergat, at the end of the peninsula for a secret military base. After all, who could object to the army if you knew what was waiting up north? The army ringed the land with barbed wire and an electric fence. The South African Defence Force emplaced a secret unit there, to train infiltrators and rehabilitate those who returned from such sorties. They designated one hill as a kind of Masada, where solemn oaths of military allegiance were be sworn. No outsider could enter, nor could anything be seen from the gate at the end of the road, but everyone knew that most of the trainees were black. And why not? When you come to think of it, who the hell else could infiltrate Africa?[19]

Although a sense of loyalty kept the syndicate quiet, the loss of Donkergat still rankled. This was their inheritance, their *erf*: never mind that their ancestors had taken it from the Khoikhoi, they, the Afrikaners, had built it up, farmed it, watered it. But what could you do if the army wanted the place? The question hung on the air. It would not go away. Unbidden, a whiff of betrayal drifted in each time guns boomed over the water.

But there was more to come. The beauty of the place proved its undoing. In 1969 the syndicate declared their land a private nature reserve and raised funds by letting the public in once a year to see the wildflowers and animals. Carpeted with daisies and stocked with introduced game, the place fell like a ripe plum into the lap of ecological conservationists. Negotiations began. The syndicate, betrayed once already by patriotism, now waited for betrayal by nature. In 1988 the Langebaan National Park was gazetted. Houses were scrutinized, water was tested. Garbage was buried and ecologically acceptable facilities designed. Maps were handed out at the gate warning people to stay in their cars, and not to trample the flowers. Scheduled hikes were led by a khaki-clad trainee, his neat khaki-socked calves twinkling as he strode along the designated trails. Semisubterranean toilets, built to resemble modest Mayan templets, were buried beneath dunes. Hamlets like Churchhaven were photographed by tourists, who stared at the hive-shaped bake ovens and the stone-walled water tanks, and at women, like Katrina, in their old-fashioned, home-made, bonnets.

The Parks Board ruled that any cat or dog seen on the road would be shot on sight to prevent rabies.

Marta rummages in the bureau. She pulls out a certificate where a cat, one Veldman, is declared male, breed ("Ras"): "house cat." He is proclaimed inoculated against rabies with a serum effective for three years. A handwritten letter from the vet. to the Parks Board declares Veldman to be free of rabies and thus entitled to run on the road. But in the event that Veldman were seen padding into the dunes, or slinking along the verge, given that he cannot declare his innocuousness for himself, he needs accreditation.

Consequently, Marta has decided to hand his documents to the Parks Board herself, binding Veldman to her, by love, food, neutrality, and law.

Last month Marta entered a raffle under the cat's name. Her ticket won. When the judges asked who Veldman might be, Marta replied that he was her boyfriend, and she was his girlie. The prize, a large tapestried handbag with shiny, pink, plastic handles, now holds pride of place on the bureau.

Proof of possession.

Chronicles of Collecting

"The Bushmen of the Kalahari Desert . . . have a few extra vertebrae that protrude and form a small but observable tail at the base of the spine."[1] This strange and false assertion was published in the United States in 1991, and it goes to show that even today some people believe that the Bushmen are not as human as the rest of us. Incongruous though it may be, it serves to contextualize a tale of Gothic practices and strange perceptions that took place in the heyday of colonialism, when, in the course of the exchange of money, diamonds, gold, spices, porcelain, cloth, and bodily fluids, certain interested parties came to cultivate an exotic tastes for native skulls, on the one hand, and European bodies, on the other. Both sides were avid to possess each other, and both became consumers, metaphorically and literally, buying and hoarding body parts, and on occasion, roasting, eating, and displaying them as well.

The geography of our brief review will circumnavigate the globe, echoing colonial ventures of that time, where primary producers from the ends of the earth were bound in commercial networks to the markets of Europe. We begin our tale at the Cape of Good Hope and circle round to Australia, Tasmania, Hawaii, Paris, and Piccadilly, before homing in on the Cape. Our tale darts from the Australian First Fleet to the Last Tasmanian, from murder in Hawaii to grave robbing in Hobart, and from pornography in Cape Town to pantomimes in London, touching briefly on the genitals of Khoikhoi women and the sparkling eyes of British men. Many though its meanderings may be, its moral is clear: What was sauce for the native goose was indisputably sauce for the European gander.

In the Age of Enlightenment and beyond, for so-called civilized colonists, amassing skulls became so commonplace as to almost be called a rage. This passion arose, in large part, from an effort to answer the larger question of whether all humans belonged to the same race or whether, as the polygenists would have it, some might belong to a more lowly order than others. Had humans been more like birds or dogs, attention might have focused on the color of their plumage and the scent between their legs. But being what they are, attention focused on the most identifiable part of the body, namely the face and head. Scientists concentrated on the shape and size of the skull and classified living, as well as extinct races, accordingly. Since the skull reflected the shape and size of the brain within, it was but a short step to assume that certain folk with bigger, longer, or rounder skulls were smarter than those with smaller ones.

Such correlations were far from perfect. The more that experts like Paul Broca perfected their protocols, the more patent was the failure of results to conform with expectations. But lack of confirmation did not hinder the pursuit of measurements. People continued to collect specimens in the firm belief that they would finally hit upon the proof that certain people were inherently closer to the apes than others. Nor was this belief confined to Western science. Indigenous people throughout the newly discovered realms sought to accommodate their newfound colonizers into the native belief systems, by taking certain aspects of their physical peculiarity as signifying something other, if not less than, human.[2]

Our venture into skullduggery begins with the aspirations of a would-be headhunter of the Age of Enlightenment, a purveyor of supplies to the new British colony at Sydney Cove, Australia. In 1789, on the day before he was due to sail from the Cape to provision the new British colony there, Capt. Edward Riou, R.N., of the frigate HMS *Guardian,* wrote a letter to Sir Joseph Banks, president of the Royal Society of Great Britain and Ireland, about the exciting promises of a Col. Robert Jacob Gordon, who, though he did not realize it at the time, was shortly to become the last commander of the Dutch garrison at the Cape of Good Hope: "I mentioned to Col. Gordon, what you did me the Honour to write about respecting Human Skulls, & the Col. who shortly means to make a journey far Northward told me he would endeavour to get some of the Hottentots and different Caffres!"[3]

This was no mere aside. The exclamation mark denotes a flourish in intent, a triumph if executed. It would be a coup to make such a collection, especially at a time when men of learning greeted new discoveries with wonder and a sense of financial expectation. For most of the eighteenth century, the famous Swedish taxonomist Carolus Linnaeus sat like God on the day of creation, naming plants and animals, as well as those best-fitted in his learned opinion to carry on scientific work in foreign lands. Heads such as those that Riou hoped to collect would be but a tiny part of vast consignments of partial and intact life forms that were shipped to London, Paris, Berlin, and Amsterdam, where they were classified, drawn, waxed, set in microscopic slides, and even, on occasion, cast in glass, to create a vast comparative compendium of biological variation on earth. Passion for collecting spread far beyond these strict scientific circles, and efforts to own an exotic skull compelled would-be collectors to finger the object of their desire, even before its owner was dead. Around the turn of the century, a customs clerk in the Northern Territory of Australia kept a watchful eye on one Flash Poll, an old Aboriginal woman, whose skull he longed to own. More successful collectors included a retired Cape Town policeman who, in 1960, was moved to donate to science one of his domestic ornaments. It was a pentagonal, Bushman skull, which had stood on his mantelpiece for many years, wired up to a red light bulb that cast a warm and at the same time scary glow through the eye sockets and dental interstices.[4]

Skulls such as those Riou hoped to collect have since become causes célèbres in the late twentieth-century efforts to reenfranchise the dispossessed peoples of the old colonial world. Aboriginal Tasmanians are a case in point, and a particularly poignant one at that. More than thirty thousand years ago, when sea levels were lower than they are today and Tasmania was joined to Australia by a land bridge, their ancestors were part of the larger continental population. Then, when the postglacial sea rose to form Bass Strait, they were isolated for ten thousand years, until the turn of the seventeenth century, when they were put on the Western map by the mariners of the Dutch East India Company. Idealized by the French, they were then invaded by the British, and by the turn of the nineteenth century, Tasmania was deemed the perfect place to hold the most recalcitrant British convicts.

The shock of contact reverberated in bullets, brutality, and disease as the Royal Navy dumped its unsavory load into the Aboriginal land. Sterility and death followed fast as reproductive tubes and lungs were strangled with foreign pathogens. Half-crazed European prisoners escaped from the fortresses that were built to protect and contain them and plunged barbarically into the world of so-called savages. It took around seventy-five years for the British authorities to declare the Aboriginal

Tasmanians extinct. The announcement was premature, if not downright inaccurate. Through no good intent on the part of the invaders, inter-marriage, concubinage, slavery, and rape served to preserve Aboriginal genes and helped to promote, in more enlightened times, a rapid bur-geoning of cultural consciousness.[5]

Today, descendants of the Aboriginal people demand reparations, and, among other things, the repatriation of their ancestral relics. An unpleas-ant skeleton in the cupboard this one: from first arrival of Europeans, human remains were shipped whole or piecemeal to the museums of Britain for scientific study. In 1869, when the supposedly last Tasmanian man on the mainland, William Lanne, died, competing headhunters battled for his corpse on behalf of the Royal College of Surgeons in London and the Royal Society of Tasmania. The surgeons struck first. Their agent beheaded Lanne and replaced the missing skull with that of a white man. Tasmanian scientists retaliated by snatching the hands and feet before burial: later they disinterred the coffin to get the rest.

William Lanne's wife, Trucanini, responding to these matters with appropriate horror, implored the Reverend Atkinson to bury her remains intact in the deepest sea. Trucanini had good reason to fear her fate. As a young woman she had helped the British conciliator, George Augustus Robinson, to round up her people and relocate them in a series of squalid settlements. Although this was seemingly done for the protection of in-digenous people, enforced containment afforded a richer medium for fatal diseases than any of the more isolated groups, left to their own devices, might have provided. Under the control of their benevolent conquerors, Tasmanians began to sicken and die with alarming speed (see fig. 29).[6]

Trucanini's role in this precipitous decline did not escape the notice of her fellows. Having been instrumental in leading the conciliator to remote tribes, to say nothing of sharing Robinson's blanket out in the bush, she must, willy-nilly, have shared his intent to concentrate people in houses and watch them die. Or so they figured. One imagines that they might also have wondered if she shared his taste for human relics. For around 1837, when the Aboriginal inhabitants of the Flinders Island settlement began dying in earnest, Robinson hit his stride. His early dia-ries show that he was always something of a collector, accumulating, as he did, the Aboriginal vocabularies and legends, but as the pace of mor-tality quickened, Robinson turned to the bones of the very people them-selves. He started with the adult mandibles and children's skulls, used as amulets against illness and pain, and graduated to skulls of newly deceased folk. This required a little more effort than amulets, for the bodies had to be decapitated, and the skulls defleshed by cooking them down. Robinson, who professed indifference to his own "earthly tabernacle," took a great interest in watching the postmortems that mutilated those of his former charges, and even acted as an agent, dispatching two of them off to the governor of Tasmania, Sir John Franklin and his wife.[7]

Although these actions paint him in a macabre light, Robinson was perfectly in line with the popular, educated thinking of his time. Some scholars go further and see him as a pioneer for Aboriginal rights who advocated that the native people be allowed to treat with their colonizers. One paints him as a working-class hero struggling in vain in a sea of British prejudice to convince his superiors that his Aboriginal charges were civilized enough to be moved from their Tasmanian death camps to more salubrious quarters on the mainland. But whatever efforts Robinson may have made on their behalf, no official move was made to mitigate the trajectory of death. Trucanini felt the cold wind of peer disapproval with each successive passing. She feared that she was cursed to witness the death of every one of her people. Her dread was fully justified. She outlived all others to assume the epithet "The Last Tasmanian," when she died in 1876. Her body was not buried at sea as she had wished, nor did it remain intact in the normal sense of the word. Instead, her bones were exhumed and packed off to the Launceston Museum, where some Victorian curator threaded them into position, and hung them out to rattle in the foyer.[8]

After he died, Robinson's ethnographic collection was shipped to Britain and sold for a song. Fruits of labors such as his could be seen in the museum of the Royal College of Surgeons in London, where rows Tasmanian skulls stood grinning on display. Scientists viewing them as strangely atavistic, speculated as to the origins of these folk. Some thought they were a Paleolithic race, others wondered whether they had come from Melanesia or the Andaman Islands. Idle speculation based on these skulls was cut short by the Second World War, when Nazi bombers inadvertently replicated a Tasmanian Aboriginal traditional practice—in fact if not in intent—by incinerating the college and cremating all the skulls. As for Trucanini, it remains a mystery as to whether her purported skeleton was truly hers. Some speculated that it came from a taller person. By 1976, however, Tasmania was caught up in the reparations of the Aboriginal Land Rights movement, and Trucanini's remains, genuine or spurious, were cremated in a state funeral. Her ashes were scattered, according to her wishes, at sea.[9]

But enough of this sorry tale, and back to our original would-be head-hunter. A watercolor shows Riou with a strong nose, thin upper lip, and large, dark eyes framed by perfectly curved brows, gazing into the distance with a certain sadness. At the time he penned his excited letter to Banks, Edward Riou was twenty-seven years old, and had been in the navy since he was twelve. A web of contacts with explorers like James Cook, Joseph Banks, and William Bligh bound him deep into the colonial enterprise. He first visited the Cape in 1776, on Cook's third, and fatal voyage, as midshipman on the *Discovery*. After Cook was killed in Hawaii, Riou transferred to the flagship *Resolution*, where he served under Captain Clerke and the master, William Bligh. It was Bligh, who, some ten years later, at the behest of Sir Joseph Banks, president of the Royal Society, set out to transport breadfruit from Tahiti to the West Indies, where their fruits would provide a cheap diet for slaves working on sugar plantations. His ship, the infamous HMS *Bounty*, called in at the Cape in 1788 and sailed thence to Tahiti and into one of the most dramatic incidents in naval history. Men mutinied and cast him adrift without a log or compass. It would have done in a lesser man, but Bligh was made of sterner stuff. He directed the castaways to row, and row they did, 5,800 kilometers to the Dutch colony of Kupang, on Timor in the East Indies. History having a way of repeating itself, Bligh endured a second mutiny, before he eventually reached Batavia. Here he became a mere passenger on the Dutch packet *Vlydt* and trans-shipped home, touching at the Cape five days after Riou posted his letter to Banks and set sail for Australia.[10]

So much for historical congruences and back to our hero at the Cape. Riou loaded his supplies and twenty convicts that he had transported from Britain and headed south to the roaring forties for a fast ride on the westerlies to Australia. He was in a hurry. The fledgling colony was starving. Aborigines stood on the edge of this newly settled continent, watching with mounting fear as birds of the sea sailed in from the Land of the Dead to disgorge their white, bloodless cargo. Things were edgy, what with the convicts, their keepers, and the vigilant watchers from the scrub. Clearly Riou had no time to waste. He sailed into the cold, southern ocean, confident of a clear summer passage, only to strike an errant iceberg on Christmas Eve. Dispatching the crew to other boats, he held an erratic course for land. Six weeks later, everyone was safely back at the

Cape, and Riou found himself swopping yarns with the crew of the *Bounty,* en route to court martials in England, and arranging pardons for his own shipment of convicts, who had helped save the *Guardian* from sinking. Presumably, he found time too to renew his acquaintance with Colonel Gordon, commander of the Cape garrison, whom, you will recall, was the would-be headhunter to Captain Riou and his patron, Sir Joseph Banks. Riou managed to salvage some of the supplies and send them on to Australia, but the *Guardian* herself was destroyed in a storm in Table Bay. Her captain sailed home to a mandatory court martial for the loss of his ship. Like Captain Bligh the previous year, Riou was honorably acquitted of this loss, and promoted to commander and post captain.[11]

Colonel Gordon blew his brains out after he surrendered his garrison to the British in 1795. His widow left his papers in Riou's care.

Riou died enmeshed in the networks in which he lived, at the battle of Copenhagen in 1801, fighting under Nelson, and alongside Bligh. Horatio Nelson put it this way: "In poor dear Riou the country has sustained an irreparable loss."[12]

And the heads? The heads were never delivered. They seem to have been lost in the rush. They are, in short, gone, setting us free to leave Riou and to turn to one of his many associates, the great British explorer Capt. James Cook.

Among Captain Cook's interests (and truly, there were many) was one he called the "great question." In 1770, Cook reached Australia, or New Holland as it was then known, in the course of his epic first voyage. Artists and naturalists charted these travels with great care, documenting every twist in a leaf, every kink in the hair of exotic natives. Cook mapped the east coast of Australia, and, noticing a mouse-colored animal—it looked like a greyhound, had it not leaped in the air like a hare; and moved like a jerboa, but was as big as a sheep, with the footprint of a goat—named it for its native appellation, "Kanguroo." This didn't make as much difference to the marsupials as did his naming of the land, "terra nullius," to the Aboriginal folk, who, by virtue of that announcement, were effectively dispossessed, by being declared mere occupants of land that no one owned. The rationalization behind this declaration was that having no apparent kings, borders, and countries, Australian Aborigines had not yet evolved the necessary level of social organization to entitle them to the land. This was the charter for centuries of oppression, unbroken by treaties or restitution, whose legal rule ended only recently, with a 1992 landmark judgment, recognizing native title to the land.[13]

Cook's classical allusions continued when he stopped en route home to water at Cape Town in March of 1771, Writing in his log, he noted that he would use this occasion to explore "the great question among natural historians, whether the women of this country have or have not that fleshy flap or apron which has been called the *Sinus pudoris*."[14]

The "great question," to which Cook was referring, concerned a reported peculiarity of Khoikhoi women, namely, their elongated labia, also called "Hottentot apron," "*tablier*," and "curtain of shame." It had been observed in the very earliest discourses on the Cape, and its functions and implications, were a source of intense speculation to everyone from the great Linnaeus, right down to the lowliest sailor. It was, in short, a great question, and the curiosity it engenders is active enough today to generate discussion in anthropology, natural history, theater, and even a chic volume on stereotypes of sexuality, race, and madness.[15]

An actual sample of the object is housed today in the Musée de l'Homme in Paris. Although this is a public institution, all curiosities are not publicly displayed. Some are banished to dusty shelves in the ethnographic section, to be shown only with great reluctance, to those petitioners ask for them by name. I was reluctant to demand outright, because I was not certain whether the word I knew for female genitalia, was acceptable, or even recognizable, in scientific circles. Instead, I asked to see the dissection of Paul Broca's brain that is reputed to sit on the shelf just below.[16]

The guide looked surprised.

"Wait a minute."

He walked away. Far down a dim corridor I noticed him gesticulating to another official. He returned, smiling gently.

"We are sorry, but we dropped Broca's brain last week."

He did not look sorry at all.

I pondered my next move, and then, remembering what the label on the genitalia read, I asked to see the "Hottentot Venus." A harried curator eventually appeared. She click-clacked down the corridors between the shelves and pointed into the gloom:

"There! See for yourself."

A plaster cast of a small woman, naked, with a very large rump, gazed sightlessly back. This was not what I was after.

I drew a deep breath and asked straight out.

She whirled on her heel, and took off down a dim passage between the storage shelves. We passed a set of bell jars containing, among other things, the severed heads of a Chinese pirate and a felon from New Caledonia. Eyes filmed with formaldehyde, peered through the cloudy wash. A flattened nose, whitened at the tip, pressed against the glass. Fine hairs floated over the hack marks on the nape of the pirate's neck.

My guide shot me a look compounded of impatience and fear. The morning's papers told of crowds of disaffected natives milling in the streets. They came from the last of the French possessions in the South Seas, to demand the restoration of their dignity and political rights. One small aspect of their discontent involved repatriation of their relics. I was quite certain they had never seen these particular examples, and watching the expression on my guide's face, was equally certain they would never do so.

I followed her anxious prompting and turned my gaze to another shelf.

The Hottentot genitalia were not immediately recognizable as such. They resembled a marine creature, an exsanguinated polyp, drifting in a pale topaz sea. The specimen carried no personal title other than "Hottentot Venus," but, given her fame, that was more than enough. They came from a Khoikhoi woman of the Cape of Good Hope. Her name, or rather, her Dutch name, was Saartjie Baartman, and she must have been a child when Riou wrote his excited letter of 1789, because twenty years later, in the full flush of womanhood, she traveled to Europe for purposes of exhibition, scientific study, and personal gain. Her chief, and most obvious asset, was her large, steatopygiac buttocks. Her hidden asset was her genitalia, which were assumed to include uncommonly long labia, dangling down to form what scientists called the "Hottentot apron." Saartjie was exhibited in Piccadilly in a cage, which offended sensitive observers. Under legal interrogation, she explained her clear understanding of the financial situation, and went on to Paris, to pose for science, as well as the general public. But chilly Europe was not the sultry Cape, and in due course, she took ill and died. Georges Cuvier's table became her last palette on this earth; his dissection of her genitals was a landmark event in centuries of speculative lasciviousness that characterized the European encounter with certain native people.[17]

The fascination of the female parts was possibly preceded, and certainly rivaled, by the belief that Khoikhoi men were monorchids, with only one testicle. Controversy bubbled over its meaning. Some said that having but one ball helped men run faster, a plausible conclusion if the owners had failed to run away fast enough to save the first. Others thought excision was practiced to cool the ardor, but this seems less plausible, given that Khoikhoi women's attentuated sexual organs were said to denote unbridled lust. Still others suggested that it was done as a method of birth control, or, conversely, to help beget sons, and the learned Grevenbroek, in a veritable cascade of misplaced logic, linked circumcision and testicular evulsion, to conclude that the Hottentots had learned this (and many of their other rites) from the Jews. When James Cook visited the Cape in 1771, he denied categorically that semicastration was a general thing, but noted, nevertheless, that those who had endured the operation, were said to be the finest warriors, and particularly skilled in throwing stones. Linnaeus, who classified Hottentots as *Homo Monstrosus Monorchides,* placed them on a side branch of human evolution. Georges Cuvier demurred. Knowing Saartjie personally, he probably felt bound to equivocate. On the one hand, she had a certain charm. He noted that she was gay, she had a good memory for faces, and she spoke Dutch, a little English, and a smattering of French. She danced, she liked music, pretty baubles, and brandy. On the other hand, her quickness reminded one of a monkey, and she had the disconcerting habit of pushing out her lips like an orang utang. If this were not enough, there was her huge backside and strange genitals. They could not be allowed to pass unnoted, so that although Cuvier saw her as fully human in most respects, some deep sense of her evolutionary position triumphed over his empirical observation. Nowhere is this more clearly seen than in his comments on her face. His illustration shows a sweet visage, a woman, with a lush, curved mouth and wide-set eyes, yet the opposite page observes that "the most disgusting part of this woman was her face, which displayed the characters of both the Negro and of the Mongole countenance in its different features." In the end, therefore, whatever he might have known of Saartjie herself, Cuvier spun a web between geography, skin color, and sexuality, to create a trope of human behavior and, by inference, human evolution where the dark venery of southern people like Saartjie yielded eventually to the pale constraints of northern ones.[18]

The point was that despite all that he knew of her accomplishments, Cuvier could not entirely shake off the animalistic implications of Saartjie's nether regions. He was, after all, descended intellectually, if not directly, from a long line of European observers, all of whom itched to

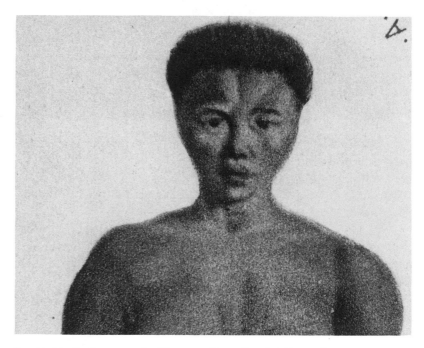

Fig. 24. Saartjie Baartman, the Hottentot Venus (South African Library, PHB, Baartman; see also Griffith 1827, facing 200)

examine the Khoikhoi sex, partly to see whether these were fully human and partly for their own sake.

Centuries of travel ethnographies are full of it: it was the thing to see. Sometimes men paid to look, sometimes they saw it for free, but each entry has its special moment. First, the sailor Wouter Schouten at the Cape in 1665: "They are avid, both men and women, for old iron, copper, tin, beads and glass rings, but above all for tobacco, for which the women will even willingly let their privy parts . . . be seen by our coarse seamen who dare to demand such of them. Truly these sailors show by this, that they are even more lewd and beastly than these wild *Hottentots*."[19]

Next, David Tappen, an old dog of eighty years, who called in at the Cape with his teenaged wife in 1682: "A Dutch woman of our ship had heard that the Hottentot women had over their privities a piece of flesh hanging such as the turkeys have in front of the head, and that this covered the vulva. She wished to examine a Hottentot woman, but this was quicker, and lifted the Dutch woman's skirt up to her navel ... the woman ... perceived us and went off, but the Hottentot woman laughed."[20] Tappen decided to see for himself: "I had often heard that if one said to them *Kutykum* they at once lifted the sheepskin and showed their little under-parts. It happened early one morning that a Hottentot woman came in front of my lodging, to whom I said *Kutykum:* she stretched out her hand and said Tabackum, at which I went and got a scrap of tobacco, and came back and gave it to her. When she had it in her hand she asked *Kutykum?* I replied Yes, and therewith she raised her sheepskin high up and let me have a good look, and then laughed and went off."[21]

Notice how the Khoikhoi laughed. It contrasted with the serious mien of travelers and scholars who stayed locked in debate of this great question. The famous, if flawed, biological statistician Francis Galton, who coined the term *eugenics,* had something to contribute here too. Following the family tradition of his cousin Charles Darwin, he traveled to remote corners of the world recording his impressions of strangers that would later be integrated into a broader view of humanity as a whole. In 1850 he visited what is now Namibia. There he met a "Venus among Hottentots," possessed of "that gift of bounteous nature to this favoured race, which no mantua-maker, with all her crinoline and stuffing, can do otherwise than humbly imitate." Galton wanted to trace her shape but was unable to speak her language or to ask his missionary host for assistance. The solution, when it appeared, constituted such a triumph of ingenuity over Victorian reticence, as to justify quoting in full:

> The object of my admiration stood under a tree, and was turning herself about to all points of the compass, as ladies who wish to be admired usually do. Of a sudden my eye fell upon my sextant; the bright thought struck me, and I took a series of observations upon her figure in every direction, up and down, crossways, diagonally, and so forth, and I registered them carefully upon an outline drawing for fear of any mistake; this being done, I boldly pulled out my measuring-tape, and measured the distance from where I was to the place she stood, and having thus thus obtained both base and angles, I worked out the results by trigonometry and logarithms.[22]

Modern scientists, taking a long, empirical look at these strange features, concluded that the Khoikhoi men were always born with two testicles and probably never evulsed them at all. They noted, too, that large rumps and elongated labia appear at puberty, with no artificial inducement. As for the function of steatopygia, Singer examined the evidence for its onset after puberty, its contribution in controlling heat loss in pregnancy, its failure to disappear with menopause, and its relationship to lumbar lordosis and concluded that we have no idea why it exists! Clearly, since sexual selection has certainly not ruled against its survival, those who have it, must perforce, like it.[23]

But whatever the scientists might say, people reading between the lines of strange encounters with these nether parts all realized that Khoikhoi women laughed when they raised their skirts. Showing their genitals was the rudest insult the natives knew, and the failure of strangers to understand this point, rendered them all the more strange.[24]

Nor were the Khoikhoi alone in their view of invaders. On the other side of the world, Pacific islanders also regarded white and bloodless strangers as something other than fully human. In 1778 Captain Cook, returned on his third voyage to Hawaii and anchored in Kealakekua Bay. After a long and lively visit, he finally departed, only to make an unscheduled return a week later for repairs to the foremast. In contrast to the earlier joyful greeting, his reappearance drew a strange hostility, marked by thefts and aggression. Tensions mounted. As Cook hastened to set sail, a confrontation developed on the beach. He managed to loose a shot at one offender, but was overwhelmed by a deadly onslaught. Cook fell beneath a welter of stabbing and battering, so deadly that his men could only mourn from the safe distance of their ship. The following evening parts of Cook's cooked and defleshed bones were formally returned to his men.[25]

Cook's passing struck deep into European visions of the noble savage. The scene was later painted by John Webber, the artist on board at the time, and also by Johan Zoffany who had narrowly missed sailing as artist on Cook's second voyage. These powerful images of death drew heavily on Benjamin West's *Death of Captain Wolfe* in its mingling of heroic pain and noble loss. Webber shows Cook an instant before the coup de grace, his right hand outstretched as though to restrain his men from retaliation. Zoffany achieved a similar message, where all the figures are struck in classical poses, the Hawaiian headgear echoing ancient Greek helmets, as the tragedy reaches classical proportions. Pantomimes and plays ran in London, Dublin, and Paris, with the stranger and native locked into webs of misunderstanding from which Cook emerged as the tragic hero.[26]

Numerous scholars have tried to reconstruct the death of Captain

Cook, searching to reveal how the worlds of the native and the stranger converged, overlapped, and finally exploded in daggers and gunfire. Sahlins argues that Cook segued into the Hawaiian domain as the unwitting reincarnation of an ancient god Lono. The Hawaiian perception of this millenarian miracle was heightened and confirmed by the way the track of the *Resolution* reenacted Lono's procession through his realm and the by the manner in which Cook's crew distributed and shared their cargo. Unaware of his role, Cook might well have survived had it not been for the intrinsic hazards of navigation that forced him to return. This broke the appointed and mandatory cycle of godly behavior and threatened the life of the king. Cook's demand that the king be held hostage to the return of a stolen boat, was therefore taken as an ominous challenge by the god to the king. It was answered by a lesser chief, rightly possessed of a valuable iron dagger, who struck the first blow, not to kill, but to stay the god temporarily, by setting him on the intended track that would bring him back to the island at the correct time, the following year. In other words, this was not murder, manslaughter, or self-defence, but rather the Polynesian way of setting things back on track.[27]s

A counterargument suggests that the myth of Cook as God emanated not from the Hawaiians but from the British themselves. Cook was worn out, and far from being the benevolent leader he has been construed to have been, had become increasingly violent and autocratic toward all men. By the time he returned to Hawaii, he had had occasion to flog almost half his crew, to cut their supply of grog, and limit their shore leaves. His summary treatment of the natives was therefore so much on a par with that of his own men that he was lucky not to have been murdered long before the final encounter on the beach.[28]

The big answers might never be clearly resolved, but there is one small detail that throws this story into sharp relief. It concerns a Polynesian belief concerning eyes, that the divine creative power of chiefs is evident in their brilliance, and their shining, which is, in turn, derived from the sun. Consequently, a distinguishing feature of gods, strangers, chiefs, and sharks, is their sparkling eyes, as opposed to commoners, whose folly gazing upon a chief would render them "burnt eyes," liable to have their eyes eaten in the course of sacrifice. Cook was said to have sparkling eyes, as were three other British victims who were massacred fourteen years later on the beach at Waimea, in Oahu. Only a few days before he was sacrificed, the young astronomer William Gooch wrote listlessly of sharks circling his boat. Gooch failed to recognize his commonality with the fish, and he died for that ignorance, not because the Hawaiians were savage and the British lacking in savvy, but because Gooch was unversed in Pacific beliefs. In hindsight then, Gooch, like Cook, might be said to have died for a somatic feature he never knew he had but which his murderers recognized in him only too well.[29]

It is of little anthropological consequence to note that sharks have flat, dead eyes, whereas Europeans have regular human eyes, because, in the eye of the Polynesian beholder, both Gooch and Cook were invested with a dangerous commonality. Likewise, there was nothing in the hind-quarters of the Cape Khoikhoi that was in anyway remarkable among their own people at the Cape of Good Hope, until a new eye turned their way. Then, the size of their backsides, the length of their labia, and the number of their testicles became an issue. The supposed somatic oddness of the Khoisan people still pushes them to animality, so that even though they did not all display the same distinctions (indeed, none of them was born a monorchid), they could all be scientifically marginalized and socially ridiculed as if they did.

In the South African Museum in Cape Town, there is a series of photographs, mostly taken in the northern Cape and filed generically as "Bushman: genitalia." It includes a few standard shots of naked women that show the thing quite blandly, as elongated labia, hanging down like tubes. Alongside these clinical examples, is a sepia-colored shot of a woman, partially clad in western dress with one foot resting on a chair. Her expression is bold, almost stern, its reproachfulness lending a air of eroticism to the purportedly scientific venture at hand. The inclusion of this picture in a scientific line-up, is strangely shocking, and it provides a new focus for a series of intimate close-ups of some perfectly normal female genitalia. These were shot in the 1920s when close-ups required a greater proximity to the subject than is demanded these days by your average telescopic lens. Given the photographer was a man, the bets are that he was also "white." This was no Francis Galton with a sextant but a white man squatting with a camera between a Khoikhoi woman's legs. However "scientifically engaged" he might have wanted to be, the photographer must have realized that there was an element of prurience in what he was doing.[30]

What we might be seeing here is a mixture of legitimate anthropology and covert pornography. The combination is perhaps not as dissonant as it sounds. For power is more than wealth, more than goods and profits.

In the end, it is physical control, control of breeding stock, and the of definition of who is who in a competitive world. Implicit in these strange close-ups in the South African Museum files is a mix of power, domination, and sexuality that has marked the colonial venture from its sixteenth-century roots until the present day.

How Saartjie would have laughed.

8

Chronicles of Leprosy

"Most Aborigines are still quite unaware of the cause of the disease. . . .
They call it 'The Big Sickness. . . . If they know they have leprosy they
usually conceal it but unlike the rest of the world they attach no stigma
whatever to it." [1]

I: 1960

The Gurrawoy mob trudged into Oenpelli Mission from the Liverpool
River in the late afternoon. Sunlight flashing between the spiny sheaves
of pandanus palms dappled their vision as they walked. They had come
across the plain, walking in single file along the path that ran between
the cliffs of the escarpment and the great stone tower of Tor Rock. Two
men went ahead, burning the dry grass to clear the passage, and plumes
of smoke hung in the air behind them. The adults carried small children
astride one shoulder, swinging the woven bags that held their possessions
in their free hand. Passing by the giant, magnetic anthills that stood like
weathered curtains on the iron pan, they finally came in sight of the
Oenpelli lagoon. Whispers, then shouts of their arrival spread. People
ran out to greet them, running their hands down the children,
and squealing for joy. The party kept moving until they reached the dry
creek bed. There they stopped, dismounted the children, lowered their
bundles, and sank onto the warm, white sand. [2]

Gurrawoy, also known as "Fred," was last man in. He stumbled along,
one foot dragging in the sand. His head was bowed, eyes fixed on his
feet, as though willing them to keep moving. Reaching the creek bed,
he looked up, a shy, almost secret smile on his heavy-featured face. It

184

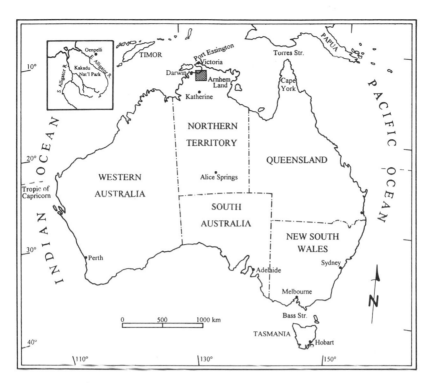

Fig. 25. Australia

softened his thick brow, transforming the leonine scowl into a gentle grimace. He sank onto a ragged blanket spread under the trees and accepted a cigarette. It was the first smoke he had seen since his mob left Oenpelli Mission a year ago, and fully six seasons of wind, rain, storms, and dry heat had since elapsed. They had gone to the Stone Country at the headwaters of the Liverpool River to complete a mortuary ceremony. Celebrations culminated at Tor Rock, where they buried the hollow log containing Uncle's bones, broken and burnished with ocher, and wrapped carefully in paper bark packages. Uncle's name had not been mentioned since he died, nor would it be spoken for the foreseeable future, but he, himself, still appeared at night—in dreams or in person—declaring himself with a soft cough from the inky darkness beyond the fire.

He often had interesting things to say.

Gurrawoy stretched. He turned to the embers smouldering in the sand and swiftly snatched a coal from the edge. Tossing it deftly from hand to hand, he lit his cigarette and drew the smoke deep into his chest. He exhaled a fine stream into the setting sun, grinned, and drew again. Around him, people sat awash in the sheer pleasure of arrival. Wood smoke curled lazily in the soft air, its sweetness mingling with another, even sweeter scent. Gurrawoy sniffed. His ears pricked at a soft hiss. Startled, he looked at his hand. The ember still smouldered in his palm, tiny bubbles forming in its small steamy circle. He gasped. Convulsively he tossed it off. His wife clapped a hand to her mouth, stifling the scream.

Gurrawoy sounded tired.

"I came to see the nurse."

Several people looked away. Coming as they did from an H.D. man, Gurrawoy's words meant only one thing: Hansen's Disease, the Big Sickness, or leprosy, had clearly penetrated deeper into his existence.

"Bad?" asked one.

Gurrawoy shrugged.

"Too much!"

He gestured, waving his hands in the air. Bony stumps tipped what had once been fingers. Small, short black boots covered his feet. They were laced tightly with double knots, as though he were a recalcitrant child who refused to keep his shoes on. His were not the only claws in evidence, nor was his the only leonine face. A grayish kerchief on Auntie's head hid the lumps that had once been ears, and coppery patches on Cousin's back peeked through a torn undershirt.

Gurrawoy sighed. He snuffed the butt of his cigarette into the sand. Across the plain, the sun sank beyond the pallid silver lagoon. A flock of white cockatoos wheeled over the water, chrome-yellow crests flashing bright against the darkening sky as they screeched to roost in the jungle.

Next day, only an hour after sunrise, the corrugated iron walls of the hospital already shimmered in the heat. Inside was cool and green, with partitions separating the ward from the office. Gurrawoy leaned against the door post until he was called. The nurse drew out a folder, scanned it, and turned to him.

"Well, Fred" (she used his Christian name), "how've you been then?"

He stared.

She smiled, cajolingly.

"Come on mate, how y'doin'?"

He thrust his hand up to show the burn. She could scent the suppuration where the tips of two fingers had fallen away. The nurse drew her breath in sharply. Rising briskly, she walked to the dispensary and returned, carrying a tray of instruments, gauze, and a towel. Gurrawoy stared at the wall as she debrided his flesh. She dabbed surgical spirit on the exposed places. He grunted now and then, to give the impression of some sensation in his hands. The nurse packed the open wounds with gauze, bandaged them, and handed him a small vial of yellow pills.

"There y' go then, mate. Three times a day!"

There was a forced upward inflection in her voice.

She turned to enter the treatment in his folder, stopped, and read: "Presenting symptoms 1932: East Arm Leprosarium 1933–47. Acute neuropathy, tendon contracture. Present status: noncontagious; burned out. Prognosis: progressive debilitation."

She bit her lip. A impatient rage rose in her throat as she swivelled round to face him.

"You've been gone a whole year. What do you people expect? You shouldn't be out there in the bush! I don't even want to think about your feet! No one to keep things clean! And what about the pills? The ointment?"

Her face grew whiter and became pinched.

"What do you want of us? And what about the kiddies? They haven't been to school for years!"

He stared.

She shrugged, turned back to the file.

Gurrawoy rose and cleared his throat.

"When will it stop?"

His voice, intended as a roar, came out high-pitched, a squeak of fear.

"Stop?"

She seemed astonished at his question.

He swallowed.

"The falling off?"

She stared, suddenly comprehending.

"Listen Fred, you spent years in East Arm. You're cured. They'd never have let you out unless it was over. You're burned out, the leprosy is gone. They explained, didn't they? It's gone. There's nothing we can do about the effects."

Gurrawoy gestured toward his son, who had trailed in from outside.

"The kiddies can't get it from you. You know that. You're burned out Fred, burned out, remember?"

She rose, and gestured toward a line of patients waiting outside.

"You must have faith."

Her eyes glazed.

"Take Jesus as your personal savior! He loves us all, even the lepers!"

Gurrawoy turned and walked slowly to the door. The vial clattered to the floor and burst open, scattering the pills over the cool stone surface. His son scooped them up and followed his father out into the blinding sun.

The evening meal, called "tea," was over. After hearty plate of boiled buffalo meat and sweet potato, eaten in the mission compound reserved for unmarried white staff, the nurse returned to her office. The roar of the generator drowned out the call of the night birds, as well as the clapping sticks that signaled a welcoming corroberree in the dry lake bed. She pulled the folder towards her and wrote:

> Gurrawoy, Fred. H.D. 1922: East Arm 1933–47; Status inactive. He came in from the Liverpool River today. He has been away from Oenpelli for a year, this against all advice. Presented with a third degree burn on palm of R. hand, plus [?] recent loss of two more terminal phalanges on same, through injury and trauma sustained in his absence. This makes a total of seven affected fingers, in addition to the severe clawing for which he has never received surgical treatment. His foot drop is more pronounced, and his toes are probably severely affected. Needs appointment for further treatment there. Patient does not use the antibiotic powder prescribed, because he left Oenpelli for the Liverpool without taking supplies. Presumably binds his feet with leaves before inserting them into his boots. Prognosis for ambulation is poor. Patient does not seem to understand the difference between being burned out and cured. When appraised of his prognosis he appeared to be depressed.

II: 1606–1925

Around the turn of the century, Paddy Cahill came up from the south to shoot buffalo at Oenpelli. He set up camp at the edge of the billabong and paid the local Kakadu natives to work as stockmen, cooks, and general helpers. Word spread. People drifted in from the plains of the South, West, and East Alligator Rivers, from the Stone Country at the headwaters of the Liverpool River, and from the valleys behind the escarpment. They camped beside the lake and harvested fish, birds, lotus lilies, and goose eggs. They slept in the open during the cool, dry nights, but when the monsoonal rains began to pelt down around December, they hiked up the twin hills that flanked the station to camp in the dry rock shelters. Arguluk Hill, a conical mound, boasted a single shelter on the

Fig. 26. Rock painting of a kangaroo, Oenpelli

top. Inyaluk had a long smooth, curve of rock, painted in pale washes of pink and orange ocher. Turtles, birds, kangaroos, and people raced across the surface, their images drawn as if they were dissected out, to show muscles, bones, and fibers. Above the cave, rock canyons formed a deep maze, scoured by hot winds and whirling leaves.[3]

Open-mouthed wonderment greeted Cahill's arrival. People lined up in neat queues for sugar and golden syrup. They listened in astonishment to the shortwave radio, and scattered at the blast of his shotgun. Their reactions may have been overdrawn, for although Cahill was the first white man to settle at Oenpelli, he was hardly the first foreign influence in these parts. Australia originally formed part of the great southern landmass of Gondwanaland, until around 38 million years ago, when it calved off and drifted north into the Tropic of Capricorn. The continental plate of Greater Australia, or Sahul, housed three land masses: New Guinea, Australia, and Tasmania. It came to rest near, but not against, Indonesia, and its failure to fetch up against land conferred a legacy of isolation upon all three masses. Birds and bats flew eastwards across the water and rats drifted over on floating spars, but otherwise Greater Australia remained aloof, biogeographically isolated from the Old World.

Locked in a subtropical world, Greater Australia forged its own unique identity. Eucalypti and casuarinas grew, interspersed with patches of ancient Gondwanic tree ferns and cycads. Pouched creatures, ranging from elephantine diprotodons through kangaroos to tiny marsupial mice browsed, grazed, and snuffled through the bush. Marsupial carnivores, named Tasmanian wolves and devils, in honor of their last outpost, tore into the flesh of more gentle herbivores. Today, taxonomists identify mammalian equivalents for most forms: Kangaroos resemble deer, Tasmanian wolves look like wild dogs, and apart from their egg laying, monotremal anteaters resemble their placental equivalents elsewhere. But for all these neat matches, one particular form never even entered the equivalence game. In all the complex course of marsupial and monotremal evolution, no creature ever slithered off a tree to stand boldly on two feet, nor did a small, human face ever peer shyly out from the warmth of its mother's pouch. Human evolution was restricted to the world of placental mammals, leaving Greater Australia to wait, until people living in China, Java, and Japan, finally floated across the sea, to land on its northern shores.[4]

Considerable speculation attends the how, where's, and when's of human arrival. Scholars first assumed that people tended to cross the Indonesian ocean during cold, low sea levels, when shorter distances between land masses presented visible destinations. Glacial climatology confounds this prediction, because offshore swamps and coral reefs shrunk when the sea was cold, thereby increasing the actual distances between landmasses at those times. In addition, effective distances probably grew then too, because monsoonal winds, which might have blown floating crafts Australia-wards, diminished in cold periods. Conversely, although the sea levels rose in warmer regimes, some compensation appeared when swamps and coral reefs expanded in the warm interstadial seas. These outgrowths shortened distances and, together with the brisk monsoonal winds, probably facilitated movements of potential colonizers across the sea.

Climatological debates notwithstanding, all agree that the first colonists had to float from shore to shore in naturally hollow bamboos, bamboo rafts, or hollow log canoes. Aboriginal people locate their ancestral moment of arrival in the Dreamtime, when a man and two sisters landed in the north and traveled across an evolving landscape to populate the country. Demographers, trying to invent the most parsimonious scenario to populate a new land, come up with one man and two wives, or a single mother, pregnant with a son. Radiocarbon dates place people in New Guinea, Australia, and Tasmania at least 35,000 years ago, and thermoluminescence dates of sand in a north Australian rock shelter, extend the earliest arrival time back, to around 55,000 years ago.[5]

The European discovery of this land began around 400 years ago when two nations bent on expanding their global influence ran neck-and-neck to report the first sighting of that hypothetical Great Southland that they figured must exist to prevent the earth from falling off its perch. The race was narrowly won by Willem Janszoon of Holland in 1606, followed by Luis Vaez Torres of Spain later that same year. Mariners of the Dutch East India Company probed "New Holland" and their names—Jan Carstensz, Gerrit Pool, and Abel Tasman—evoke the VOC listings at the Cape of Good Hope. And well they might, for Australia and the Cape became bound within a new network, in 1610, when Hendrik Brouwer discovered that the quickest way to reach Batavia and the Spice Islands was not via India but on the wings of the roaring forties, sailing from the Cape of Good Hope, west toward Australia, and then bearing hard north for the Straits of Sunda and Java.

The only hitch was to make sure to hang that left turn before striking the foaming reefs and needle rocks of west Australia. Seventeenth-century mariners plotted their direction by the stars and a compass and calculated their latitude using the altitude of the polestar, and an astrolabe or quadrant in conjunction with the position of the sun. But until the invention of the Harrison chronometer in the late eighteenth century, calculations of longitude were made without astronomical readings, by dead reckoning. This involved estimating the direction and distance traveled from a previously known position, through a combination of readings from the compass and the log. "Dead," was often the watchword, as numerous wrecks of East Indiamen on the west Australian coast attest.

Some passengers drowned on the needle-sharp reefs, others stayed behind on the beach, while small parties went north to Batavia for help. Some castaways lived to tell the tale, some were massacred by Aboriginal people, and others disappeared completely, crew, passengers, and cargo, all gulped into the maw of the Great Southland.[6]

William Dampier, who landed briefly on the west Australian coast in 1688, brought the Aboriginal people most memorably to European minds in his famous comparison with their Khoikhoi counterparts at the Cape of Good Hope:

> The inhabitants of this country are the miserablest people in the world. The Hodmadods of Monomatapa, though a nasty people, yet for wealth are gentlemen to these; who have no houses and skin garments, sheep, poultry, and fruits of the earth, ostrich eggs, etc., as the Hodmadods have; and setting aside their human shape, they differ but little from brutes. . . .
>
> I did not perceive that they did worship anything. . . .
>
> How they get their fire I know not. . . .
>
> These people speak somewhat through the throat, but we could not understand one word that they said.[7]

Aboriginal folk watched Dampier through fly-blown eyes. Their thoughts went unrecorded, as did those of other people living on the northern coast, who hosted numerous visitors when their rattan-sailed praus washed ashore from Indonesia, on the northwest monsoon. Around the late seventeenth century, crews sailed annually from the Celebes port of Macassar to the land they called "Marege" on the north Australian coast, to harvest trepang or sea cucumbers, for sale as aphrodisiacs in the markets of Indonesia. Divers brought the great slugs up in rattan baskets, eight to ten at a time, then boiled them in great cauldrons, and dried them out on long racks. Their seasonal visits were imprinted in archaeological sites and archives. Today, exotic tamarind trees, ruined stone smokehouses, and scatters of porcelain, earthenware, and glass mark the position of Macassan camps on north Australian shores. Aboriginal paintings on rock walls and bark show praus and curved Asian knives, and crumbly ledgers in the old Batavian archives at Jakarta list shipments of trepang and tortoiseshell. Some argue that these visitors brought smallpox to an otherwise unexposed population, but there is no disputing the songs, ceremonies, genetic markers, dugout canoes, iron spear heads, loanwords, and dialects that stamp the mark of Indonesia on this, the southernmost limit of its maritime trading realm.[8]

In the early nineteenth century, the British built a series of forts along the north Australian coast. Their cities were already well established far-

ther south: Sydney, in Port Jackson harbor, at the site of the landing of
the First Fleet in 1788; then Adelaide, Perth, and Hobart on the island
of Tasmania. All enjoyed climates reminiscent of their mild, English
motherland. The same could not be said of the north. Here, outwardly
verdant parklands masked a monsoonal regime that proved a siren for
prospective colonists from more temperate zones. The British forts were
short-lived. The last one, Victoria, lay in a sultry hollow behind the
beach at Port Essington, smack in the middle of the preferred habitat of
sand flies, flying ants, mosquitoes, snakes, centipedes, roosting birds, and
land crabs. The nights were particularly unpleasant. Stars shone as though
in mocking anticipation of the sun, while fearsome drones, clicks, and
hisses punctuated the still darkness. A quiet evening at home by the par-
affin lamp drew a wild, jostling guest-line of insects, shoving to die in
heaps of powdery wings and rasping claws. A stroll on the beach drew
murderous passengers, malaria-bearing mosquitoes, giant flies, and tiny
black sand flies whose fiery toxins generated weeping welts and buboes
hard as rocks.

A Cornish builder erected conical chimneys, and later, Capt. George
Lambrick, R.N., buried his wife and babies in their shadow. Officers
toasted rotten food, deliberately dispatched from Sydney, with glasses of
Chateau Margaux, inadvertently dispatched from London. They grew
preoccupied with saving cows and with whether the navvies should
speak directly to the commander's wife or not? "Port Essington," wrote
Thomas Huxley to his mother, "is about the most useless, miserable, ill-
managed hole in Her Majesty's dominions." He had tripped off the bark
Rattlesnake for a short visit in 1848. His diary picked up the thread: "The
place deserves all the abuse that has ever been heaped upon it. . . . there
is as much petty intrigue, caballing and mutual hatred as if it were the
court of the Great Khan. . . . It is worse than a ship and it is no small
comfort to know that this is possible."[9]

The Great Equalizer silenced all whining. Moving in like an angry
pimp, he propeled men from etiquette into reality by way of dysentery,
typhoid, and malaria. Survivors hacked shallow graves in the rock-hard
laterite. The natives watched impassively from their camps at the edge of
the settlement. They stole surreptitious glimpses at themselves in broken
mirrors, noting carefully their new red headbands. Foraging in cesspools
and refuse pits, they fashioned murderous scrapers from the glass prunts
of Mr. Rothschild's finest harvest. They sang garbled hymns and learned
strange words.[10]

"We were electrified," wrote Ludwig Leichhardt on hearing a native near Port Essington in 1845 say, "Commandant!" and "what's your name?!!!!" Leichhardt had traveled some 5000 kilometers from Brisbane on the eastern coast of the continent. Before him lay the Alligator Rivers plain. Pillars of smoke wreathed the great magnetic anthills. The flats teemed with hunter-gatherers who harvested water chestnuts, lotus hearts, and goose eggs from the shrinking swamps, set fish and crab traps at the river crossings, and speared fish, geese, and wallabies. Groups, five hundred strong, came to inspect Leichhardt's camp, greeting the strangers, or "Balanda" (Hollanders), with "Perikot, nōkot" (Very good, no good). They whistled at his weary horses and made desultory attempts to steal the gear. They jostled their plump babies on their hips, and fanned themselves with goose wings. They let it be known that they were quite familiar with the doings at Port Essington, cackling, mewing, quacking, and grunting to imitate the sounds they had heard at the British outpost. Some shuddered as they pointed out the tracks of the "Anaborro," or buffalo, whom they called "devil-devil." [11]

Twenty years later, whites were no longer welcome on the Alligator plains. In February 1866, an exploratory party of men, sheep, horses, and mules, led by John McKinlay, set off to explore the land from Darwin to the East Alligator River. It was not the best time to travel, because the monsoonal rains were in full force. A diary kept by the second in command, John Edmunds, started with startling prescience: "I have constructed a rain gauge."

There was plenty to measure.

It rained, it squaled, it poured. Sheep rotted from the feet up, and horses struggling through the mire, burst their hearts and dropped in their tracks. The sodden party ate their erstwhile mounts, for after all, what goes around, comes around, or so they say. The natives watched, and sensing disaster, drew nearer. McKinlay advanced slowly through the mud and water, bickering about longitude. The Aborigines whooped, danced, and shot menacing looks at the mud-booted men. At the East Alligator River the whites stopped with their backs to the proverbial wall. The natives pressed closer. They lit fires, they laughed, and they taunted from the trees. Spears whistled through the smoke.

McKinlay strafed the jungle with gunfire.

Howls shivered through the paperbarks and bounced off the cliffs.

Clearly, the time, had come.

McKinlay stopped debating exactly *which* Alligator River he had reached and began to build a raft. Edmunds took notes. He chiseled into a tree: " MK 41 Made punt of horsehides & tent & start'd down river 7 to 29 June 1866 dig in track for bottle 8 feet S.W. R.H.E." On another tree he cut, "Natives trecherous," taking time to correct his original spelling by inserting a pedantic *A* in "trecherous," in case future travelers misunderstood. In direct counterpoint, Aboriginal witnesses, who memorialized the event in their own blood, apparently commemorated it in a more artistic way as well, in rock paintings of men mounted on strangely marsupial-looking horses, strung about with reins and pack-bells.[12]

McKinlay sailed to safety. Feral animals, grazing on the banks watched him pass by. These were descendants of domesticated animals, released when the British abandoned their coastal settlements. They included cats, dogs, pigs, deer, horses, and a handful of Asian water buffalo. Most grunted, spat, and snarled in their newfound niches, but the buffalo flourished apace. They exploded into the friendly ecosystem of a vast coastal swamp. The immense herds caught the attention of the European hides market, and around 1891 a buffalo shooter called Paddy Cahill materialized on the plain. In 1906 he established a camp and a dairy herd alongside the permanent billabong at Oenpelli, the traditional home of the Kakadu people and entered anthropological history.[13]

Oenpelli was remote, yet by the standards of the day it was easily accessible. The hostile warriors of McKinlay's time had settled down. Horses brought visitors 300 km overland from Darwin, and steamers sailed up the East Alligator River from the northern shore. Cahill played host to numerous inspectors and officials and also to Aboriginal watchers like Elsie Masson, future wife of the famous anthropologist Bronislaw Malinowski, and Walter Baldwin Spencer, a famous zoologist, who came to the Northern Territory as chief protector of Aborigines in the Northern Territory. From 1912, Spencer held dominion over all Aborigines and part-Aborigines, and by extension over everyone else as well. The Aboriginals Act of 1910, and the Aboriginal Ordinance of the following year, empowered him to control and protect his charges by deportation, relocation, and threats. It was a mandate rooted in racism, emanating in part from the anti-Asian laws of South Australia, and it enabled Spencer to abrogate the civil rights of numerous groups. He rooted Malays, Whites, and Chinese out of Aboriginal camps in order to prevent "mixed marriages." He let it be known that he would be happy to deport the Chinese en masse. He shifted Aboriginal people into more sanitary compounds, interpreted their perceptions in the courts, and behaved, in general, very much like the paternalistic authoritarians who, at that very moment, were busily setting up the structures of a future apartheid state in South Africa. There, no one was given to the irony of styling themselves "protector" of anyone else, but this technicality was of no consequence to either Spencer or his many charges. A practical and energetic man, his new job gave him the chance to do exactly what he wanted to do—collect new animals and continue fieldwork among exotic people. Booted, jodphured, and laced to the gills, this model of anthropological inquiry landed at Paddy Cahill's homestead by the lagoon at Oenpelli in the dry season of 1912.[14]

"You," wrote Cahill later, "are the only one that I know, who thoroughly understands the natives and the right way to treat them." Cahill underestimated himself. In a series of letters that he penned to Spencer between 1913 and 1921, this Irish buffalo skinner emerges as a compassionate and prescient man, whose affection for the land and its people glows on every page. He was interested in everything the natives did, and he treated them as equals, eschewing hand-outs and insisting that they exchange wild honey, fish, or eggs for clothes, food, and medicine. He insisted that the men stop beating their women and emphasized his point with his fists when the need arose. In a marked departure from the contemptuous renaming of native people worldwide, Cahill always called everyone by their native names, making certain that he spelled them as they were pronounced. Where Aboriginals were concerned, he was hot-tempered, opinionated, and he loved them dearly; where Spencer was concerned, he was obsequious to the point of nausea, bowing and scraping to the Great Man's every request, and considering it a rare honor, to be allowed to enhance Spencer's already towering reputation with his own copious field notes and specimens.[15]

Spencer described Kakadu daily life, ceremonies, beliefs, and rituals. His reports set the Kakadu people firmly in a Stone Age amber, and his findings here and elsewhere became the subject of intense anthropological debate. Scholars pondered who married whom, and what they called one another. Did they have gods? More realistic observers, hearing what buffalo skinners, prospectors, and settlers called the natives, stopped wondering what they called each other and grew fearful for their future.[16]

Cahill wrote to Spencer:

> I believe in doing all that I can for the natives, but their future frightens me. If the mission people could only make the native ambitious so that he could be made to live in a house & do anything for a living, except tre-

panging or hunting or be a hand on a plantation, then it would be a kindness to teach their women civilized habits, learn them to read and write cook and be clean, but to instil the love of housekeeping into any woman and then turn them over to a nomadic native & for the women to go back to their usual way of life, then I say it is an injustice to any woman and anything but a kindness.[17]

As things turned out, Cahill might have done better to be more idealistic. But he was no Jean-Jacques Rousseau penning the Noble Savage in the bistros of Paris but a buffalo skinner, now also styled "protector," trying to make a living on the plains of the Alligator Rivers. His position was not as safe as he imagined. One morning at breakfast, Mrs. Cahill and the hired hand suddenly fell, writhing, to the ground. The butter they were spreading so liberally on their home-baked bread was laced with strychnine. Cahill moved fast. He pumped the poison from the victims and emptied the water bags. He shook with rage and fear. He bellowed for justice.

The perpetrator came forward immediately. He was Romula, Cahill's right-hand man. Come to think of it, he agreed that the water bags were poisoned. Cahill turned on Romula, hit him on the head, and chained him up. Romula countered, shouting that his actions stemmed directly from Cahill's infringement on a man's need to fight with spears and on his right to beat his wife. Cahill took no notice. In Darwin, the judge listened carefully to Romula's admission of guilt. He had heard already heard something of the summary way in which Cahill dealt with miscreants. He bent closer, listening intently, as Romula, on the advice of his fellow felons, shifted his plea to "Not Guilty." The judge had heard these things before. He ordered a new trial, and dispatched Romula to Fanny Bay jail to think things over. Romula weighed his options, and fled to the bush before he received any more justice.[18]

Back at Oenpelli, Cahill penned the entire tale to Spencer and, indignation notwithstanding, decided to stay. People all around depended on him to cure their coughs, pain, lameness, and imminent death, which he did with a mixture of honey, quinine, tincture benzoin, and water. Sufferers flocked to Oenpelli for the "cure." It soothed their throats, but inadvertently it also killed them, because it was one of many such magnets that drew them to the settlement in sufficiently large numbers to harbor and perpetuate the new pathogens. By 1920, Cahill noted that "the people S.S.W. of Oenpelli, got the influenza and died in scores, only a few of a once numerous tribe, are now living." If Spencer read this letter, he never addressed its sad implications. He remained preoccupied with the finer points of Aboriginal custom and belief, questioning the distracted Cahill with dogged persistence: What was the kin tie between the two men who danced the goanna corroberri? Whose wife placed the leaves across the path? Where was the black kangaroo pelt that Cahill promised to ship down to Melbourne?[19]

As the pool of Aboriginal informants shrank before Cahill's eyes, Spencer's reputation soared. Growing wiser each day, he also waxed romantic; perhaps his endless inquiries into the private lives of savages sparked a savage interest in his own. Leaving Mrs. Spencer behind in Melbourne, he sailed for London. With him went a young lady as secretary. In 1929 they traveled to the tip of South America in Darwin's footsteps, to try to elucidate the threads that bound all southern hemisphere foragers in a common savage world. There were three tribes in Tierra del Fuego, the Ona, the Yahgan, and the Alacaluf. Spencer, arriving in winter, found that there were almost no natives to be seen. Disease had thinned their ranks. He dispatched emissaries to roust out some informants. One old woman eluded him, dying even as his mendicant boat beached up on her shore. Others succumbed, climbing into the boat. Huddled in guanaco cloaks, they squatted obligingly by what the secretary called the "great man's fire," and arranging sticks and stones to represent their kin, they recited their beliefs in a mantra of anthropological babble. Spencer's young assistant wrote everything down. Outside, the south polar wind howled. Rain lashed the small windows and trickled through the cracks in tiny frozen tears. The Tierra del Fuegans smoked, coughed, and spat. Their babies wheezed and snuffled down their mothers' hoods.

Spencer caught a cold.

He gasped, and clutched his chest.

Drawing a deep breath, he sat up, and died.

His assistant was as surprised as he.[20]

A world away the natives of Oenpelli hacked phlegm from deep in their chests. Their ears exuded pus.

"Runny ear?" said the nurse.

"Influenza!" barked the doctor.

"Hmm?" said the expert, palpating the nodular radial nerve. His eye fell on the nonsweating, hypopigmented coppery patches on the back. "Hansen's disease?"

With their diseased feet tracing grooves in the sand, the lepers of Oenpelli slouched toward Mr. Cahill's remedy. Having already succumbed in large numbers to the initial onslaught of foreign pathogens, the remedy did them no great harm, although where leprosy was concerned, it did them no good either. Faces grew large and leonine, ears festered, fingers and toes grew numb and dropped off. Doctors, ignoring centuries of Indonesian contact in the north, traced the origin of this plague to a handful of Chinese laborers who had come to scratch the tiny lodes of gold in Pine Creek a few decades earlier, in 1874. The authorities descended on the Chinese quarter of Darwin and declared it to be even worse than the black parts of Cape Town. Efforts were made to evict the shanty dwellers; outraged, one refused to do the administrator's laundry any longer. Chinatown burned to the ground repeatedly, but leprosy resurged, rising phoenixlike from the flames, to flourish in towns and in distant bush camps.[21]

It could now be defined: Doctors differentiated "Indeterminate" from the more recognizable "Tuberculoid," with its localized invasion of skin and peripheral nerves, as opposed to "Leprotamous," with its generalized invasion of the body. Pictures were circulated so that lepers might be recognized, and isolated in the lazarets, such as the one on the East Arm of Darwin harbor. The bush folk figured out their options and hid in the vast hinterland. There, far from the Protector, the Flying Doctor, and the Bush Nurse, leprosy bloomed slowly but most inventively.[22]

III: 1964

When Gurrawoy heard that archaeologists were coming back to Oenpelli, he smiled his quiet secret smile. After his release from East Arm Leprosarium, he had returned to his people. Oenpelli was now a mission station, located within the borders of the vast protective Arnhem Land Reserve. A year after Gurrawoy came home, a large party of Australian and American scientists arrived at the Mission. They camped by the billabong, caught birds and wallabies, skinned them, and packed the fur and feathers into tissue paper. They fished in the lake and streams and bottled their catch in alcohol and mentholated spirits. Some climbed the hills and hammered at the rocks, placing the chips in labeled bags. Two of them camped with a party of people at the waterfall and weighed every scrap of food snared, hunted, gathered, and eaten. Others trudged up Arguluk and Inyaluk to dig into the dirt floors of their caves. They shoveled the fine, gray dust into sieves, which they shook until a cloud hung over the entire hilltop. Whooping with joy, they retrieved stone spears, old sticks, and even the painted bones of dead people.[23]

One night, as the scientists sat around their fire, Gurrawoy limped up and introduced himself. They nodded. Their radio crackled and spat. Gurrawoy laughed: "Judy Garland," he offered. "Wizard of Oz?"

The leader gasped.

"I heard her at East Arm," he explained.

The faces grew stony in the orange glare. Involuntarily they looked around for help.

"What the hell," shrugged the leader, "you're burned out, aren't you?"

Now, fifteen years later, Gurrawoy recalled their frozen smiles and the fear in their eyes, as he watched the new party drive in. The Landrover was plastered with mud. They had misjudged the position of the East Alligator River, and, bickering in much the same style as McKinlay's party a century earlier, had plunged down the sandy embankment into the incoming tidal bore. Their shouts reached the opposite bank where two of Gurrawoy's cousins were watching for alligators. The cousins stayed perfectly still, crouching near the small, smoky fire they had lit to deter mosquitoes. The people in the truck panicked. One threw the door open, flooding the cabin. Another clambered onto the roof. Cursing, they grabbed a block and tackle and winched the truck across the river. They slapped at the insects leaving patches of blood on their bare skins. The truck bucked like a wild horse. It moved slowly across the causeway and up onto the far bank. Finally, the engine caught and trundled off, steam and smoke farting from the exhaust.

Gurrawoy's cousins laughed till tears rolled down their cheeks, then loped back to Oenpelli to tell the tale. Gurrawoy smiled, his small, secret smile, and kept an eye on the archaeologists. He watched them drive off in a different direction each morning. They trudged up the hills, screaming as they blundered unseeingly into green ant nests. One tore his trousers off, clawing wildly as the tiny pincers nipped his privates. They sank small, deep holes into the floors of caves, keeping the excavated relicts in small, labeled bags. One stumbled across a King Brown snake. He shrieked and leaped high up into the air with both legs folded tight beneath him. Children watching these antics from afar rolled laughing on the ground.

Gurrawoy smiled quietly. He waited.

A few days later they approached his camp, two men and a rangy-looking woman in men's clothes. The leader pulled a pack of cigarettes from his shirt pocket and offered them around. Most people took a handful, but Gurrawoy took only one. He snapped a match on his shoe, and offered the leader a light.

"You the same as the 1948 mob?" he ventured.

The leader gasped, smiled, and stuck out his hand.

"Pleased to meet'cha!"

Gurrawoy extended a fist terminating in a few keratic points that may, or may not, have been nails.

It was gratifying to watch the leader's expression freeze as he slowly palmed the proffered shake.

By nightfall they had smoked two packs of cigarettes and had polished off a fair amount of brandy. The Mission allowed no grog on its land whatsoever, but, nevertheless, a silver flask was surreptitiously passed round. Gurrawoy's portion was poured into a cup. He noticed that it was a hefty slug and decided to forget the implications. Then they began to talk about work. The deal was that the woman wanted to dig in caves and needed a friend, guide, mentor, and informant. Gurrawoy looked at her through slit eyes. She was young, intense, with a loud voice. He wondered. The people would laugh at him having a woman boss.

Suddenly a moth fluttered into her hair. She screamed and beat at her head. Tears came to her eyes.

Gurrawoy smiled.

A pushover!

IV: 1964

Gurrawoy surveyed his domain. He and the cousins had now been working for the archaeologist woman for three weeks. They were camped in the shade of an immense boulder near the East Alligator River. A short distance away, in the lee of another rock, stood the archaeologist's camp, and between the two, the cave that she was excavating. He remembered coming here as a child and climbing the rocks to watch the birds roosting in the dark trees that lined the river. He reached into his shirt pocket for a Rothman's Kingsize, knelt over the small fire, and drew deeply. Things could be worse. The work was boring, the pay was indifferent, but the perks were good. Pretty good, even. All the cigarettes they wanted, all the food they could eat and no questions asked, even when they demanded more syrup only one day after she had given them a five-pound can. He intended to keep things this way. He reminded her regularly that he was the only man left who could remember the old days. He assured her that he was probably the only man there willing to work for a woman, explaining that he had spent so much time in the white man's world that he was able to handle the shame. With each exchange, his eye fell longingly on another particular item in her store.

She understood.

Gurrawoy now had a case of bully beef, six tins of spaghetti, a shovel, a box of torch batteries, and a large ball of string. In addition, discussions about the final disposition of the camera, the radio, the tape recorder, and the ranging poles had begun.

He smiled to himself.

The archaeologist squatted at the edge of the excavation and looked down. Digging makes for great muscle development in the trowel hand. Dirt mingles with sweat. Shoulders ache from shaking sieves, intravertebral discs weaken and tear. There are nice inferences to be made: A small hearth set with fire-cracked stones marks the place where two crabs and three clams baked dry while their cook turned to some other task. A splinter of bone, broken in midshaft, with polish at its tip, betrays that it was used as an awl, to bore holes in skin or wood. A clamshell, its margin worn to a fine polish, once scraped the shaft of a spear. The count of stone chips tells how many blows it took to fashion a spear point from a large pebble core, and the radioactive decay of a fragment of charcoal, how many years have past since the fire burned. These are islands of fresh air in a fug of repetition. All day, sorting bone from stone, joints from shafts, flakes from cores, over and over again, until the past resonates its obvious message:

"We were here: we ate shellfish, we ate crabs, we hunted possums, we chipped stone, we were here."

It's not a job for everyone.[24]

The archaeologist habitually wore men's clothes. She spent a great deal of time trying to jump-start the Landrover, which had never recovered from its dunking in the salty river. Her four workmen regarded her with some considerable bemusement. Despite her incorporation in their kinship system as Gurrowoy's sister, her gender was indeterminate. Her clothes declared her to be a man, but on the rare occasions that she drove to Oenpelli to fetch her mail, she would stop just short of the gate, walk to the back and immerse herself under the faucet of the water tank at the

Fig. 27. Making stone tools for archaeological study, Oenpelli, 1964

side of the truck. The men watched her strip and step into a short dress. Smoking, singing, and braying with laughter, she would swing back into the cabin and race along the rutted track into the station, transformed, as it were, by this strange baptism, into an ordinary white woman.

Gurrawoy was slow and clumsy this morning. He rolled his swag—a blanket, a groundsheet, and a small, stained pillow— into a bundle, and stretched. Senseless though they were to the touch, his feet ached with a dull, remote pain. They were cold in their thick socks. His hands were gnarled. Their dead joints had fallen off years ago, and hard calluses now grew where nails and pads had once been. He manipulated his shoelaces with thumbs held awkwardly against his palms, frowning with the effort to tie them tightly. Walking stiffly to the site, he wondered at its yield. So far, only old bones from meals, fires, the odd stone spear.

The rock shelter lay crisscrossed with strings, anchored at various points by spikes sunk deep into the ground. A square hole gaped darkly in the middle of the cave, its walls striped with bands of gray-white ash, lenses of charcoal, and fragile lenses of paperbark. The archaeologist stood back from the hole, then stepped widely into its depths, to avoid breaking the fragile, clean-cut section. Reaching for a trowel in her back pocket, she began to scrape away. She ladled the earth into a bucket, swung it up into waiting hands, and caught an empty one in exchange. The men tipped the earth into a sieve, shook the dust out, and squatted over the residues of broken bones, stones, and charcoal. They extracted the finds as delicately as if they were selecting sweets at a church social. Everyone smoked. The woman occasionally sang. Now and then she would leap out of the hole and inspect the finds, asking for identifications and native names: where does this shell come from? what is this animal? how do you use this bone point? To men whose childhood had been spent hunting possums and spearing fish, she seemed utterly ignorant. Yet you had to hand it to her for sheer persistence, digging away, sunrise to sunset, week after week, with little change to show for it all. A mad person, no doubt, whatever else she might be. The men stole sideways glances at the alarm clock, ticking loudly on the edge of the trench, watching, as its hands moved maddeningly slowly round to tea time.

Gurrawoy noticed the bone in the last sieve before lunch. It was more spongy than the others. He recognized it immediately as a human fingerbone. Although it made him shiver at first, he was not at all surprised to see it there. It was customary to retrieve human bones after their initial burial, to decorate them, and to repack them into the dusty recesses of rock defiles and shelters. He himself had often handled bones in mortuary rituals. They wrapped the body in bark, placing it on a platform, and returned years later, to finish the business. The bones were coated with ocher, some were smashed, others placed in a hollow log. The time that elapsed between death and final burial allowed everyone, wherever they might be traveling, to hear the news and to come in for the final ceremony. In a man's life he might witness several such events every year, and he never forgot each moment.[25]

She had clearly shoveled this small relic out, unrecognized. He palmed it clumsily, clenching its smallness into his abbreviated hand, terminal claws turned in, like the paw of a flying fox. As he rose, he heard her call out: "Wow!"

She was crouched over a pile of bones. They were patently human. Not a burial in the normal sense of the word but a heap of secondarily buried remains packed in shredded paperbark. She brushed the dust away, sketched and photographed the packing, and then cleaned the bones so that they lay exposed as a crisscrossed heap. Some bore traces of ocher, others shone as though they had been carried around and nurtured for a long time. The men stopped working. They formed a small circle around her and watched in silence. This was no one they knew; nevertheless, their discomfort grew as they watched her disturb the sacred things, wrap them in tissue and tin foil, and pack them carefully into a larger paper bag.

Gurrawoy stood in silence, his swollen face impassive and shut. Suddenly he wished he had never seen her, the truck, the tins of food, the batteries, even the tape recorder. A wave of shame and hate boiled up at her and her kind. Clutching the fingerbone, until its knobs bit into his palm, he started back toward his camp, taking small, dragging steps in his tightly laced boots.

Thoughts rushed in like the great bore of the East Alligator River, a wash of foam and dust.

His eyes smarted.

He clutched it tight, this perfect finger, from the time before men's hands lost their feeling.

V: 1964–80

Fifty years after Cahill and Spencer sat on the veranda at Oenpelli to contemplate the world of the Aboriginal savage, the Aborigines were still wards of the state. A large directory defined "ward" as someone who is unable to act in their own interest, and listed each such person by name. Access to the Reserve was barred to non-Aboriginals, and would-be visitors had to run the gauntlet of bureaucratic procedures and a mandatory chest X-ray before being issued with a pass. In 1964, the indigenes graduated from wards to citizens. A new act empowered them to vote and to make some decisions about life in their traditional lands. They also had to register their dogs and pay for a license.

Some felt strongly about this matter. One man strode into the camp by the Oenpelli billabong and shot every one of his fourteen curs.

"Puck them and their pucking vote!" he declared.

A decade later, the great magnetic anthills turned out to be beacons of betrayal, because their steep walls contained uranium, dredged up from the underlying soil by millions of termites. Where buffalo guns once blazed, geiger counters now crackled, heralding the arrival of Multinational Investors, followed by Supervising Scientists, and Resident Anthropologists. The Aborigines of Oenpelli became Traditional Landowners of Mining Territory. Beer can in hand, they sat through solemn hearings about their rights and their prospective royalties, weaving home later in their long-wheel-based Landrovers, accelerators fixed at 80 kilometers per hour. Foam slopped over their knees as the boom box slammed into country blues.[26]

The region was declared the Kakadu National Park. The Office of the Supervising Scientist was set up to monitor the effects of commercial development. They measured the dust raised by vehicles on the roads, the seepage from retention ponds at the uranium mines, and the effects of chemically treated soil on the termites it was meant to deter, as well as the other wildlife who passed through its shield. Six-legged frogs leaped from contaminated ponds near termite-free houses: they looked like green spiders.[27]

The parks people decided to rehabilitate the environment. Buffalo were shot on sight. Free from their ravages, the lush swamp vegetation regenerated. With it came birds, fish, turtles, geese, and alligators, their jaws wreathed in menacing smiles. A tourist with his video camera stood on the banks of the East Alligator River, near McKinlay's last stand, stolidly filming a fisherman hook a barramundi, or giant perch. As his camera whirred, an alligator slithered up from the yellow waters, and snatched the fisherman away. The camera continued to roll, through flurried foam, shrieks, jaws, teeth, tangled line, and leaping perch.

Then silence.

The entire episode replayed that night on the Northern Territory Nightly News.

The interviewer leaned forward sympathetically.

"After this," he said, "would you ever want to go back to Kakadu again?"

The photographer, a builder from Melbourne, seemed nonplussed.

"Would I ever? Too right mate!"
He smiled, a wolfish grin.

VI: 1982

Oenpelli is hot and silent in the late Dry. Tin cans, plastic bags, the occasional dead dog lie rotting on the paths. Where decades earlier Spencer recorded a line of women wending up the hills at dusk to escape the mosquitoes, now a line snakes tiredly at six o'clock to the Social Club near the old banyan tree. Beer is sold only in open cans to discourage solitary boozing at home. There are twenty four to a flat. Everyone drinks as fast as possible before the place shuts down at nine o'clock.

Two old women watch a video of *The Boys from Brazil*. Vicious rottweilers tear at the throats of mustachioed men, all of whom happen to be identical clones of Adolf Hitler. The men claw at the ravening teeth with lacerated hands. The thunderous cadences of the Horst Wessel Song drown their dying shrieks. The women watch impassively. One nods knowingly: "Good hunting dog that!"

As closing time approaches, they begin the slow walk home. The moon rises on pale-walled shacks, painting ghostly garbage heaps, and reflecting off the silver beer cans piled in a long trench. Shouts erupt from one shack as a man beats his wife. Thuds, screams, curses. Running feet. Night sweeps back, and silence returns, broken only by the birds at dawn. Crows caw as the sun rises on another hot day. A boy sniffs petrol from a rusty can. Women slump against their doorways; their men stay stuporous until sunset, when they stir, and start the slow walk back to the club.[28]

Some feet still drag. Some hold their beer can in both hands, to cope with their old, abbreviated digits and their recent tremors. These days dapsone takes care of leprosy so fast it makes the old-fashioned sulphones look like homeopathy. Only the older people are physically impaired, and no one stays contagious for long.

Everyone is burned out.

9

Chronicle of a Bushman

"Kagga Kamma . . . Place of the Bushmen. An evocative name, a magical situation. Imagine yourself amidst the rugged beauty of the Cedarberg mountains, inhaling the crisp Karoo air, in the company of a large variety of game, and, unbelievably, several families of stone-age Bushmen that have returned here to the home of their ancestors."[1]

The semidesert region of southern Africa, called the Kalahari, stretches across the northern Cape, from Namibia to Botswana. In 1937, seventy-seven hunter-gatherers from the southern region journeyed 800 kilometers east to participate in the celebrations being held at the Empire Exhibition in Johannesburg. Here, they danced and sang to twanging bows and drums, coaxed fires from vibrating sticks, and watched their audience, as spectators gazed with immense curiosity at what were supposedly the last living remnants of the purest Bushmen (fig. 28).[2]

Among them was !amg!aub, and his brother Isak, sons of old Makai. !amg!aub was known to the Boers as "Regopstaan," an Afrikaans soubriquet that translates literally as "Rightupstanding."

There too was old Uyeb.

Old Uyeb is said to have danced himself to death on this occasion.[3]

More than fifty years later, some forty descendants of these people left their home in the red dunes that form part of the Kalahari Gemsbok National Park, on the edge of the Kalahari Desert and relocated themselves 750 kilometers south on a farm in the Cedarberg Mountains of the southwest Cape. Their purpose, it was said, was to to recreate a Bushman world in a landscape allegedly scoured of hunters more than two centuries earlier (see fig. 7).

The linkages that bind these events together reveal something about hunters and something, too, about ourselves.

Fig 28. Bushmen at the Empire Exhibition, Johannesburg, 1936–37 (South African Library, INIL 2984)

Let's start with old Uyeb. He was an elder, a dancer, and among his people he was probably also a shaman who knew how to enter trance. If he deliberately tranced himself into a netherworld beyond the Empire show in Johannesburg, who could blame him? For people like Uyeb were descended from folk who were systematically hounded and hunted off their land by the northward sweep of colonial farmers. It is not known whether Uyeb's direct ancestors once lived in the southern Cape, but links in language, material possessions, and beliefs suggest that they all once shared a common culture. European colonists labeled such indigenous people with a wide variety of names, of which "Bushmen," and "Hottentots" have survived the hazards of memory and usage to remain in common parlance.

It is likely that the early settlers intended that "Bushmen" cover hunters, and "Hottentots," refer to folk with a similar economy who also herded sheep and cattle, but these distinctions have turned out to be problematic. All native peoples of the Cape seem to have been bound into an interactive network that allowed them to forage, herd, trade, and steal each other's stock. Early travelers tended to label particular groups according the activity in which they were engaged when seen, but this does not mean that someone out hunting did not return to his small flock of sheep at night. Nor do archaeological sites occupied after the appearance of domesticated animals here about 2,000 years ago resolve the issue further. They often contain bones of domesticated animals comingled with those of wild ones, making it impossible to decide whether the residues were left by hunters who generally ate game but occasionally preyed on domesticated sheep, or herders out on a hunting expedition who took time out to consume one of their own stock. The written history of Bushmen living in and around the Kalahari documents their rapid integration into wider networks of trade and labor. Over the past century they traded in ivory and skins, worked as herders for local pastoralists and Boer settlers, and bred with many of the people they encountered in the course of these matters. Bushmen also occasionally preyed on sheep and hunted on newly declared farms. For these intrusions they were brutally beaten, or shot, and on occasion had their ears sliced off by bounty hunters.[4]

Ironically enough, we are indebted in large part for our current knowledge of Bushman beliefs to the relentless operations of the colonial system of justice. Tentacles of law, reaching far and wide, periodically gathered up Bushman felons in their grasp and dispatched them to prisons, to punish them more effectively for crimes committed against the European invaders. Around 1870 some /Xam Bushmen, from the region around Kenhardt, in the northern Cape, found themselves way down south, in Cape Town. They were incarcerated within the great crenelated walls of Breakwater Prison, from which they emerged regularly to smash rocks for the new harbor wall. A certain Wilhelm Heinrich Immanuel Bleek, formerly of Berlin, lived in the city at that time. He was a linguist and philologist and a scholar of Hebrew grammar. What was more, he was cousin to the famous Ernst Heinrich Haeckel, a German zoologist, who is perhaps best known for his observation that ontogeny recapitulates phylogeny, or, as Gould so aptly puts it, that every individual as it matures, metaphorically climbs its own family tree, by passing through its adult ancestral forms, in their correct, evolutionary order. Where paleontology was concerned, Haeckel probably drew on his cousin's familiarity with philology to argue that in the same way a child learns to speak as he grows, so the rational language of men only appeared after they had been present on earth for some time. He invented a hypothetical human ancestor that might have appeared as far back as the Miocene period and dubbed him *Pithecanthropus alalus,* the "Speechless ape-man." He went on to suggest that these primeval *Alali* were succeeded by a Genuine or Talking men. Haeckel placed the origin of true *Homo* in tropical Africa, Asia, or even on the vanished continent of Lemuria, now lying deep below the Indian Ocean. The force of his argument inspired a young Dutch doctor named Eugene Dubois to ship out to the Dutch East Indies, and search for fossil evidence of this scheme. In a sequence of astonishingly lucky events, Dubois discovered the first specimen of a genuine human ancestor, in Java, in 1891. Whether it had spoken or not, it had certainly walked upright, and Dubois commemorated this singular feature, as well as its putative ancestor, by naming it *Pithecanthropus erectus.*[5]

Flawed though Haeckel's ideas may have been, they were clearly landmarks in the science of human origins. Likewise, his cousin Wilhelm Bleek also cultivated a sense of what was important in anthropological circles. He arranged for some of the Bushmen to come and live in his back yard, to teach him their language, their legends, and life stories. After the Great Man died in 1875, his sister-in-law, Lucy Lloyd, continued the work he had begun, and later his daughter, Dorothea, joined the enterprise. Together, they left us a record of the words and souls of these beleaguered people. They interviewed shamans or medicine men who claimed to control health, game, rain, and misfortune. The power of the shaman, shared by other potent forces such as eland and pubescent girls, was called "*n/um.*" It was activated while dancing into a trance, during which time people shivered, sweated, bled from the nose, and released their spirit to travel either in the form of an animal or as an element such as wind and rain. Medicine men described the nether regions that they visited in trance; they told how they changed their form and substance and how they journeyed over vast distances to control a world far beyond the newly acquired realm of the invader. One such shaman was //kabbo, whose name meant "dream," and who, while in a state of trance, could cause the rain to fall. In the more immediate world of colonial times, he was captured while eating a springbok and indicted for stealing a sheep.[6]

For all that Bleek learned of the Bushmen, //kabbo learned a great deal too about the world of his captors as he planned his return home. "He only awaits the return of the moon," said //kabbo, sitting in Bleek's house, in the winter of 1873, "that he may return, that he may examine the water pits; those at which he drank. . . . I shall go to drink at home.

For the children will have probably fetched water. . . . For I have sat waiting for the boots, that I must put on to walk in; which are strong for the road. . . . For, it is a great road; it is long. . . . I must remain at my own place. . . . It is there that I sit waiting for the gun; . . . For, a gun is that which takes care of an old man; It satisfies a man with food in the very middle of the cold."[7]

When all the transcriptions were done, Dorothea Bleek visited the northern Cape, to see the places that the informants had described. She studied the Bushmen who traveled to the 1937 Empire show and watched as their lives became increasingly involved in the scientific discourse of those times. She must have been familiar with the introduction to her father's and aunt's book on folklore, where the famous historian George McCall Theal posited the Bushmen as a race that had made little advance since the long-ago days when their members shot flint arrows at reindeer in France. Likewise, she must have read his sad conclusion, that "there is no longer room on the globe for palaeolithic man." This view of Bushmen, as the last heirs of prehistoric hunters, now rapidly disappearing from the world, is patent in some of her possessions, now housed in the voluminous Bleek archives. They include people no one had ever seen, like Uncle Ernst's hypothetical *Pithecanthropus alalus,* people other ethnographers saw often, like William Lanne, the last Tasmanian man, and Trucanini, the Last Tasmanian, as well as many Bushmen, that she herself saw often, who worked with her father and aunt, and lived in their back yard in Cape Town (fig. 29).[8]

"This 3,700 ha nature reserve lies 260 km from Cape Town. . . . A stay here is the perfect escape from your daily routine. . . . A unique experience for visitors is the privilege to step into the world of authentic Bushmen. Here they let you share in their age-old skills of hunting and fire-making, and in the beauty of their handicrafts, dancing and story-telling."[9]

As time passed, Bushman existence centered on the waterholes of their sandy homelands, in places renamed by the invaders, like Twee Rivieren, on the edge of the Kalahari Gemsbok National Park. Here, people classified linguistically as "San," and colloquially as "Bushmen," were reclassified within the constraints of apartheid taxonomy according to their pale yellow skin, as "Colored." They lived off meager earnings as laborers and guides, receiving a small government pension when they grew old. Commercial film crews, looking for new twists to their African

Fig. 29. Portraits in the Bleek collection. Note Trucanini, the Last Tasmanian, *second left;* Haeckel's *Pithecanthropus alalus,* center rear, and William Lanne, the last Tasmanian man, *far right.* (South African Library, MSC 57, 27)

adventure movies, recognized their possibilities as hunters and shamans in a modern make-believe world, and they moved swiftly to make a series of films. "The Poisoned Butterfly" aired in South Africa, where Pieter de Waal, a farmer in the southwestern Cape, watched his television screen with mounting interest. Instead of being mystified by the repeated fade-outs behind the eyes of the shaman, he saw the Bushmen actors as people with nothing much else to do. Up north, in the Cedarberg Mountains, he had a large farm with nothing much to yield. An idea grew. He would visit the Gemsbok Park and meet the Bushmen. He would make them a proposal, and with any luck, they would come down and live on the farm. There they would recolonize a land once owned by prehistoric hunters. They would earn a living by making weapons and crafts for sale, and he would make enough money from the tourists to hang on to the land. The Bushman kids would go to school, their parents would have a home, and together they would all move confidently into the new century.[10]

Next morning, the idea looked just as good as it had the night before. De Waal phoned the TV producer. He made an appointment with the man on whose farm the Bushmen were then living. He got into his truck and drove north. Words like "exhibitionistic" popped into his mind. "Exploitative!" said the interviewer from the liberal press. "Atavistic too," said an anthropologist. De Waal stepped on the gas. He crossed the Orange River, named in 1777, by the last Dutch commander of the Cape garrison, not for its muddy hue but for the Dutch national stadtholder of the House of Orange. Pausing for a brief look around, de Waal headed into the Kalahari.[11]

At the farm he parleyed with Regopstaan's son, Dawie Kruiper, the leader of the Bushmen. The family had taken the name "Kruiper" (Creeper), though everyone used each other's Bushmen names when talking among themselves. De Waal explained his proposition.

Dawie listened carefully. He nodded.

"Let's go!"

A few weeks later, twenty-eight Bushmen went south. Dawie and his brother Hendrik, their wives and relatives, all heaved their bundles into the trunk and piled into the buses. Old Regopstaan stayed behind. He said he was too old to travel anywhere. Dawie craned his neck, watching as the bent figure faded from sight. The buses were on the road for two days. Flat land gave way to hills, and then to mountains. The buses wound their way around the rocky slopes and swung on to a high plateau ringed with peaks. Grotesque pillars of rock rose out of the red earth, yellow proteas bloomed on the slopes.

De Waal pointed to a sandy flat, abutting on some reddish cliffs as the bus drew up.

"Here we are!"

He spread his arms in welcome. A huge grin wreathed his weathered face.

The people stepped gingerly off the buses. Piles of reeds, freshly cut for windbreaks, lay on the sand. A heap of packaged food was stacked neatly against the rocks. Dawie took a deep breath of the hot, mountain air and laughed out loud.

Back in the Gemsbok Park, old Regopstaan felt the palpable silence of their departure. He felt mystified by the world of white men. He had always foraged in the veld for food, but some years earlier he and his old father Makai were jailed for shooting a gemsbok outside the game reserve. Released, they were then invited to hunt *inside* the reserve, where one might have thought animals would be even more protected. Not surprisingly, things had not worked out well, and the Bushmen were ordered to stop hunting altogether. Their dogs were shot, and a game ranger provided them with two gemsbok a week for food. Regopstaan still pondered the matter in complete bewilderment. He began to reconsider the entire matter of staying and changed his mind. Together with a score of other relatives, he traveled south to join the rest of his people at Kagga Kamma.[12]

Other would-be immigrants soon followed. Small pick-up trucks chugged back and forth between Gemsbok Park and Kagga Kamma, bringing friends and family. Oom Piet de Waal watched carefully, anxious in case troublemakers joined the group. One evening a truck pulled in. A man clambered out and walked over to the welcoming blaze. Firelight flickered over his scarred face. A woman looked startled: "It's Bylkapper!" she gasped.

"Bylkapper" means "Axe chopper," even "Axeman." The cicatriced face bore witness to numerous encounters with equally skilled opponents. Bylkapper grinned, a little nervously. His trip south had taken far longer than he anticipated, owing to a spot of sheer bad luck on the way down. A few months earlier he had hitched a ride from the Gemsbok Park, in the back of a pick-up heading south. The truck lurched over the unmade roads until it hit the National highway. Gathering speed, its headlights cut through a black, moonless waste. Suddenly pinpoints flashed in the distance, and lights and sirens declared a police roadblock, part of a massive national security check aimed at would-be terrorists. The truck pulled up. A soldier strode up, shining his torch into the cabin and over the blanketed shape in the back.

"Everyone out!" he shouted.

The passengers disembarked clumsily onto the gravel verge. The torch flashed again and again, then paused on Bylkapper's furrowed face.

The soldier grinned.

"Aii," he yelped, "Bylkapper?"

Bylkapper smiled weakly. He recognized the soldier from a disciplinary patrol that had passed through the park the previous year.

The soldier's memory was no less sharp. Without ceremony he reached into the Bushman's pocket and drew out a packet of *dagga,* or marijuana.

"Christ!" said the soldier, "You again?"

He pointed to the massive fortified Casspir at the side of the road.

"Wait there, man."

Kagga Kamma was not what Bylkapper had expected. People had to get up in the morning in order to greet the first tourist bus of the day.

They had to act like hunters, whittling bows, and shooting arrows. Sometime, they had to wear skin breechclouts, even beads. Even at night sobriety reigned, and the women were uniformly unfriendly. De Waal was adamant that his was to be a brief visit, and after a few weeks, Bylkapper concurred.

He took the next ride home.

"After many decades, the bushmen have come home to the original hunting grounds of their ancestors. Numerous Bushman rock paintings—relicts from the ancient San tribes who lived a long time ago can be found on Kagga Kamma. Most of these rock paintings range from more than two thousand to approximately six thousand years old."[13]

The Cedarberg Mountains, in which Kagga Kamma is situated, are renowned for their rock formations. Wind and water have carved the sandstone into pillars and cavities. Some form arches, others lie in attenuated, stratified humps, looking like the fossilized spine of a mud-bound reptile. Prehistoric people camped in the rock shelters for many thousands of years, and archaeologists now excavate their hearths, stone scrapers, broken bones, and ochers that lie embedded in the earthen floors. The rock walls are decorated with faded paintings, pale yellow, red, and black, traces of animals and people. Some are realistic, down to the digging sticks held in women's hands, and hunters' quivers bristling with arrows. Buck, baboons, and snakes festoon the walls, and even elephants are rendered in perfect detail, down to the fine tufts at the end of their tails. Intermingled with this realism are strange and unfamiliar images. Here, as elsewhere in southern Africa, humans are occasionally depicted in grotesque postures, with rigid arms extending backwards, as if in flight. Men, perfect in all other respects, sometimes have the hooves and heads of the great eland antelope. Here and there eland appear with their hair standing on end. Some have blood dripping from their noses, others sport a strange red line, running upward from their heads. Then too, large animals, like well-executed elephants, stand incongruously, framed in boxes.[14]

At first scholars tended to ignore these oddities, or else simply to label the eland men as hunters disguised to deceive their prey. But over the past decade a new theory has been formulated, linking the art to the beliefs of living San hunters of the Kalahari and to myths recorded by Bleek and his followers a hundred years ago. Scholars now interpret the art as part of a widespread and long-lasting belief system that was formulated by the artists to explain their world and their operating position within it. The rock paintings are seen as the product of myths and visions experienced in trance, or death, where men and animals interchange shapes and roles, bleeding from their noses and extending their power, or *n/um,* in a line from their heads as this potency is achieved. Large powerful creatures like eland and elephants that help control rain are enclosed in boxes or decorated with wavy lines to depict the vision changes experienced in trance.[15]

It is an attractive, integrated synthesis, but it is unprovable, because the artists who made the rock paintings are long gone, and modern Kalahari folk, who recite myths and who trance today, live in a flat and sandy desert where there are neither rocks nor paintings. Nevertheless, the ancient art has its repercussions today. Doppies is the son of Dawie Kruiper. He is twenty years old. He looks like a tiny bikie in his tight jeans, black leather jacket, and dark wrap-around glasses. Only when he lifts the glasses and smiles, and a grin crinkles from his high cheekbones to his shining, slanted eyes, does Doppies resemble his grandfather, old Regopstaan. Ever since he arrived, Doppies has wandered freely over the farm, looking at the prehistoric paintings. He discovered some reddish stones in the river bed, which he ground into powder and mixed with fat to form a paste. Using this pigment he began, slowly at first, to draw pictures of animals on the rock walls behind his camp. A single small giraffe and a few buck now glow beneath one of the overhangs. Doppies thinks they are identical to the faded drawings in the caves.

He is not completely correct here, because his drawings show no contorted dancers and no dots. His animals have no strange lines rising from their heads, their hides are smooth, and no blood leaks from their noses. Even the large giraffe stands free, unfettered by a box of any sort.

For until he came to Kagga Kamma, Doppies had never painted, nor had he ever seen rock art. He had therefore not linked the fragmentary myths of his childhood with this or any other art. If the anthropologists are right, and the prehistoric paintings encode myth and trance, then it is clear that Doppies, seeing only the superficial appearance of the ancient paintings, copies their form but not their substance. In time, some anthropologist may tell him the inner message, and initiate this elected heir of prehistoric Cape hunters into the world behind the drawings on their walls of weathered rock. Then, if Doppies draws a bleeding eland with its hair standing on end, or an elephant emboxed, the past will merge with present and the theories of anthropologists will become true.

"Make your conference a rewarding experience in the rugged natural surroundings of Kagga Kamma." [16]

One morning, about six months after the first group arrived, people rose slowly. It had been a bitterly cold night. Glancing through the narrow slits in their reed-walled shacks, they noticed that the distant mountains gleamed white. Shocked and surprised, they stumbled outside, only to fall into foot-high drifts of icy powder. Small white flakes drifted through the thin pale air and fell softly onto their upturned faces. It stung briefly, then washed down their cheeks.

No one had ever seen snow in their lives.

Some have no intention of seeing it again.

People recall how the red dunes stood clean and clear against the blue Kalahari sky. Old Regopstaan wants to be buried there in the dunes. Tucking his balaclava around his cheeks, he lights a pipe, and squints at the small shacks clustered in the lee of the contorted rocks. The dull, persistent pain below his ribs has worsened, but he knows that if he goes to hospital it will kill him dead. His sons, on the other hand, recall their homeland with considerably less nostalgia. Now that they have a steady income from the tourists, they realize how insurmountable was the poverty and hopelessness of their former life.

Dawie Kruiper has decided that he wants to make his home here, at Kagga Kamma. He wants his grave to lie in the lee of these rocks. He sits in the sun, carving the kudu horn that de Waal provided to make arrowheads. Around him the hum of the settlement rises and falls. Children call and laugh as they chase each other up the rocks. His small daughter, Oulip, sits nearby, the tip of her tongue protruding in concentration as she grinds ostrich eggshell into beads.

Dawie looks up: "When the snow melted I said this. Listen this is what I said. Yesterday evening I heard it. . . . I called all the children together. I said 'listen.' The little birds, the brown birds. Listen how they beat their little wings. The cold days are over. Feel it, feel the wind. The days will grow warm. I said that. I did." [17]

FIRST CERES BUSHMAN IN 250 YEARS

Proud Bushmen parents Hendrik, 40, and Fytjie Kruiper, 35, yesterday celebrated the birth of a son at the Kagga Kamma game farm—the first Bushman born in the Ceres area in 250 years. Mekai [sic] was named after his great-grandfather. The tribe visited Cape Town earlier this year . . . (An informant said). "They wanted to see the sea, see how their ancestors are depicted in a Bushman exhibit in the S.A. Museum, visit the castle and spend some of the money they have earned." [18]

In 1994, Dawie Kruiper traveled to Geneva to tell a United Nations conference on the predicament of indigenous folk, how he and his people were saved from extinction by moving to Kagga Kamma. He spoke of forgiveness, of reconciliation with former oppressors, who would now help the Bushmen to forge a brighter future, but if his published words are any guide, it seems that underneath his magninimity, lingers a gentle sense of retribution, that what goes around, must surely come around:

"[In] Cape Town . . . Van Riebeek's statue is messed on all day by birds. That's his eternal punishment while the Bushman statue is protected from rain and wind behind the glass in the South African Museum, just as we are protected at Kagga Kamma."[19]

10

Conclusion

My friend Jane hosts a "Hunter's Feast" each year, to serve some of the game and fowl that her husband and his friends have shot and snared. Twenty-five guests appear, all glowing with good will. Tables are laid with green-checked cloths, and flowered centerpieces feature carved duck decoys. Three wineglasses sparkle in the candlelight at each place setting. A serving table groans with game pie, springbok stew, braised guinea fowl, and roasted boar. Dishes of yams, rice, and greens, stand alongside small bowls of relishes like tangy jellies, stewed peaches, and apricots in cloves and cinnamon syrup.

The wines are chosen with care. Guests sip before they drink, though everyone drinks deep and long as they demolish plate after plate. The men are farmers, business men, lawyers, and doctors. Most of them hunt on odd weekends. They have been friends for ever and ever. Some played rugby together, first at Rondebosch Boys High or Bishops, then later for the university teams or local clubs. They share holidays, compete in the Durban-Mauritius yacht race, and watch rugby or cricket on Saturday afternoon, depending on the season of the year. Their wives usually go along, and if they don't, they sometimes find themselves traded in for a new one, or else they trade in their man for something more to their taste.

Tonight a glow pervades the room. The talk is loud and full of laughter. Jane pedals at the pianola and guests, leaning back for a breather, sing along.

Then one man, dark hair smooth on his head, face flushed, begins: "A joke," he bellows, "I've got a bloody good joke!"

The roar subsides.

"Just listen!"

People smile. He is a famous raconteur, but he waits, running his finger around the rim of his glass until he has everyone's full attention. Then he begins to speak, slowly, in Afrikaans, curling his tongue around the words in a lazy drawl that evokes smiles even before the story gets under way.

"The ships come sailing into the bay. Full sails. There are three of them. You know them, the *Dromedaris,* the *Reijger,* and the *Goede Hoope* . . ."

People settle in. They get the drift of the story. He is talking about the first settlers to come to the Cape, in the first fleet, under the first commander, Jan van Riebeeck. The year is 1652.[1]

". . . and maybe there are also the *Nina* and the *Pinta* and the *Santa Maria,* but who the fuck cares? They sail into the bay, cheering. Everyone's waving. Hello! Hello! And there, right in the middle of the bay, there, believe me, there is the little island. It's Robben Island, but Nelson Mandela isn't there. No, no, no. Not yet. Instead, there's this girl on the island."

Nudges and winks. The joke is getting off at a lope.

"So this girl, O man but she's lovely with her golden skin and her tits and that bum, she's the best thing they've ever seen, she waves to the *Reijger,* and she calls to them, and hell man, one of the ship heaves to and anchors there, right off Robben Island.

"And she beckons to them again. So a couple of men let a boat down and they row ashore, and hell, they throw her one. And what the hell, another. And another."

Laughter. Nudges and winks.

Wine circulates again.

"So then this ship sails off and the next one, the *Goede Hoope,* arrives. And she waves again, and hell, she's lovely, and again, they throw her one!"

More laughter. A woman looks knowingly at her husband's grin. He catches her glance and looks away.

"And then, then the last ship of the line now sails in. The flagship, *Dromedaris,* with the commandant aboard, him, Johhhhan . . ."

He drawls the word loud and long.

"Johan van Riebeeck, he sees her and as a welcome, even he, he throws her one. And then he says, 'Thank you,' because he is the commandant, and he says, 'Thank you, Eva,' because that's her name now, see?"

Nods all round.

"And they sail into the shore.

"A couple of months later, some men are still on the ships, and they look out, and there's a small rowboat coming toward them from Robben Island. And they look, and they watch, and it's her, Eva! And she's rowing and rowing, and she draws up alongside, and she calls out to them: 'Where's the *Kaptein*?'

"And the men see she's gone a bit fat. She's big now, you know, she's got these great tits and this big belly, and they put her off, but she doesn't want to hear, and she calls out again. So they call him: 'Ay, Johann van Riebeeck,' they call him, 'where the hell are you, man?'

"And he comes to a porthole, and sticks his head out and calls to Eva: 'Yes? What you want?'"

The audience straighten up for the punch line.

"And she sails right up to him, him, the commandant, and she leans out and she shouts."

The raconteur knows his audience. He waits.

"And she leans over, leans over so he can see all the way down to the bloody Promised Land . . ."

He pronounces it "Promisslen."

"And she says . . ."

He waits again. His listeners draw in their breath.

"'You, you with that bloody great ship around your neck? You!'

"Eva looks him full in the face. Straight out. She shouts: '*Jou ma se moer!*' Your mother's womb!"

Notes

Bibliography

Index

Notes

Chapter 1: Introduction:

1. See, for example, Boorstin 1985; Crosby 1986. For post-office stones, see Raven-Hart 1967, facing 101; Schoonees 1991. For a general summary of VOC routes, see Bruijn, Gaastra, and Schöffer 1987, 56–76.

2. This anecdote was related by Jim Deetz, ca. 1988. For the archaeology of Parting Ways, see Deetz 1977, 138–54.

3. For the first human colonization of Australia, see Roberts, Jones, and Smith 1990; for America, see Bednarik 1989; Bray 1988; Dillehay and Collins 1988; Guidon and Delibrias 1986. For a population growth-rate study, see McArthur, Saunders, and Tweedie 1976. For Phoenicians in South Africa, see Herodotus 4.42.2–4, and for Australian contact, Macknight 1986; Mulvaney 1989. For general works on the impact of endemic diseases, see Butlin 1983; Dobyns 1983, 1993; Krech 1981; McNeill 1989; Martin 1978; Ramenofsky 1987; Stannard 1989, 1992. For critical discussions of the problems regarding computation of carrying capacity in prehistoric societies, see Nordyke 1989; Schmidtt 1989. The tale of the Arctic factor appears in Burch 1978.

4. Algemeen Rijksarchief VOC 4111, folio 107–17 (Dec. 18, 1729). Arguments that indigenous people were rarely, if ever, in the area at this time (Smith et al. 1991, 90; Yates and Smith 1993, 53), are dispelled by the correspondence from the VOC post that documents continual interactions between indigenes and colonists there around that time (Schrire 1990).

5. Bainbridge 1991; Coetzee 1983. The quotation comes from Coetzee 1992, 99.

6. For details, see chapters 4 and 5.

7. For references to this massacre see chapter 4, note 12; chapter 5, notes 5 and 6. For Kees, Elphick 1985, 129.

8. Dening 1986, 117.

Chapter 2: Chronicle of a Childhood

1. The information about Reb Yehuda Leb Schrire (1851–1912) that follows is drawn from several sources, chief of which is an undated autobiographical account

entitled "The history and happenings, reasons and adventures, from the day of my birth, to the day of my death, with a short critique in a clear language, in songs and prose, in remembrance for all time," henceforth referred to as Schrire ca. 1910. The manuscript, a small black notebook, contains 150 eight-line Hebrew stanzas in meticulous handwriting. It came into my father's possession on the death of his mother. It is clearly not a diary but a memoir transcribed in Cape Town around 1910. The quotations used here come from a preliminary translation. Other sources include his Hebrew novel (Schrire 1879), and a brief, untitled, undated account by his son Harry. For a brief history of Sherira Ben Hanina Gaon, see M. H. 1972.

2. Shimoni 1980, 7–8. For a definitive biography of Sammy Marks, see Mendelsohn 1991.

3. See Schrire, ca. 1910, verses 28–30.

4. For the use of *Khoikhoi,* see chapter 3, note 22.

5. These inferences are drawn from Raper and Boucher 1988, 33; Cullinan 1992, 170–71; Penn 1988.

6. Cullinan 1992, 183–85.

7. Ross 1991.

8. For District Six, see Franck, Manuel, and Hatfield 1967, 1; Small and Wissema 1986.

9. Schrire ca. 1910, verse 58. Glass negatives of some of the photographs of the Boer War, taken by M. Schrire, are housed in the Cape Archives Depot, Schrire Collection, SH1–27.

10. For a history of the business enterprises described here, see Kaplan 1986, 308–24. For documentation of Rebecca Mauerberger's interest in Zionism, see letter from Theodore Herzl to Rebecca Mauerberger, June 13, 1901, The Nahum Goldman Museum of the Jewish Diaspora, Tel Aviv., neg. no. EXH. 42.3c.29.11. For her other Zionist activities, including attendance at the Sixth Zionist Congress in Basle (1903), see Kedourie 1979, 298, plate 40; Herrman 1929, 75. For Reb Schrire's founding of the first Zionist group in Africa, see Gitlin 1950, 43.

11. For a general discussion of the Immigration Restriction Act of 1902, see Shain 1983, 15–32. The quotation used here is found in Shain 1983, 30. For an overall summary of anti-Semitism in South Africa, see Shain 1994.

12. These cartoons and others like them, are reproduced in Shain 1981, 1983, 1994. They appeared in the *Owl:* Dec. 12, 1902; Nov. 1, 1901; May 6, 1904; Sept. 26, 1902, and Nov. 14, 1902. It is worth noting that the tone of these cartoons was not sufficiently offensive to deter several Jewish firms from advertising in the *Owl,* as is witnessed in May 24, 1901; March 4, 1904 and June 17, 1904.

The origin of Hoggenheimer appears in Pallister, Stewart, and Lepper 1988, 48–49; and Shain 1981. Where the etymology of *smous* is concerned, Shain 1992, 187, note 4, suggests that it may derive from a corruption of Moses, or from the German *Mauschel,* a Jewish trader, or even from the German *Schmuss* (Yiddish colloq. *shmooz*) for talk or patter.

13. An interesting recent argument is discussed in Adhikari 1992.

14. For a more extensive and affectionate description of this school, see L. Gordon 1992.

15. Schrire 1956.

16. Herrman 1929, 77.

17. The quotation about the royal visit comes from the *Cape Argus,* Feb. 17, 1947. For other details, see Higham and Moseley 1991, 136–37.

18. See, for example, Furlong 1991 and a review of this work by Shain 1992, 194–95.

19. UNESCO 1972, 15–29; Brookes 1968.

20. For a revisionist view of the festival, see Rassool and Witz 1993; see also Schrire 1984b, 5.

21. The song may be translated as follows: "And do you hear the mighty thunder? / Over the veld it comes soaring widely."

22. Schrire 1966, 1972.

23. For references to this raid, see Pakenham 1992, 1–5.

24. See UNESCO 1972, 100–116. The refusal of a post to Archie Mafeje is documented in UNESCO 1972, 111. He was co-author of a landmark study on township life (Wilson and Mafeje, 1963).

25. For a history of this school of British anthropology, see Kuper 1973. For the early work of Monica Wilson, see Hunter 1936.

26. For a brief biography of Goodwin, see Deacon 1989. Other works referred to here include Burkitt 1928; Goodwin and Van Riet Lowe 1929. For an assessment of these works, see Schrire et al. 1986, 123; Shaw 1991.

27. For Sharpeville, see Phillips 1961, 3; Pogrund 1990, 129–47. For reference to Jordan, see Phillips 1961, 170–71; to Kgosana, see Phillips 1961, 161–73; Pogrund 1990, 138–39.

28. See Drennan 1953; Singer and Wymer 1968.

29. See Dart 1925, 1957; Brain 1958, 10–12; Leakey, Tobias, and Napier 1964.

30. Singer and Wymer 1982, 5–8.

31. Archives of the Jagger Library, MS. 04.03.03, 3.

32. For autobiographical and biographical works, see Daniel 1986; Clark and Wilkinson 1986; Clark 1989. Examples of Higgs's research may be found in Higgs 1972; for excavations at Haua Fteah, see McBurney 1967.

33. See Daniel 1986, 97–100.

34. For biographical studies of Golson, see Gathercole 1993; Groube 1993; Mulvaney 1993; Spriggs and Jones 1993.

35. Opinions about Australian archaeology at this time may be found in Mulvaney 1961, 1993.

36. See Murray and White 1981; Mulvaney 1960; Jones 1968; White 1972; Wright 1971.

37. For a brief and succinct discussion of Aboriginal cosmology in relation to the land, see Tonkinson 1980.

38. Schrire 1982. Some exposition of this work appears in chapter 8.

39. See Peterson and Langton 1983.

40. For an updated view of Aboriginal sacred sites, see Maddock 1991. The cynical view of politicians is attributed to Rhys Jones, in Davidson 1991, 255. For views on the uranium-impact project, see Harris 1980; Schrire 1985; Tatz 1982, 118–90.

41. The assassination of Verwoerd and his treatment at Groote Schuur is documented in Botha 1967, 1–9.

Chapter 3: Chronicles of Contact

1. Boorstin 1985, 179–98, 220–23; Crosby 1986, 57.

2. See, in addition to sources quoted above, Boxer 1977, 1979; Braudel 1985, 1986; Curtin 1985; Wallerstein 1980; Wolf 1982.

3. For the Siamese diamonds, see Elphick 1985, 207. For an exposition of *Hottentot*, see note 22.

4. I have embellished here a throwaway line offered to me by Carl Hoffman at the University of Pennsylvania in 1984.

5. The Australian reaction may be found in Cook 1846, 205; Swain 1993, 114–15. The Arctic version emanates from a Netsilik Inuit story told in 1948 about the 1829 encounter between native people and the expedition led by Sir John Ross to the Boothia Peninsula, as told in Weibe 1989, 89–91. The Hawaiian story, found in Sahlins 1981, is embellished in chapter 7.

6. The allusion to Narcissus appears in Ten Rhyne 1933, 139.

7. See, for example, Butlin 1983; Crosby 1972, 122–64; Dobyns 1983, 1993; Krech 1981; McNeill 1989; Martin 1978; Stannard 1989, 1992. For the ecological impact of European invasion in northeastern America, see Cronon 1983.

For the debate concerning the spread of syphilis, see Baker and Armelagos 1988; Crosby 1972. For a counterargument that syphilis may have been present in France in the third to fifth centuries A.D., see Pàlfi et al. 1992.

8. Strictly speaking, since the Cape of Good Hope divided the realms of the two companies, the VOC should not have encompassed the west coast of South Africa within its realm. For trade networks, see Boxer 1977, 198–214; 1979, 11–14; Bruijn, Gaastra, and Schöffer 1987, 173–94; Parker 1978; Ross 1991. For the uses of mercury, or quicksilver, in mining and gilding and its shipment in stoneware flagons, see Sténuit 1974, 239–43. For particular shipwrecks, see Green 1977a, 169–72; Sténuit 1978; Werz 1993, 37.

9. For reference to missionary training, see Boxer 1977, 134; for slavery in general, Boxer 1979, 238–41. For Cape slavery, see Armstrong and Worden 1989; Ross 1983; Shell 1994.

10. For Formosa, see Hauptman and Knapp 1977; for Banda, Boxer 1977, 99, 239; for the Moluccas, Boxer 1977, 99. Pepper appears in Boxer 1977, 198–99, and its use in the preservation of meat, in Boorstin 1985, 195.

11. The quotation regarding porcelain comes from Chatwin 1988, 52. For the Dutch trade in China and Japan, see Boxer 1979, 174–75; Woodward 1974, 9–31, 53–80.

12. The history of the Dutch in Brazil is taken from Boxer 1957. Analysis of the art appears in Joppien 1979 and Van den Boogaart 1979. For descriptions of these portraits as an ethnography or human map of the country, see Alpers 1984, 163–64; Joppien 1979, 302.

13. The ascription of the paintings in European art comes from Joppien 1979, 302. For the rest of this section on Brazil, see Boxer 1957, 112–58. For the section on the departure of Johan Maurits from Brazil, ibid., 156–57.

14. Arrack is a strong alcoholic beverage of the Near and Far East, distilled from a mash of rice and molasses or from the juice of the coconut palm. Elphick 1985,

165–66, insists that trade in alcohol was relatively minor in South Africa and that it never had the same initial devastating effect here as in North America.

15. This is a amalgam of punishments typical of those meted out in ancien-régime days.

16. The seminal paper on this subject is Cann, Stoneking, and Wilson 1987. For the recent controversy about the existence of Mitochondrial Eve, see Frayer et al. 1993; Klein 1994; Maddison 1991a,b; Maddison et al. 1992; Templeton 1993; Thorne and Wolpoff 1992; Vigilant, et al. 1991. For a discussion of the integrity of mt DNA, see Zouros et al. 1992.

17. The finds at Border cave appear in Beaumont, De Villiers, and Vogel 1978; Grün, Beaumont, and Stringer 1990. Finds at Klasies River Mouth cave appear in Singer and Wymer 1982; Klein 1989.

18. Reference to the Israeli finds appears in Ahrensburg 1989; Bar Yosef et al. 1992; Shea 1989. For Asian material, see Thorne and Wolpoff 1992; Wolpoff 1989.

19. Deacon 1984.

20. For the antiquity of sheep in southern Africa, see Sealy and Yates 1994. Group identity is a hotly debated issue in the field of hunter-gatherer studies. Some seminal arguments appear in Elphick 1985; Klein 1986; Marks 1972; Schrire 1980, 1984a; Smith 1983, 1986, 1990; Solway and Lee 1990; Wilmsen and Denbow 1990.

21. For first callers at the Cape, see Raven-Hart 1967. For Phoenicians, see Herodotus 4.42.2–4; O'Sullivan 1990. A comprehensive series of accounts of early travels to the Cape appears in Raven-Hart 1967, 1971.

22. For discussion of the term *Hottentot,* see Elphick 1985, xv; Maingard 1935. When I use the term here, I do so to echo, in the appropriate context, its use by early colonists, in referring to the indigenous pastoral hunter-foragers that they encountered at the Cape from the seventeenth century onwards. The derogatory implications that attended later on its usage are not intended here (see Bredenkamp 1991; Newton-King 1991). Elsewhere, the term *Khoikhoi* is used throughout in reference to these people (see Smith 1990, 3, note 1).

23. The prayer is found in Bruijn, Gaastra, and Schöffer 1987, 167, and the natural selection process, 162. For statistics, 162–72; Ross 1991, 179. For further particulars of ships, see Bruijn, Gaastra, and Schöffer 1979a,b.

24. For Van Riebeeck's problem, see Thom 1952, xxiii–xxiv. A reprint and translation of this Dagregister, or diary, is available in Van Riebeeck 1952, 1954, and 1958. For details about the early settlement, see Elphick and Giliomee 1989; Robertson 1945.

25. For the increase of indigenous herds, see Mentzel 1921, 56; 1944, 212–13. For colonial land use, see Guelke 1989.

26. For trade, see Elphick 1985, 164–66, and for guns on wet days, 112; Dapper 1933, 13; Ten Rhyne 1933, 133.

27. Loosely translated from Van Riebeeck 1958, 196.

28. Eva's name first appears in 1656, in Van Riebeeck 1954, 4, note 2. A short biography is found in Malherbe 1990. For the reference to "lady into fox", see Garnett 1923. For reference to "vixen" and "skins," see Cape Archives, C1876, 307–8, (Nov. 22, 1663), translated in Leibbrandt 1901:81; Moodie 1960, 271.

29. For a history of Robben Island, see De Villiers 1971. The Oppenheimer

reference is Pallister, Stewart, and Lepper 1988, 77. Eva's biography draws on Elphick 1985, 96, 104–9, 111–15, 121–22, 177, 200–205, 213; Leibbrandt 1901, 266–68.

30. Sara's case appears in Moodie 1960, 315–16, and 315 note 1. For additional information, see Elphick 1985, 184, 203, 205, 213.

31. The plague is documented in Elphick 1985, 231–34; Valentyn 1726, 51–52; 1971, 217–19. The classical names appear in Leibbrandt 1896a, 258.

32. For the spread of Khoikhoi people, see Penn 1989, 4; 1990. For Eva's children, see Barnwell 1946, 101–2; Elphick 1985, 203.

33. The quotation here is from Marks 1972, 77.

Chapter 4: Chronicle of a Dig

1. For excavations of the Fort de Goede Hoop, see Abrahams 1987, 1993; Potgieter and Abrahams 1984. For a history of the castle, see Fransen and Cook 1980, 39–40; Picard 1972; Ras 1959. For the archaeology of the castle see Hall 1992, 386–90.

2. Sleigh 1993, 411–68.

3. Portuguese crosses are documented in Axelson 1973, and references to the Saldanha Bay post in Axelson 1977. The oldest fortress discussion appeared in the *Argus,* Oct. 31 1973: "This may be SA's oldest fortress," by Florence Short.

4. Reference to Captain Kidd appears in Raven-Hart 1971, 424. Piracy in 1693 is documented in Cape Archives, LM 12, 33–38, (May 3–10, 1693), and in 1699, in Leibbrandt 1896a, 9–10; 1896b, 113. A popular account of these events appears in Burman and Levin 1974, 39–44.

5. The establishment of the post in 1669 is documented in the official diary, as translated in Leibbrandt 1901, 274. Its final abandonment, in 1732, is documented in Sleigh 1993, 456–57; Cape Archives, C336, 404 (May 12, 1732); C432, 106 (May 2, 1730). Sources on the French intervention appear in Leibbrandt 1901, 203–12; Raven-Hart 1971, 94–101.

Details regarding maps of the post are as follows. Among the earliest maps in the Cape Archives is one drawn by the Company surveyor, Peter Potter, around 1660, which plots a series of anchorages and waterholes lying along the shore (Cape Archives Catalog of Maps, M1/84). The post that was established in 1669 after the French tried to take the bay in 1666 first appears as a "Compagnies Post" on maps attributed to the early eighteenth century (Cape Archives Catalog of Maps, M1/1176; M1/1177a,b). The watering place where the French first planted their arms in 1666 is noted in the mid-eighteenth century too (Cape Archives Catalog of Maps, M1/1172), but the two entities became erroneously conflated when post was misnamed a "French fort." The earliest appearance of this error is Valentyn's map, Cape Archives Catalog of Maps, M1/1183, which features a "France schants." Although Valentyn only published it in 1726 (Valentyn 1726; 1971, facing 34), its other place-names suggest that it may have been drawn in, or before, 1710 (see Serton 1971, 11–13). Two subsequent maps by Van der Aa, one dated to 1713 (Norwich 1983, 282, no. 212), and the other to 1729 (Tooley 1963, 9, plate 10), perpetuate this "Fort Francois." Finally, Kolben's map, published two years later, shows a track from the

Dutch fort at Table Bay to a French one at Saldanha Bay (Kolben 1731, 2: facing 1; see fig. 9).

Maps such as these, confusing the Dutch post and a French fort, appeared while the original outpost was still in operation, and they persisted long after the post was abandoned in 1732, as may be seen in De L'Isle's map of 1740–56 (Norwich 1983, 288, no. 218), and two later maps by Bellin, one published in 1764 (Tooley 1963, 13, plate 21), and the other, in 1781 (Norwich 1983, 292, no. 222) with their "Fort et Etab. des Francois abandonné."

The cartographic fiction of a French fort disappeared in the later eighteenth century. In a series of maps dating from 1786–96, the original outpost is termed "Oude Post" or "VOC post," as opposed to the new post, which is labeled "Nieuwe Post," "DE Comp. Post," or "Company's Post" (see Cape Archives Catalog of Maps, M1/874, M1/888, M1/951, M1/954, M1/1331, and M1/1396). Barrow, who visited the post, makes the same distinction, referring as he does to "Oude Post" and "Post House" (Barrow 1802). By 1803 the bay where the original post stood was labeled "Old Post House Bay" (Raymond 1867, facing t.p.) and this name continued in use into the nineteenth century (see Cape Archives Catalog of Maps, M4/31). It later became "Kraal Bay," possibly due to the misidentification of the ruined outpost as a Khoikhoi kraal (Green 1970, 92).

6. Kaplan 1986, 309; chapter 2, note 10.

7. For information about the syndicate, see Die Oude Post Syndikaat 1984 and chapter 6.

8. Noël Hume 1991, 34–41, 76–83.

9. A preliminary analysis of the skeleton was made in the field by Alan Morris, Department of Anatomy and Cell Biology, University of Cape Town, in 1987. A more detailed analysis is now under way.

10. For differential burial of common sailors and prominent people at sea, see Bruijn, Gaastra, and Schöffer 1987, 167.

11. Noël Hume 1991, 356–57.

12. For documentary accounts of the massacre and its aftermath, see Leibbrandt 1902, 142–49; Moodie 1960, 329–31; chapter 5, notes 5 and 6. For a summary and analysis see Elphick 1985, 117–37. The temporary abandonment of the post after the massacre of 1673 is documented in Böeseken 1959, 116; 1961, 98–99; Sleigh 1993, 423–25.

13. For "Kaaps" see Small and Wissema 1986, 6.

14. The list cited here is drawn from Algemeen Rijksarchief, VOC 4004, folio 591v–592v (May 31, 1669). It is reproduced with a few slight amendments, such as grouping like things together under headings. I am grateful to Robert Ross and Remco Raben for locating and translating this document. Where measures are concerned, a *mas* is gold weight of approximately 38 gm, and a *mengel* is almost one liter.

15. The information about Wreede comes from Moodie 1960, 271, and Spohr 1963, though Goodwin 1952, 86–87, is skeptical of Wreede's skills. For reference to Kling, see Hoge 1946, 206; Cape Archives, LM 10, 644 (Mar. 18, 1687); Hendrick, Cape Archives, LM 20, 121 (Nov. 4, 1729). For further details, see Bruijn, Gaastra, and Schöffer 1987, 152–57; Schrire 1990.

16. For Khoikhoi cooperation see Leibbrandt 1901, 324; Raven-Hart 1971, 100.

For antagonism to Gonnema, see Leibbrandt 1902, 89. For the massacre of 1673 and its aftermath see note 12. For the identification of Kees himself, see Elphick 1985, 129.

17. The meaning of various names of indigenous groups is discussed in Gordon 1984, 196; Parkington 1984; Schrire 1980. Modern anthropologists, leery of the derogatory nature of *Bushman,* use what they imagine to be a more ethnically acceptable term, *San,* and combine it with *Khoikhoi,* to produce *Khoisan* as a catchword for all the indigenous non-Bantu speakers in southern Africa. Recently, *Bushman* has come back into favor, as seen in Griffin 1994, 13. Historically speaking, *Sonqua,* was used at the time of the massacre to describe hunters who preyed on the stock of others. See also chapter 9, note 1.

For reference to hereditary enmity, see Böeseken 1959, 153; Moodie 1960, 344. For one instance of antagonism toward the local Hottentots, see Cape Archives, LM 9, 2 (Jan. 6, 1677). The reoccupation of the post in 1685 is documented in Sleigh 1993, 425, and its relocation in 1732, in Sleigh 1993, 456–57. See also Cape Archives, C 336, 404 (May 12, 1732), and C432, 106 (May 2, 1730).

The aftermath of these events is discussed in Penn 1989, 1991; Schrire 1990, 1991, 1992; Yates and Smith 1993.

18. The discussion that follows is based largely upon published papers about Oudepost I, including Schrire 1987, 1988, 1990, 1991; Cruz-Uribe and Schrire 1991; Schrire et al. 1990; Schrire, Cruz-Uribe, and Klose 1993.

19. The relative densities of various artifact groups are listed in Schrire, Cruz-Uribe, and Klose 1993, 28. For information about garbage disposal of this sort, see Deetz 1977, 125–26. Slate pencils appear in Green 1977a, 228, and Stanbury 1974, nos. 4202–5. For references to the pattern of metal use, see Faulkner and Faulkner 1987, 135–61.

20. For reference to the earliest pottery works, see Böeseken 1973, 222. The analysis of the *Batavia* cargo may be found in Green 1975; Stanbury 1974.

21. The figures come from Schrire, Cruz-Uribe, and Klose 1993, 26. For private trade, see Boxer 1977, 201–6, 244–45, 249, 254–55. The allusion to *porcella* is taken from Chatwin 1988, 102.

22. See Harrington 1954. For an extensive analysis of the Oudepost pipes, see Schrire et al. 1990. For pipe typology in general, see Deetz 1988; Duco 1987, and for reference to the specific heel stamp in question, Duco 1982, 58, no. 126.

23. For a comprehensive study of Later Stone Age artifacts, see Deacon 1984. The geology of Oudepost appears in Flemming 1977. For a general description of Kasteelberg, see Klein 1986; Klein and Cruz Uribe 1989; for the archaeology of a nearby indigenous midden, see Robertshaw 1977, 1978. The controversy about the Oudepost artifacts appears in Schrire and Deacon 1989, 1990; Schrire 1992; Smith et al. 1991; Wilson et al. 1990.

24. For colonial artifacts in South African rock shelters, see Westbury and Sampson 1993. For glass artifacts in South Africa, see Clark 1977; Deacon 1986, 143; Goodwin 1945. For glass artifacts being produced during his visit to the Australian desert, see Gillen 1968, 271. For glass and porcelain points in Australia, see Flood 1983, 188; Mulvaney 1969, plate 46, a–d; White and O'Connell 1982, 112, 114, 125. For Tasmania, see Murray 1993, 513.

25. For the Oudepost silcrete gun flints, see Schrire and Deacon 1989, 108–9. For linkage of actual Khoikhoi people and stone artifacts, see Smith et al. 1991, 89; Wilson et al. 1990, 123, vs. Schrire and Deacon 1990; Schrire 1992.

26. Cruz-Uribe and Schrire 1991; Schrire 1990.

27. Proclamations concerning game appear in sources such as Böeseken and Cairns 1989, 14–16, and repeatedly in Jeffreys 1944. The Dutch meat lists are Algemeen Rijksarchief, VOC 4098, folio 309; 4101, folio 101; 4104, folio 106–13; 4107, folio 175; 4111, folio 134; 4115, folio 849; 4117, folio 913; 4120, folio 1183.

28. For the famous exchange of 1660, see Van Riebeeck 1958, 196. Examples of species counts from late prehistoric sites near Oudepost appear in Avery and Underhill, 1986, 350–51. The preliminary counts of the Oudepost birds were made by G. Avery at the South African Museum, Cape Town.

29. For an analysis of the dump, see Schrire, Cruz-Uribe, and Klose, 1993. For the coin itself, Schrire and Meltzer 1992, 104.

30. For information on the post at Groene Kloof, or Mamre, see Sleigh 1993, 494–509. Examples of bartering of sheep appear in Cape Archives, LM 11, 928 (May 20, 1692), importing sheep from Groene Kloof, in Cape Archives, LM 24: 127 (Mar. 19, 1727), and treatment of offal, in Cape Archives, LM 23, 3–4 (Jan. 15–16, 1723). This information is integrated in Schrire 1990.

31. The relative size of the Cape cattle industry in the early eighteenth century is documented in Mentzel 1944, 205–6, and their late importation, in Van Ryneveld 1942, 103–5.

32. The Oudepost beads are described in Karklins and Schrire 1991.

33. I am indebted to Greg Dening 1992, 62–63, for the idea of a cliometric moment. For Elphick's moment, see Elphick 1985, 160, and for Khoikhoi stock loss, 38.

34. The listing of bead colors appears in a consignment sent to the Namaqua people in November 1661, in Van Riebeeck 1958, 432–33.

35. For the carved eggshell, see Schrire 1988, 223–24.

Chapter 5: Chronicle of an Outpost

1. This chapter owes much to Coetzee 1983. The Khoikhoi view of the Dutch as "birds of passage" comes from Elphick 1985, 87. Reneging on contracts is documented in Elphick 1985, 124. For the positing of the Khoikhoi by historians, see Marks 1972. For a brief positing of Khoikhoi by colonists, and vice versa, see Schrire 1988, 215–17.

2. Moodie 1960, 317–18.

3. The chronicle is drawn directly from the official diary, or Dagregister, of the Cape for the years 1673 (Cape Archives: C1879), and 1676 (Cape Archives: VC7). The translation used is Leibbrandt 1902, which has been checked against the original manuscript by Bruno Werz, Department of Archaeology, University of Cape Town, and amended where necessary: C1879, 10 (Jan. 8, 1673); Leibbrandt 1902, 105. C1879, 12 (Jan. 10, 1673); Leibbrandt 1902, 105. C1879, 12 (Jan. 11, 1673); Leibbrandt 1902, 105. C1879, 17 (Jan. 16, 1673); Leibbrandt 1902, 107. C1879, 20 (Jan.

20, 1673); Leibbrandt 1902, 107. C1879, 21–22 (Jan. 23, 1673); Leibbrandt 1902, 107–8. C1879, 24 (Jan. 25, 1673); Leibbrandt 1902, 108. C1879, 36 (Feb. 10, 1673); Leibbrandt 1902, 111.

For the outward voyage of the *Hellevoetsluys,* see Bruijn, Gaastra, and Schöffer 1979a, 178–79.

4. Drawn from the following entries in the Dagregister, as follows: C1879, 42 (Feb. 20, 1673); Leibbrandt 1902, 112. C1879, 88 (Mar. 14, 1673); Leibbrandt 1902, 118. C1879, 89 (Mar. 15, 1673); Leibbrandt 1902, 119. C1879, 100 (Mar. 20, 1673); Leibbrandt 1902, 120.

5. Drawn from the following entries in the Dagregister, as follows: C1879, 161–62 (June 18, 1673); Leibbrandt 1902, 139. C1879, 163 (June 21, 1673); Leibbrandt 1902, 139. C1879, 165 (June 29, 1673); Leibbrandt 1902, 140. C1879, 170 (July 10, 1673); Leibbrandt 1902, 141. C1879, 171 (July 11, 1673); Leibbrandt 1902, 142. C1879, 173–74 (July 14, 1673); Leibbrandt 1902, 142–43. C1879, 181 (July 24, 1673); Leibbrandt 1902, 145.

6. Drawn from the following entries in the Dagregister and the Court Records, as follows: C1879, 210–11 (Aug. 11, 1673); Leibbrandt 1902, 154, and Cape Archives, CJ1, 831–32, (Aug. 11, 1673). The court case specifies charges against Jan Nielse of Stockholm, Wouter Larois of Gorcum, Dauwe Jansz. of Beeq, Jan Ples of Felsburgh, and Nicolaes Jansz. of Fredrickstat, on charges of vagabondage and desertion. Nielse confirmed the charge made by the other four, that he induced them to desert, but all were nevertheless, held responsible for their own actions. C1879, 211 (Aug. 12, 1673); Leibbrandt 1902, 154. C1879, 214–16 (Aug. 20, 1673); Leibbrandt 1902, 155–56.

7. This section draws heavily for its descriptions of Dutch behavior, but not for the sequence of events as I see them, on the writings of Grevenbroek 1933.

8. Drawn from the following entries in the Dagregister, as follows: VC7, 340–41 (Oct. 27, 1676); Leibbrandt 1902, 289. VC7, 345–51 (Nov. 1, 1676); Leibbrandt 1902, 289–91.

9. Drawn from the following entries in the Dagregister, as follows: VC7, 376–77 (Nov. 11, 1676); Leibbrandt 1902, 295–97. VC7, 380–81 (Nov. 15, 1676); Leibbrandt 1902, 298. VC7, 381–82 (Nov. 19, 1676); Leibbrandt 1902, 299.

10. This section is freely adapted from the diary of Governor Simon van der Stel, in Van der Stel 1932, 1979. For an analysis of toponymy, see Guelke and Shell 1992.

11. Gonnema died in late 1685 (Van der Stel 1932, 155), and Oedesson or Oedasoa in 1689 (Elphick 1985, 133). The death of both chiefs hastened the decline of the Cochoqua.

12. This section is drawn from Valentyn 1973, 15–57, as follows: Title, 15; Oct. 20, 1705, 17; Oct. 21, 1705, 19; Oct. 26, 1705, 25–27; Oct. 30, 1705, 31; Nov. 4, 1705, 41. The chief Hannibal mentioned here succeeded Oedasoa in 1689 (Elphick 1985, 133). Many authors, including Parkington 1984, 163–65, concerned with the names of native people, have noted how *Bushman* is used to denote brigands, not hunters, in Valentyn 1973, 41. For further comments and interpretation, see Penn 1989.

13. See Editorial Notes and News 1953, item 1.

Chapter 6: Chronicle of a Hamlet

1. For Saldanha's visit, see Raven-Hart 1967, 8, and for Spilbergen's impressions, 25–29. For a summary of early travelers, see Burman and Levin 1974.

2. For Ólafsson, see Raven-Hart 1967, 110. De Flacourt's impressions appear in Raven-Hart 1967, 172–77. The quotation comes from 175.

3. The *Haarlem* episode appears in Bruijn, Gaastra, and Schöffer 1987, 109; Elphick 1985, 87–89. For details about Deshima, see Woodward 1974, 18; for Banda, see Boxer 1977, 99. Van Goens's visit is documented in Boxer 1977, 246; Van Riebeeck 1954, 9–11.

4. Boxer 1977, 208.

5. Conflict is documented in Elphick 1985; Marks 1972. The spread inland may be found in Penn 1989, and discussion of toponyms, in Guelke and Shell 1992.

6. The joke appears in Boxer 1977, 229.

7. Raven-Hart 1971, 94–101; Leibbrandt 1901, 203–12.

8. The establishment of the post appears in Leibbrandt 1901, 274. See also chapter 4, note 5.

9. Reconstruction of the life on the outpost is based largely on excavations at Oudepost I, 1984–87, and on archival materials relating to its operation. See chapter 4 and Schrire 1990.

10. For the history of the post, see chapter 4, notes 12 and 17. For changes of place-names in the area, see chapter 4, note 5.

11. See Burman and Levin 1974, 57–64. The map referred to here is from the Cape Archives Depot, M748.

12. Boxer, 1977, 205.

13. For the history of British occupation, see Freund 1989, and for the Boer War, Pakenham 1992.

14. For the shift to Oostenwal (now mapped as Oosterwal), see Burman and Levin 1974, 91. Mention of Oostenwal also appears in Green 1958, 34. For a history of the Oudepost Syndicate, see Die Oude Post Sindikaat 1984. I am grateful to Mr. P. Haumann of Fransch Hoek, Cape, and Mrs J. Klose of Cape Town for information about the syndicate, and for the document.

15. Green 1973, 242–51.

16. Brookes 1968; UNESCO 1972, 19–29.

17. I am indebted for this account to the son of the last agent at the post who related it at a meeting of the National Parks Board at Geelbek, in 1991. For a discussion of the etymology of *smous,* see chapter 2, note 12.

18. See Die Oude Post Syndicate 1984.

19. For an account of members of this unit who were captured on maneuvers in Angola in 1985, see Soule, Dixon, and Richards 1987. Other details were learned during an escorted, and well-controlled, visit by C. Poggenpoel and myself to Donkergat in 1985, under the watchful eye of Commandant Venter, who, if memory serves, is the unnamed "commanding officer," pictured with a repatriated hero, in Soule, Dixon, and Richards 1987, 160.

Chapter 7: Chronicles of Collecting

1. Marks 1991, 8.

2. For the historical context of these studies, see Stocking 1987. For development of craniology, see Gould 1981, 73–112;

3. A biographical sketch of Riou appears in Ffolliott 1981, 504–5; Nash 1990, xv–xxxix. The quotation appears in Riou 1990, 33.

4. Flash Poll's problems appear in Searcy 1907, 57–58.

5. Tasmanian sea-level changes are discussed in Blom 1988; Chappell 1993; Jones 1977. For a history of Aboriginal people there, see Ryan 1981.

6. For details about the lives of William Lanne and Trucanini, see Ellis 1981, 133–44; Murray 1993, 513–16.

7. Trucanini's dealings are related in his extensive diaries, in Robinson 1966. Her intimacy with Robinson appears in Ellis 1981, 38–39. For Robinson's interests in relics, see Rae-Ellis 1988, 129–31.

8. For a spirited, and convincing, exoneration of Robinson in the light of Rae-Ellis's accusations, see Ryan 1988, for indications of Trucanini's feelings, see Rae-Ellis 1988, 132–33. For treatment of her remains, see Ellis 1981, 154–56, and plate 27, facing 56.

9. The sale of Robinson's goods appears in Rae-Ellis 1988, 262–65. Early views of the origins of the Tasmanians are discussed in Kirk and Thorne 1976; Sollas 1924, 107–32; and in its broader intellectual context, Jones 1992. The final disposition of Trucanini's skeleton is related in Ellis 1981, 158–72; Hubert 1989, 150.

10. For a portrait of Riou, see Nash 1990, facing xxii, and for his relationship with Cook, Nash 1990, xvi. Cook's voyages are described in Beaglehole 1968, 1974. Riou's presence on the third voyage is noted in Beaglehole 1974, 499. For an account of Bligh, see Dening 1992, and for the close call between Bligh and Riou, Nash 1990, xxv.

11. The Australian Aboriginal reaction appears in Cook 1846, 205; Swain 1993, 114–15; chapter 3, note 5. For Gordon's estate, see Nash 1990, xxxviii.

12. Ffolliott 1981, 504.

13. The allusion to "Kanguroo" appears in Cook 1846, 234, 240–41. For a recent statement about *terra nullius,* see Treaty 88 Campaign 1988. The landmark judgment, recognizing native title to land, is *Eddie Mabo and Ors. Plaintiffs vs. The State of Queensland, Defendant,* High Court of Australia, June 3, 1992.

14. Cook 1846, 327.

15. Examples of writings on this subject include R. J. Gordon 1992; Gould 1982; Altick 1978, 268–72; Gilman 1985, 76–108.

16. Gould 1982, 24.

17. For Baartman's story, see note 15.

18. Cited reasons for testicular evulsion include faster running, in Raven-Hart 1971, 19; cooling the ardor, 1971, 56; birth control, Raven-Hart 1967, 122–23; more sons, Valentyn 1973, 63. For relationship of Hottentots and Jews, see Grevenbroek 1933, 209, and for Cook's observations, 1846, 326. For classification, see Linné (Linnaeus) 1767, 29, and for Cuvier's impressions, Griffith et al. 1827, 196–201. The quotation is ibid., 200.

19. Raven-Hart 1971, 85.

20. Ibid., 240.

21. Ibid., 238.

22. Galton 1890. The "Venus" is Galton 1890, 53. The crinolines, and the extended quotation, 54.

23. Singer 1978, 120–24.

24. R. J. Gordon 1992, 193.

25. For an account of Cook's death, see Beaglehole 1968, 301–7; 1974, 637–77.

26. Joppien and Smith 1988, 126–27; Smith 1985, 108–23. For a detailed analysis of the mutual incorporation of European and Pacific islander cultures, especially with regard to pantomimes and shows, see Dening 1986.

27. For expositions of these ideas, see Sahlins 1981, 9–32; 1987, 104–35; Dening 1982.

28. For Cook as tyrant, see Dening 1982, 430, and for a full exposition, Obeyesekere 1992.

29. For references to sharks, and burned or sparkling eyes, see Dening 1988, xviii–xix, 89, 94; Fornander 1969, 2:25; Sahlins 1981, 20; 1987, 18–19. For Gooch's watching sharks, see Dening 1988, 88.

30. The photographs in question are catalogued as SAM nos. 655, 655A, 1278–1307. They were taken by J. Drury, modeler to the museum, who made a large series of live casts for the South African Museum between 1907 and 1924. For particulars, see Drury and Drennan 1926, and for a comprehensive overview of this subject and an account of how the live cast collection was made, see Davison 1991, 139–67; 1993.

The particular photograph described here is now missing. I saw it in the South African Museum in 1991. It was housed in a folder that contained those numerous other shots of female genitalia attributed above. When I returned the following year to check its acquisition number, the file was gone. My initial inquiries met with blank denial that any such pictures had ever been in the collection. When I persisted, I was told that since (but not on account of) my previous visit, all anatomical photographs had been placed in a special place to prevent them being used for pornographic purposes. A search of the newly hidden material failed to reveal the particular photograph that I was after, but it did elicit considerable concern from a senior curator, who was loath to imagine that the photographer (presumably Mr. Drury), should ever be construed to have operated in a prurient way.

Chapter 8: Chronicles of Leprosy

1. Northern Territory Medical Service of the Australian Department of Health 1970, vii–viii.

2. Cole 1975.

3. Ibid., 15–17.

4. For a bestiary of extinct Australian fauna, see Murray 1984. For ancestral populations in Asia, see Brown 1987; Thorne and Wolpoff 1992.

5. Early possible migration routes from Indonesia appear in Birdsell 1977. For a current overview of sea-level changes, see Chappell 1993. For bamboo rafts, see

Birdsell 1977, 143–44; Thorne and Raymond 1989. For Aboriginal views of creation and colonization, see Stanner 1965; White and Lampert 1987. Demographic theories appear in Birdsell 1953, 1967, 1977; White and O'Connell 1982, 74–83. For calculations of population growth in island migrations, see Levinson, Ward, and Webb 1972; McArthur, Saunders, and Tweedie 1976; Ward, Webb, and Levinson 1976. For a current overview of the Pleistocene colonization of Greater Australia, see Allen 1993. For radiocarbon dates for early human settlement in New Guinea, see Groube et al. 1986; in island Melanesia, Allen et al. 1988; in Tasmania, Cosgrove 1989; Cosgrove, Allen, and Marshall 1990. The north Australian thermoluminescence dates appear in Roberts, Jones, and Smith 1990.

6. For the earliest sightings of Australia, see Frost 1987; Mulvaney 1989, 8–17. The details and implications of Brouwer's sea passage, discovered in 1610, appear in Bruijn, Gaastra, and Schöffer 1987, 70–72; also in Boxer 1977, 197–98; Green 1977a, 4–6. For navigational problems, see Green 1977b, 9–12; for a collection of navigational instruments found in a VOC wreck of 1653, see Sténuit 1974, 226–35; for dead reckoning, see Boorstin 1985, 149; for Australian shipwrecks, see Green 1975, 1977a,b.

7. Major 1859, 102, 104.

8. Macknight 1969, 1976, 1986. For loanwords, Walker and Zorc 1981; for arguments about a north coast Creole, Urry and Walsh 1981; for the introduction of smallpox, Macknight 1986, 69.

9. The history of British settlements in north Australia appears in Flynn 1979; Lockwood 1977; Mulvaney 1989, 68–74; Spillett 1979. For Cornish chimneys at Port Essington, see Allen 1973, 50–51. The Lambricks appear in Allen 1967, 129; Spillett 1979, 142. The wine bottles are documented in Allen 1967, 130–31; the cows in Huxley 1936, 115. The letter is found in Huxley 1901, 47, and his diary is Huxley 1936, 114–15.

10. Allen 1967, 133–34.

11. For a history of Leichhardt's travels, see Webster 1980; for a review of contact on the Alligator Rivers plain, Keen 1980; Schrire 1982, 18–27. For the greeting, see Leichhardt 1964, 502; for the Aboriginal patois, Leichhardt 1964, 495, 502–3, 522–24. Their animal sounds, appear in Leichhardt 1964, 523. The "devil-devil" reference appears in Mitchell Library, MS. C.155, 421.

12. A summary of the McKinlay expedition and its aftermath is found in Lockwood 1977, 24–29. The rain gauge appears in South Australian Archives, Edmunds MS, 1, the inscription, 46. For the putative rock art, see Chaloupka 1979.

13. For feral animals, see Calaby 1980, 328–32; Letts 1979; McKnight 1976, 78, 83. For contact in the Oenpelli region, see Keen 1980. For Cahill, see Cole 1975, 15; Schrire 1982, 19.

14. Masson 1915; Spencer 1914, 1928. Spencer's mandate is appears in Mulvaney and Calaby 1985, 280–304, where the similarities with apartheid are noted, 286.

15. Mulvaney and Calaby 1985, 302–4, are in agreement with this assessment of Cahill. The Cahill letters are Australian Institute of Aboriginal Studies, MS 9568, the admiring quotation, 7 (Oct. 30, 1913).

16. Spencer 1914, 1928.

17. Australian Institute of Aboriginal Studies, MS 9568, 3 (Nov. 18, 1916).

18. For a summary of the Romula trial, see Lockwood 1977, 221–22. Cahill's account appears in Australian Institute of Aboriginal Studies, MS 9568, 1–9 (Oct. 10, 1917).

19. The cure appears in Australian Institute of Aboriginal Studies, MS 9568, 6 (Oct. 10, 1917). For influenza, see 4 (July 27, 1920), for the pelt, 1 (Nov. 24, 1921).

20. This section is drawn from Marett and Penniman 1931; Mulvaney and Calaby 1985, 406–18. For Darwin's footsteps, Marett 1931, 45; for the old woman, Spencer 1931, 59–60.

21. The origin of leprosy in the Northern Territory is discussed in Cook 1966, 561; 1970, 128–29; Flynn 1979, 19–34; Stack 1983, 5–6. Historical references to leprosy in the Northern Territory include Breinl 1912, 51; Breinl and Holmes 1915, 4; Cook 1927, 48–51; Holmes 1913, 3. For reference to the squalor and burning of Darwin's Chinatown, see Holmes 1913, 6, 8; Lockwood 1977, 79. For Holmes's comparisons of Chinatown and Cape Town, see Lockwood 1977, 150.

22. For a comprehensive overview of leprosy in the Northern Territory, see Hargrave 1975. See also Northern Territory Medical Service of the Australian Department of Health 1970. For a harrowing account of official policy on leprosy in the Northern Territory and Queensland, see Saunders 1990. The decline of this disease is tabulated in Government Documents, Canberra 1978, 1346–47. For medical personnel, see Fenton 1982; Kettle 1967.

23. After Cahill left in 1924, the government handed the station over to the Church Mission Society. The reserve was proclaimed in 1931. In 1948 a major scientific expedition worked at Oenpelli. See, for example, Mountford 1960. For the archaeology carried out by this group, see McCarthy and Setzler 1960.

24. The technical aspects of this section may be found in part in Schrire 1982, 1984c.

25. For accounts of Aboriginal burial customs, see Berndt and Berndt 1964, 386–419; Hiatt 1969.

26. Fox, Kelleher, and Kerr 1977; Toohey 1981.

27. Australian National Parks and Wildlife Service 1980. For impact studies, see Supervising Scientist for the Alligator Rivers Region Annual Report 1980.

28. For current perspectives on racism and Aboriginality, see Thiele 1991.

Chapter 9: Chronicle of a Bushman

1. Kagga Kamma publicity pamphlet 1, 1991. The term *Bushman,* formerly thought to have pejorative connotations, has recently come back into use, especially since the term *San,* which was considered innocuous, carries similar derogatory implications among certain Bushman groups. For many years anthropologists were vehement about correct usage, but recently Megan Biesele, a Kalahari specialist, announced at an international conference, that as far as the Namibia Bushmen themselves are concerned, *Bushman* will do just fine (see Griffin 1994, 13). The use made of *Bushman* in this essay, is therefore done in accord with current usage, with no disrespectful connotations.

2. See Dart 1937, 159; Steyn 1984, 117.

3. Steyn 1984, 117.

4. For a comprehensive discussion of the names, economy, and integrity of the groups discussed here, see Elphick 1985; Klein 1986; Klein and Cruz-Uribe 1989; Marks 1972; Schrire 1980, 1984a, 1992; Smith 1983, 1986, 1990; Solway and Lee 1990; Wilmsen and Denbow 1990. For a poignant rendition of these encounters into poetry, see Watson 1991.

5. For details of some of the Bushmen who were taken to the Breakwater Prison, see Bleek and Lloyd 1911; Deacon 1986, 1988; Theal 1911. I thank Bleek's great-granddaughter, P. Scott, for confirming his kinship with Haeckel. For an elucidation of Haeckel, see Gould 1981, 113–14. For his theory of human evolution, see Haeckel 1879, 181–3; 1914, 398–99.

6. Examples include Bleek 1875; Bleek 1924; Bleek and Lloyd 1911. For Bushman beliefs regarding shamans, animals, and power, see Bleek 1929, 1931, 1932a-c, 1933a,b, 1935. For //kabbo, see Bleek and Lloyd 1911, 290–316; Deacon 1986, 141–43; 1988, 134, 137.

7. //kabbo's account is drawn from Bleek and Lloyd 1911, 305, 313, 315, 317.

8. See Theal 1911, xxx-xxxi. The photographs were recently sent back to South Africa from New Zealand. They are now housed in the South African Library, MSC 57; 27. I am indebted to Karel Schoeman, of the South African Library, Cape Town, for drawing my attention to them. For Lanne and Trucanini, see chapter 7, notes 6–9.

9. Kagga Kamma publicity pamphlet 1, 1991.

10. This section is drawn from an interview with Mr. de Waal, Aug. 12, 1991.

11. Raper and Boucher 1988, 33.

12. Steyn 1984, 117–18.

13. Kagga Kamma publicity pamphlet 2, 1991.

14. Johnson 1979; Parkington 1989.

15. Lewis-Williams 1981, 1983; Lewis-Williams and Dowson 1988, 1990; Lewis-Williams, Dowson, and Deacon 1993.

16. Kagga Kamma publicity pamphlet 2, 1991.

17. Interview with Mr. Dawie Kruiper, Aug. 5, 1991.

18. *Cape Times,* Aug. 31, 1991.

19. *Sunday Times Cape Metro,* Feb. 27, 1994.

Chapter 10: Chronicle of a Joke

1. The Commandant's account of the arrival of the first settlers at the Cape appears in Van Riebeeck 1952, 18–26

Bibliography

Published Sources

Abrahams, G. 1987. Seventeenth and eighteenth century glass bottles excavated from Fort de Goede Hoop, Cape Town. *Annals of the South African Cultural History Museum* 1, 1:1–38.

———.1993. The grand parade, Cape Town: Archaeological excavations of the seventeenth century Fort de Goede Hoop. *South African Archaeological Bulletin* 48:3–15.

Adhikari, M. 1992. The sons of Ham: Slavery and the making of coloured identity. *South African Historical Journal* 27:95–112.

Almensburg, B. 1989. New skeletal evidence concerning the anatomy of Middle Palaeolithic populations in the Middle East: The Kebara skeleton. In *The human revolution: Behavioural and biological perspectives on the origins of modern humans*, ed. P. M. Mellars and C. B. Stringer, 165–71. Edinburgh.

Allen, J. 1967. The technology of colonial expansion: A nineteenth-century military outpost on the north coast of Australia. *Industrial Archaeology* 4:111–37.

———.1973. The archaeology of nineteenth-century British imperialism: An Australian case study. *World Archaeology* 5, 1:44–60.

———.1993. Notions of the Pleistocene in Greater Australia. In *A community of culture: The people and prehistory of the Pacific*, ed. M. Spriggs, D. E. Yen, W. Ambrose, R. Jones, A. Thorne, and A. Andrews, 139–51. Occasional papers in prehistory, no. 21. Canberra.

Allen, J., C. Gosden, R. Jones, and J. P. White. 1988. Pleistocene dates for the human occupation of New Ireland, northern Melanesia. *Nature* 331:707–9.

Alpers, S. 1984. *The art of describing: Dutch art in the seventeenth century*. Pbk. ed. Chicago.

Altick, R. D. 1978. *The shows of London*. Cambridge.

Australian National Parks and Wildlife Service. 1980. *Kakadu National Park plan of management*. Canberra.

Armstrong, J. C., and N. A. Worden. 1989. The slaves, 1652–1834. In *The shaping of South African society, 1652–1840*, ed. R. Elphick and H. Giliomee, 109–183. Pbk, rev. ed. Middletown, Conn.

Avery, G., and L. G. Underhill. 1986. Seasonal exploitation of seabirds by late Holocene coastal foragers: Analysis of modern and archaeological data from the western Cape, South Africa. *Journal of Archaeological Science* 13:339–60.

Axelson, E. 1973. *Congo to Cape: Early Portuguese explorers.* London.

————.1977. A summary of the history of human settlement at Saldanha Bay. *Transactions of the Royal Society of South Africa* 42, pts. 3 and 4:215–21.

Bainbridge, B. 1991. *The birthday boys.* London.

Baker, B. J., and G. J. Armelagos. 1988. The origin and antiquity of syphilis: Paleo-
pathological diagnosis and interpretation. *Current Anthropology* 29, 5:703–37.

Barnwell, P. J. 1946. *Visits and despatches (Mauritius, 1598–1948).* Port Louis, Mauritius.

Barrow, Sir J. 1802. *An account of travels into the interior of southern Africa, in the years
1797 and 1798.* New York.

Bar Yosef, O., B. Vandermeersch, B. Ahrensburg, A. Belfer-Cohen, P. Goldberg, H.
Laville, L. Meignen, Y. Rak, J. D. Speth, E. Tchernov, A.-M. Tellier, and S.
Weiner. 1992. The excavations in Kebara Cave, Mt. Carmel. *Current Anthropology*
33, 5:497–550.

Beaglehole, J. C. 1968. *The exploration of the Pacific.* Pbk. 3d ed. Stanford.

————.1974. *The life of Captain James Cook.* Stanford.

Beaumont, P. B., H. de Villiers, and J. C. Vogel. 1978. Modern man in sub-Saharan
Africa prior to 49,000 B.P.: A review and evaluation with particular reference to
Border Cave. *South African Journal of Science* 74:409–19.

Bednarik, R. G. 1989. On the Pleistocene settlement of South America. *Antiquity*
63:101–11.

Berndt, R. M., and C. H. Berndt. 1964. *The world of the first Australians.* London.

Birdsell, J. B. 1953. Some environmental and cultural factors influencing the struc-
turing of Australian Aboriginal populations. *American Naturalist* 87:171–207.

————.1967. Preliminary data on the trihybrid origin of the Australian Aborigines.
Archaeology and Physical Anthropology in Oceania 2, 2:100–155.

————.1977. The recalibration of a paradigm for the first peopling of Greater Australia. In *Sunda and Sahul: Prehistoric studies in Southeast Asia, Melanesia, and Australia,* ed. J. Allen, J. Golson, and R. Jones, 113–67. London.

Bleek, D. F. 1924. *The mantis and his friends.* Cape Town.

————.1929. Bushman folklore. *Africa,* 2:302–13.

————.1931. Customs and beliefs of the /Xam Bushmen. Part 1: Baboons. *Bantu
Studies* 5, 2:167–79.

————.1932a. Customs and beliefs of the /Xam Bushmen. Part 2: The lion. *Bantu
Studies* 6, 1:47–63.

————.1932b. Customs and beliefs of the /Xam Bushmen. Part 3: Game animals.
Bantu Studies 6, 3:233–49.

————.1932c. Customs and beliefs of the /Xam Bushmen. Part 4: Omens, wind-
making, clouds. *Bantu Studies* 6, 4:323–342.

————.1933a. Beliefs and customs of the /Xam Bushmen. Part 5: The rain. *Bantu
Studies* 7, 3:297–312.

————.1933b. Beliefs and customs of the /Xam Bushmen. Part 6: Rain-making.
Bantu Studies 7, 4:375–92.

————.1935. Beliefs and customs of the /Xam Bushmen. Part 7: Sorcerors [*sic*]. *Bantu Studies* 9, 1:1–47.

Bleek, W. H. I. 1875. *A brief account of Bushman folk-lore and other texts. Second Report concerning Bushman Researches, presented to both Houses of the Parliament of the Cape of Good Hope, by command of his Excellency the Governor.* Cape Town.

Bleek, W. H. I., and L. C. Lloyd. 1911. *Specimens of Bushman folklore.* London.

Blom, W. 1988. Late Quaternary sediments and sea-levels in Bass Basin, southeastern Australia: A preliminary report. *Search* 19:94–96.

Böeseken, A. J., ed. 1959. *Resolusies van die Politieke Raad, Deel II, 1670–1680, Suid-Afrikaanse Argiefstukke.* Cape Town.

————.1961. *Resolusies van die Politieke Raad, Deel III, 1681–1707, Suid-Afrikaanse Argiefstukke.* Cape Town.

————.1973. *Dagregister en briewe van Zacharias Wagenaer 1662–1666, Suid-Afrikaanse Argiefstukke: Belangrike Kaapse Dokumente, Deel II.* Pretoria.

Böeseken, A. J., and M. Cairns. 1989. *The secluded valley: Tulbagh, 't Land van Waveren.* Cape Town.

Boorstin, D. J. 1985. *The discoverers: A history of man's search to know his world and himself.* Pbk. ed. New York.

Botha, J. 1967. *Verwoerd is dead.* Cape Town.

Boxer, C. R. 1957. *The Dutch in Brazil 1624–1654.* Oxford.

————.1977. *The Dutch seaborne empire 1600–1800.* Pbk. ed. London.

————.1979. *Jan Compagnie in war and peace 1602–1799. A short history of the Dutch East India Company.* Hong Kong.

Brain, C. K. 1958. The Transvaal ape-man-bearing cave deposits. *Transvaal Museum Memoir 11*, 1–131. Pretoria.

Braudel, F. 1985. *The structures of everyday life: The limits of the possible.* Vol. 1 of *Civilization and capitalism, 15th-18th century.* Pbk. ed. New York.

————.1986. *The wheels of commerce.* Vol. 2 of *Civilization and capitalism, 15th-18th century.* Pbk. ed. New York.

Bray, W. 1988. The Palaeoindian debate. *Nature* 332:107.

Bredenkamp, H. C. 1991. Die Khoisan en vakterminologie na *The Oxford History of South Africa:* 'n Historiografiese dilemma. *South African Historical Journal* 25:61–76.

Breinl, A. 1912. Report on health and disease in the Northern Territory. In Report of the preliminary scientific expedition to the Northern Territory. *Bulletin of the Northern Territory* 1:32–53.

Breinl, A., and M. J. Holmes. 1915. Medical report on the data collected during a journey through some districts of the Northern Territory. *Bulletin of the Northern Territory* 15:1–5.

Brookes, E. H. 1968. *Apartheid: A documentary study of modern South Africa.* London.

Brown, P. 1987. Pleistocene homogeneity and Holocene size reduction: The Australian human skeletal evidence. *Archaeology in Oceania* 22, 2:41–67.

Bruijn, J. R., F. S. Gaastra, and I. Schöffer. 1979a. *Dutch-Asiatic shipping in the 17th and 18th centuries.* Vol. 2, *Outward-bound voyages from the Netherlands to Asia and the Cape (1595–1794).* The Hague.

————.1979b. *Dutch-Asiatic shipping in the 17th and 18th centuries.* Vol. 3, *Homeward-bound voyages from Asia and the Cape to the Netherlands (1597–1795).* The Hague.

244   *B i b l i o g r a p h y*

————.1987. *Dutch-Asiatic shipping in the 17th and 18th centuries.* Vol. 1, *Introductory volume.* The Hague.

Burch, E. S., Jr. 1978. Caribou Eskimo origins: An old problem reconsidered. *Arctic Anthropology* 15, 1:1–35.

Burkitt, M. C. 1928. *South Africa's past in stone and paint.* Cambridge.

Burman, J. and S. Levin. 1974. *The Saldanha Bay story.* Cape Town.

Butlin, N. G. 1983. *Our original aggression: Aboriginal populations of southeastern Australia 1788–1850.* Pbk. ed. Sydney.

Calaby, J. H. 1980. Ecology and human use of the Australian savanna environment. In *Human ecology in savanna environments,* ed. D. R. Harris, 321–37. London.

Cann, R. L., M. Stoneking, and A. C. Wilson. 1987. Mitochondrial DNA and human evolution. *Nature* 325:31–36.

Chaloupka, G. 1979. Pack-bells on the rock face: Aboriginal paintings of European contact in north-western Arnhem Land. *Aboriginal History* 3, 1–2:92–95.

Chappell, J. 1993. Late Pleistocene coasts and human migrations in the Austral region. In *A community of culture: The people and prehistory of the Pacific,* ed. M. Spriggs, D. E. Yen, W. Ambrose, R. Jones, A. Thorne, and A. Andrews, 43–48. Occasional papers in prehistory, no. 21. Canberra.

Chatwin, B. 1988. *Utz.* Pbk. ed. London.

Clark, G. 1989. *Prehistory at Cambridge and beyond.* Cambridge.

Clark, J. D. 1977. Interpretations of prehistoric technology from ancient Egyptian and other sources. Part 2: Prehistoric arrow forms in Africa as shown by surviving examples of the traditional arrows of San Bushmen. *Paleorient* 3:127–50.

Clark, J. D., and L. P. Wilkinson. 1986. Charles Brian Montague McBurney (1914–1979): An appreciation. In *Stone-Age prehistory: Studies in memory of Charles McBurney,* ed. P. Callow and G. N. Bailey, 7–25. Cambridge.

Coetzee, J. M. 1983. The narrative of Jacobus Coetzee. In *Dusklands.* Pbk. ed. Harmondsworth.

————.1992. Jerusalem Prize acceptance speech (1987). In *Doubling the point: Essays and interviews,* ed. D. Attwell, 96–99. Cambridge, Mass.

Cole, K. 1975. *A history of Oenpelli.* Darwin.

Cook, C. E. 1927. *The epidemiology of leprosy in Australia.* Canberra.

————.1966. Medicine and the Australian Aboriginal: A century of contact in the Northern Territory. *Medical Journal of Australia* 1, 14:559–65.

————.1970. Notable changes in the incidence of disease in Northern Territory Aborigines. In *Diprotodon to detribalisation,* ed. A. Pilling and R. A. Waterman, 116–30. East Lansing, Mich.

Cook, J. 1846. *The voyages of Captain James Cook in two volumes.* Vol. 1. London.

Cosgrove, R. 1989. Thirty thousand years of human colonization in Tasmania: New Pleistocene dates. *Science* 243:1703–5.

Cosgrove, R., J. Allen, and B. Marshall. 1990. Palaeo-ecology and Pleistocene human occupation in south central Tasmania. *Antiquity* 64:59–78.

Cronon, W. 1983. *Changes in the land: Indians, colonists, and the ecology of New England.* New York.

Crosby, A. W. 1972. *The Columbian exchange: Biological and cultural consequences of 1492.* Westport, Conn.

————.1986. *Ecological imperialism: The biological expansion of Europe, 900–1900.* Pbk. ed. Cambridge.

Cruz-Uribe, K., and C. Schrire. 1991. Analysis of faunal remains from Oudepost I, an early outpost of the Dutch East India Company, Cape Province. *South African Archaeological Bulletin* 46:92–106.

Cullinan, P. 1992. *Robert Jacob Gordon, 1743–1795: The man and his travels at the Cape.* Winchester.

Curtin, P. D. 1985. *Cross-cultural trade in world history.* Pbk. ed. Cambridge.

Daniel, G. 1986. *Some small harvest: The memoirs of Glyn Daniel.* London.

Dapper, O. 1676. *Naukeurige Beschrijvinge der Afrikaensche Gewesten.* Amsterdam.

————.1933. *Kaffraria or land of the Kafirs, also named Hottentots (1668),* trans. I. Schapera. In *The Early Cape Hottentots,* ed. and trans. I. Schapera and B. Farrington, 6–77. Van Riebeeck Society 14. Cape Town.

Dart, R. A. 1925. *Australopithecus africanus:* The man ape of South Africa. *Nature* 115:195–99.

————.1937. The hut distribution, genealogy and homogeneity of the /'Auni/ ≠Khomani Bushmen. *Bantu Studies* 11, 3:159–74.

————.1957 The osteodontokeratic culture of *Australopithecus prometheus. Transvaal Museum Memoir 10,* 1–105. Pretoria.

Davidson, I. 1991. Archaeologists and Aborigines. *Australian Journal of Anthropology* 2, 2:247–58.

Davison, P. 1991. Material culture, context and meaning: A critical investigation of museum practice, with particular reference to the South African Museum. Ph.D. diss., Department of Archaeology, University of Cape Town.

————.1993. Human subjects as museum objects. A project to make life-casts of "Bushmen" and "Hottentots," 1907–1924. *Annals of the South African Museum* 102, 5:165–83.

Deacon, J. 1984. Later Stone Age people and their descendants in southern Africa. In *Southern African prehistory and paleoenvironments,* ed. R. G. Klein, 221–328. Rotterdam.

————.1986. "My place is the Bitterpits": The home territory of Bleek and Lloyd's /Xam San informants. *African Studies* 45, 2:135–55.

————.1988. The power of a place in understanding southern San rock engravings. *World Archaeology* 20, 1:129–40.

————.1989. Introducing Goodwin's legacy. *South African Archaeological Society Goodwin Series* 6:3–5.

Deetz, J. 1977. *In small things forgotten: The archaeology of early American life.* Garden City, N.Y.

————.1988. American historical archeology: Methods and results. *Science* 239:362–67.

Dening, G. 1982. Sharks that walk on the land: The death of Captain Cook. *Meanjin* 41, 4:427–37.

————.1986. Possessing Tahiti. *Archaeology in Oceania* 21, 1: 103–18.

————.1988. *History's anthropology: The death of William Gooch.* New York.

————.1992. *Mr. Bligh's bad language: Passion, power and theatre on the "Bounty."* Cambridge.

De Villiers, S. A. 1971. *Robben Island: Out of reach, out of mind. A history of Robben Island.* Cape Town.

Die Oude Post Sindikaat. 1984. *Geskiedenis en ontstaan van die Oude Post Sindikaat en Postberg natuurreservaat.* MS:1–4.

Dillehay, T. D., and M. B. Collins. 1988. Early cultural evidence from Monte Verde in Chile. *Nature* 332:150–52.

Dobyns, H. F. 1983. *Their number become thinned: Native American population dynamics in eastern North America.* Pbk. ed. Knoxville.

————.1993. Disease transfer at contact. *Annual Review of Anthropology,* 22:273–91.

Drennan, M. R. 1953. A preliminary note on the Saldanha skull. *South African Journal of Science* 50:7–11.

Drury, J., and M. R. Drennan. 1926. The pudendal parts of the South African Bush race. *Medical Journal of South Africa* 22:113–17.

Duco, D. H. 1982. *Merken van Goudse pijpmakers 1660–1940.* Poperinge.

————.1987. *De Nederlandse kleipijp: Handboek voor dateren en determineren.* Leiden.

Editorial Notes and News 1953. *South African Archaeological Bulletin* 8:89.

Ellis, V. R. (see also Rae-Ellis) 1981. *Trucanini: Queen or traitor?* New, exp. ed. Canberra.

Elphick, R. 1985. *Khoikhoi and the founding of White South Africa.* Pbk. ed. Johannesburg.

Elphick, R., and H. Giliomee, eds. 1989. *The shaping of South African society, 1652–1840.* Pbk. rev. ed. Middletown, Conn.

Faulkner, A., and G. F. Faulkner. 1987. *The French at Pentagoet 1635–1674: An archaeological portrait of the Acadian frontier.* Augusta. Maine.

Fenton, C. 1982. *Flying doctor.* Pbk. ed. Melbourne.

Ffolliott, P. M. 1981. Riou, Edward. *Dictionary of South African Biography.* Durban.

Flemming, B. W. 1977. Depositional processes in Saldanha Bay and Langebaan Lagoon. *Council for Scientific and Industrial Research Professional Series* 2. Stellenbosch.

Flood, J. 1983. *Archaeology of the dreamtime.* Honolulu.

Flynn, F. 1979. *Northern gateway.* Pbk. ed. Marrickville.

Fornander, A. 1969. *An account of the Polynesian race (first pub. 1820) now three vols in one.* Rutland, Vt.

Fox, R. W., G. G. Kelleher, and C. B. Kerr. 1977. *Ranger uranium environmental inquiry: Second report.* Canberra.

Franck, B., G. Manuel, and D. Hatfield. 1967. *District Six.* Cape Town.

Fransen, H., and M. A. Cook. 1980. *The old buildings of the Cape.* Cape Town.

Frayer, D. W., M. H. Wolpoff, A. G. Thorne, F. H. Smith, and G. G. Pope. 1993. Theories of modern human origins: The paleontological test. *American Anthropologist* 95, 1:14–50.

Freund, W. M. 1989. The Cape under the transitional governments, 1795–1814. In *The shaping of South African society, 1652–1840,* ed. R. Elphick and H. Giliomee, 324–357. Pbk., rev. ed. Middletown, Conn.

Frost, A. 1987. Towards Australia: The coming of the Europeans 1400 to 1788. In *Australia to 1788,* ed. D. J. Mulvaney and J. P. White, 369–411. Broadway, N.S.W.

Furlong, P. J. 1991. *Between crown and swastika: The impact of the radical right on the Afrikaner Nationalist Movement in the fascist era.* Hanover, N.H.

Galton, F. 1890. *Narrative of an exploration in tropical South Africa being an account of a visit to Damaraland in 1851.* 3d ed. London.

Garnett, D. 1923. *Lady into fox.* New York.

Gathercole, P. 1993. Cambridge: History, archaeology and politics. In *A community of culture: The people and prehistory of the Pacific,* ed. M. Spriggs, D. E. Yen, W. Ambrose, R. Jones, A. Thorne, and A. Andrews, 1–5. Occasional papers in prehistory, no. 21. Canberra.

Gillen, F. J. 1968. *Gillen's diary: The camp jottings of F. J. Gillen on the Spencer and Gillen expedition across Australia 1901–1902.* Adelaide.

Gilman, S. L. 1985. *Difference and pathology: Stereotypes of sexuality, race, and madness.* Ithaca.

Gitlin, M. 1950. *The vision amazing: The story of South African Zionism.* Johannesburg.

Goodwin, A. J. H. 1945. Some historical Bushman arrows. *South African Journal of Science* 41:429–43.

———.1952. Commentary on "Jan van Riebeeck and the Hottentots." *South African Archaeological Bulletin* 7:86–91.

Goodwin, A. J. H., and C. van Riet Lowe. 1929. The stone age cultures of South Africa. *Annals of the South African Museum* 27:1–289.

Gordon, L. 1992. *Shared lives.* Cape Town.

Gordon, R. J. 1984. The !Kung in the Kalahari exchange: An ethnohistorical perspective. In *Past and present in hunter gatherer studies,* ed. C. Schrire, 195–224. Orlando, Fla.

———.1992. The venal Hottentot Venus and the great chain of being. *African Studies* 51, 2:185–201.

Gould, S. J. 1981. *The mismeasure of man.* New York.

———.1982. The Hottentot Venus. *Natural History* 10:20–24.

Green, J. N. 1975. The VOC ship *Batavia* wrecked in 1629 on the Houtman Abrolhos, Western Australia. *International Journal of Nautical Archaeology and Underwater Exploration,* 4, 1:43–63.

———.1977a. The loss of the Verenigde Oostindische Compagnie Jacht *Vergulde Draeck,* Western Australia 1656. Parts 1 and 2. *British Archaeological Reports Supplementary Series* 36. Oxford.

———.1977b. Australia's oldest wreck: The historical background and archaeological analysis of the wreck of the English East India Company's ship *Trial,* lost off the coast of Western Australia in 1622. *British Archaeological Reports Supplementary Series* 27. Oxford.

Green, L. G. 1958. *South African beachcomber.* Cape Town.

———.1970. *A giant in hiding.* Cape Town.

———.1973. *In the land of the afternoon.* Cape Town.

Grevenbroek, J. G. 1933. *An elegant and accurate account of the African race living around the Cape of Good Hope commonly called Hottentots (1695),* trans. B. Farrington. In *The Early Cape Hottentots,* ed. and trans. I. Schapera and B. Farrington, 172–299. Van Riebeeck Society 14. Cape Town.

Griffin, B. 1994. CHAGS 7. *Anthropology Newsletter* 35, 1:12–14.

Griffith, E. et al. 1827. *The animal kingdom arranged in conformity with its organization, by the Baron Cuvier.* London.

Groube, L. M. 1993. "Dig up those moa bones, dig": Golson in New Zealand, 1954–1961. In *A community of culture: The people and prehistory of the Pacific,* ed. M. Spriggs, D. E. Yen, W. Ambrose, R. Jones, A. Thorne, and A. Andrews, 6–17. Occasional papers in prehistory, no. 21. Canberra.

Groube, L., J. Chappell, J. Muke, and D. Price. 1986. A 40,000 year-old human occupation site at Huon Peninsula, Papua New Guinea. *Nature* 324:453–55.

Grün, R., P. B. Beaumont, and C. B. Stringer. 1990. ESR dating evidence for early modern humans at Border Cave in South Africa. *Nature* 344:537–39.

Guelke, L. 1989. Freehold farmers and frontier settlers, 1657–1780. In *The shaping of South African society, 1652–1840,* ed. R. Elphick and H. Giliomee, 66–108. Pbk. rev. ed. Middletown, Conn.

Guelke, L., and R. Shell. 1992. Landscape of conquest: Frontier water alienation and Khoikhoi strategies of survival, 1652–1780. *Journal of Southern African Studies* 18, 4:803–24.

Guidon, N., and G. Delibrias. 1986. Carbon-14 dates point to man in the Americas 32,000 years ago. *Nature* 321:769–71.

Haeckel, E. 1879. *The evolution of man: A popular exposition of the principal points of human ontogeny and phylogeny.* Vol. 2. New York.

———.1914. *The history of creation or the development of the earth and its inhabitants by the action of natural causes.* Vol. 2. 6th ed. New York.

Hall, M. 1992. Small things and the mobile, conflictual fusion of power, fear, and desire. In *The art and mystery of historical archaeology: Essays in honor of James Deetz,* ed. A. E. Yensch and M. C. Beaudry, 373–99. Boca Raton, Fla.

Hargrave, J. C. 1975. Leprosy in the Northern Territory of Australia, with particular reference to the Aborigines in Arnhem Land and the arid regions of the Northern Territory. M.A. diss., University of Sydney.

Harrington, J. C. 1954. Dating stem fragments of seventeenth and eighteenth century clay tobacco pipes. *Quarterly Bulletin. Archeological Society of Virginia* 9, 1:1–5.

Harris, S., ed. 1980. *Social and environmental choice: The impact of uranium mining in the Northern Territory.* Canberra.

Hauptman, L. M., and R. G. Knapp. 1977. Dutch-Aboriginal interaction in New Netherland and Formosa: An historical geography of Empire. *Proceedings of the American Philosophical Society,* 121, 2:166–82.

Herbert, Sir T. 1634. *A relation of some yeares travaile, begun 1626. Into Afrique.* London.

Herrman, L. 1929. A history of Capetown Jewry. In *The South African Jewish Yearbook. Directory of Jewish Organisations and Who's Who in South African Jewry 1929, 5689–90,* ed. M. De Saxe, 45–78. Johannesburg.

Hiatt, B. 1969. Cremation in Aboriginal Australia. *Mankind* 7, 2:104–19.

Higham, C., and R. Moseley. 1991. *Elizabeth and Philip: The untold story of the queen of England and her prince.* New York.

Higgs, E. S., ed. 1972. *Papers in economic prehistory: Studies by members and associates of the British Academy major research project in the early history of agriculture.* Cambridge.

Hoge, J. 1946. Personalia of the Germans at the Cape, 1652–1806. *Archives Year Book for South African History* 9. Cape Town.

Holmes, M. J. 1913. Report of the Medical Officer of Health for the year ending 31st Dec., 1912. *Bulletin of the Northern Territory* 6:3–21.

Hubert, J. 1989. A proper place for the dead: a critical review of the "reburial" issue. In *Conflict in the archaeology of living traditions,* ed. R. Layton, 131–66. London.

Hunter, M. (Wilson). 1936. *Reaction to conquest: Effects of contact with Europeans on the Pondo of South Africa.* Oxford.

Huxley, J., ed. 1936. *T. H. Huxley's diary of the voyage of H.M.S. "Rattlesnake."* New York.

Huxley, L., ed. 1901. *Life and letters of Thomas Henry Huxley,* Vol. 1. New York.

Jeffreys, M. K. 1944. *Kaapse Plakkaatboek. Deel I, (1652–1707), Kaapse Argiefstukke.* Cape Town.

Johnson, R. T. 1979. *Major rock paintings of Southern Africa.* Cape Town.

Jones, R. 1968. The geographical background to the arrival of man in Australia and Tasmania. *Archaeology and Physical Anthropology in Oceania* 3, 3:186–215.

———.1977. Man as an element of a continental fauna: The case of the sundering of the Bassian bridge. In *Sunda and Sahul: Prehistoric studies in Southeast Asia, Melanesia and Australia,* ed. J. Allen, J. Golson, and R. Jones, 317–86. London.

———.1992. Philosophical time travellers. *Antiquity* 66:744–57.

Joppien, R. 1979. The Dutch vision of Brazil. Johan Maurits and his artists. In *Johan Maurits van Nassau-Siegen 1604–1679: A humanist prince in Europe and Brazil,* ed. E. van den Boogaart, in collaboration with H. R. Hoetink and P. J. P. Whitehead, 297–376. The Hague.

Joppien, R., and B. Smith. 1988. *The art of Captain Cook's voyages.* Vol. 3. *Text: The voyage of the "Resolution" and "Discovery" 1776–1780.* New Haven.

Kagga Kamma publicity pamphlet, 1991. 1, 2. Cape Town.

Kaplan, M., assisted by M. Robertson. 1986. *Jewish roots in the South African economy.* Cape Town.

Karklins, K., and C. Schrire. 1991. The beads from Oudepost I, a Dutch East India Company outpost, Cape, South Africa. *Beads* 3:61–72.

Kedourie, E., ed. 1979. *The Jewish world: Revelation, prophecy and history.* London.

Keen, I. 1980. The Alligator Rivers Aborigines: retrospect and prospect. In *Northern Australia: options and implications,* ed. R. Jones, 171–86. Canberra.

Kennedy, R. F. 1975. *Catalogue of prints in the Africana Museum.* Vol. 1: A-K. Johannesburg.

Kettle, E. 1967. *Gone bush.* Sydney.

Kirk, R. L., and A. G. Thorne. 1976. Introduction. In *The origin of the Australians,* ed. R. L. Kirk and A. G. Thorne, 1–8. Canberra.

Klein, R. G. 1986. The prehistory of Stone Age herders in the Cape Province of South Africa. *South African Archaeological Society Goodwin Series* 5:5–12.

———.1989. Biological and behavioural perspectives on modern human origins in southern Africa. In *The human revolution: Behavioural and biological perspectives on the origins of modern humans,* ed. P. M. Mellars and C. B. Stringer, 529–46. Edinburgh.

————.1994. The problem of modern human origins. In *Origins of anatomically modern humans,* ed. M. H. Nitecki and D. V. Nitecki, 3–17. New York.

Klein, R. G., and K. Cruz-Uribe. 1989. Faunal evidence for prehistoric herder-forager activities at Kasteelberg, western Cape Province, South Africa. *South African Archaeological Bulletin* 44:82–97.

Kolben, P. 1727. *Naauwkeurige en uitvoerige beschryving van De Kaap de Goede Hoop.* Vol. 2. Amsterdam.

————.1731. *The present state of the Cape of Good Hope: or, A particular account of the several nations of the Hottentots.* Vol. 2. London.

Kolbe(n), P. 1745. *Beschreibung des Vorgebürges der Guten Hoffnung.* Reprint of 1719 edition. Frankfurt.

Krech, S., III, ed. 1981. *Indians, animals, and the fur trade. A critique of the "Keepers of the game."* Athens Ga.

Kuper, A. 1973. *Anthropologists and anthropology: The British school 1922–1972.* London.

Leakey, L. S. B., P. V. Tobias, and J. R. Napier. 1964. A new species of the genus *Homo* from Olduvai Gorge. *Nature* 202:7–9.

Leibbrandt, H. C. V. 1896a. *Precis of the Archives of the Cape of Good Hope: Journal, 1699–1732.* Cape Town.

————. 1896b. *Precis of the Archives of the Cape of Good Hope: Letters Despatched. 1695* [sic]*–1708.* Cape Town.

————.1901. *Precis of the archives of the Cape of Good Hope: Journal, 1662–1670.* Cape Town.

————.1902. *Precis of the archives of the Cape of Good Hope: Journal, 1671–1674 and 1676.* Cape Town.

Leichhardt, L. 1964. *Journal of an overland expedition in Australia from Moreton Bay to Port Essington, a distance of upwards of 3000 miles during the years 1844–1845. (1847).* London. Fascimile ed., Public Library of South Australia.

Letts, G., Chairman. 1979. *Feral animals in the Northern Territory: Report of the Board of Enquiry.* Darwin.

Levinson, M., R. G. Ward, and J. W. Webb. 1972. The settlement of Polynesia: A report on a computer simulation. *Archaeology and Physical Anthropology in Oceania* 7, 3:234–45.

Lewis-Williams, J. D. 1981. *Believing and seeing: Symbolic meanings in southern San rock paintings.* London.

————.1983. *The rock art of southern Africa.* Cambridge.

Lewis-Williams, J. D., and T. A. Dowson. 1988. The signs of all times: Entoptic phenomena in Upper Palaeolithic art. *Current Anthropology* 29, 2:201–45.

————.1990. Through the veil: San rock paintings and the rock face. *South African Archaeological Bulletin* 45:5–16.

Lewis-Williams, (J.) D., T. A. Dowson, and J. Deacon. 1993. Rock art and changing perceptions of southern Africa's past: Ezeljagdspoort reviewed. *Antiquity* 67:273–91.

Linné, C. 1767. *Systema naturae.* 13th ed. N.p.

Lockwood, D. 1977. *The front door: Darwin 1869–1969.* Pbk. ed. Adelaide.

McArthur, N., I. W. Saunders, and R. L. Tweedie. 1976. Small population isolates: A micro-simulation study. *Journal of the Polynesian Society* 85:307–26.

McBurney, C. B. M. 1967. *The Haua Fteah (Cyrenaica) and the stone age of the southeast Mediterranean.* Cambridge.

McCarthy, F. D., and F. M. Setzler. 1960. The archaeology of Arnhem Land. In *Records of the American-Australian scientific expedition to Arnhem Land, 1948.* Vol. 2, *Anthropology and nutrition,* ed. C. P. Mountford, 215–95. Melbourne.

Macknight, C. C., ed. 1969. *The farthest coast: A selection of writings relating to the history of the northern coast of Australia.* Melbourne.

———.1976. *The voyage to Marege': Macassan trepangers in Northern Australia.* Melbourne.

———.1986. Macassans and the Aboriginal past. *Archaeology in Oceania* 21, 1:69–75.

McKnight, T. L. 1976. *Friendly vermin: A study of feral livestock in Australia.* Berkeley.

McNeill, W. H. 1989. *Plagues and peoples.* Pbk. ed. New York.

Maddison, D. R. 1991a. The discovery and importance of multiple islands of most-parsimonious trees. *Systematic Zoology* 40, 3:315–28.

———.1991b. African origin of human mitochondrial DNA reexamined. *Systematic Zoology* 40, 3:355–65.

Maddison, D. R., M. Ruvolo, and D. L. Swafford. 1992. Geographic origins of human mitochondrial DNA: Phylogenetic evidence from control region sequences. *Systematic Biology* 41, 1:111–24.

Maddock, K. 1991. Metamorphosing the sacred in Australia. *Australian Journal of Anthropology* 2, 2:213–32.

Maingard, L. F. 1935. The origin of the word "Hottentot." *Bantu Studies* 9, 1:63–67.

Major, R H., ed. 1859. *Account of the observations of Captain William Dampier on the coast of New Holland, in 1687–88,* . . . In *Early voyages to Terra Australis, now called Australia,* 99–107. London, The Hakluyt Society 25.

Malherbe, V. C. 1990. *Krotoa, called "Eva": A woman between.* Cape Town.

Marks, R. L. 1991. *Three men of the Beagle.* New York.

Marks, S. 1972. Khoisan resistance to the Dutch in the seventeenth and eighteenth centuries. *Journal of African History* 13, 1:55–80.

Marett, R. R. 1931. Memoir. In *Spencer's last journey. Being the Journal of an expedition to Tierra del Fuego by the late Sir Baldwin Spencer,* ed. R. R. Marrett and T. K. Penniman, 14–46. Oxford.

Marett, R. R., and T. K. Penniman, eds. 1931. *Spencer's last journey. Being the Journal of an expedition to Tierra del Fuego by the late Sir Baldwin Spencer.* Oxford.

Martin, C. 1978. *Keepers of the game: Indian-animal relationships and the fur trade.* Berkeley and Los Angeles.

Masson, E. R. 1915. *An untamed territory: The Northern Territory of Australia.* London.

Mendelsohn, R. 1991. *Sammy Marks: "The uncrowned king of the Transvaal."* Cape Town and Athens, Ohio.

Mentzel, O. F. 1921. *A complete and authentic geographical and topographical description of the famous and (all things considered) remarkable African Cape of Good Hope. (1785),* trans. H. J. Mandelbrote. Van Riebeeck Society 4. Cape Town.

———.1944. *A complete and authentic geographical and topographical description of the fa-*

mous and (all things considered) remarkable African Cape of Good Hope. (1787), rev. and ed. H. J. Mandelbrote, trans. G. V. Marais and J. Hoge. Van Riebeeck Society 25. Cape Town.

M. H. 1972. Sherira Ben Hanina Gaon. *Encyclopedia Judaica* 14:1381–82.

Moodie, D., comp., trans., and ed. 1960. *The Record; or A series of official papers relative to the condition and treatment of the native tribes of South Africa.* Reprint of 1838–42. Amsterdam and Cape Town.

Mountford, C. P., ed. 1960. *Records of the American-Australian scientific expedition to Arnhem Land, 1948.* Vol. 2, *Anthropology and nutrition.* Melbourne.

Mulvaney, J. 1960. Archaeological excavations at Fromm's Landing on the lower Murray River, South Australia. *Proceedings of the Royal Society of Victoria* 72:53–85.

———.1961. The stone age of Australia. *Proceedings of the Prehistoric Society* 27:56–107.

———.1969. *The prehistory of Australia.* London.

———.1989. *Encounters in place: Outsiders and Aboriginal Australians 1606–1985.* St. Lucia.

———.1993. From Cambridge to the bush. In *A community of culture: The people and prehistory of the Pacific,* ed. M. Spriggs, D. E. Yen, W. Ambrose, R. Jones, A. Thorne, and A. Andrews, 18–26. Occasional papers in prehistory, no. 21. Canberra.

Mulvaney, D. J., and J. H. Calaby. 1985. *"So much that is new": Baldwin Spencer, 1860–1929, a biography.* Melbourne.

Murray, P. 1984. Extinctions downunder: A bestiary of extinct Australian Late Pleistocene monotremes and marsupials. In *Quaternary extinctions: A prehistoric revolution,* ed. P. S. Martin and R. G. Klein, 600–628. Tucson.

Murray, T. 1993. The childhood of William Lanne: Contact archaeology and Aboriginality in Tasmania. *Antiquity* 67:504–19.

Murray, T., and J. P. White. 1981. Cambridge in the bush? Archaeology in Australia and New Guinea. *World Archaeology* 13, 2:255–63.

Nash, M. D. 1990. The last voyage of the Guardian: an introduction. In *The last voyage of the Guardian, Lieutenant Riou, Commander 1789–1791,* by E. Riou, ed. M. D. Nash, xv–xxxix. Van Riebeeck Society II, 20. Cape Town.

Newton-King, S. 1991. Comment. In "Die Khoisan en vakterminologie na *The Oxford History of South Africa:* 'n Historiografiese dilemma", by H. C. Bredenkamp. *South African Historical Journal* 25:74–76.

Noël Hume, I. 1991. *Martin's Hundred.* Rev. and exp. pbk ed. Charlottesville, Va.

Nordyke, E. C. 1989. Comment. In *Before the horror: The population of Hawai'i on the eve of Western contact,* by D. E. Stannard, 105–13. Honolulu.

Northern Territory Medical Service of the Australian Department of Health. 1970. *Leprosy in Northern Territory Aborigines: A short guide for the field staff in the diagnosis, treatment and management of leprosy in Aborigines.* i–x, 1–14. Canberra.

Norwich, O. I. 1983. *Maps of Africa: An illustrated and annotated carto-bibliography.* Johannesburg.

Obeyesekere, G. 1992. *The apotheosis of Captain Cook: European mythmaking in the Pacific.* Princeton.

O'Sullivan, B. 1990. A report on drilling and trenching on the Woltemade Flats, Cape Town, in 1988 and 1989. *South African Journal of Science* 86:487–88.

Pakenham, T. 1992. *The Boer War.* Pbk. ed. London.

Pàlfi, G., O. Dutour, M. Borreani, J.-P. Brun, and J. Berato. 1992. Pre-Columbian congenital syphilis from the Late Antiquity in France. *International Journal of Osteoarchaeology* 2:245–61.

Pallister, D., S. Stewart, and I. Lepper. 1988. *South Africa Inc.: The Oppenheimer empire.* Pbk. rev. ed. London.

Parker, J. 1978. *The world for a market-place: Episodes in the history of European expansion.* Minneapolis.

Parkington, J. E. 1984. Sonqua and Bushmen: Hunters and robbers. In *Past and present in hunter gatherer studies,* ed. C. Schrire, 151–74. Orlando, Fla.

———.1989. Interpreting paintings without a commentary: meaning and motive, context and composition in the rock art of the western Cape, South Africa. *Antiquity* 63: 13–26.

Penn, N. 1988. Review of *Robert Jacob Gordon: Cape travels, 1777 to 1786,* by R. J. Gordon, ed. Peter E. Raper and Maurice Boucher. *South African Historical Journal* 20:166–72.

———.1989. Labour, land and livestock in the Western Cape during the eighteenth century. In *The angry divide: Social and economic history of the Western Cape,* ed. W. G. James and M. Simons, 2–19. Cape Town.

———.1990. *Droster* gangs of the Bokkeveld and the Roggeveld, 1770–1800. *South African Historical Journal* 23:15–40.

———.1991. "Excavating archives at Oudepost": A riposte. *Social Dynamics* 17, 1:101–5.

Peterson, N., and M. Langton, eds. 1983. *Aborigines, land and land rights.* Canberra.

Phillips, N. (C.) 1961. *The tragedy of apartheid: A journalist's experiences in the South African riots.* London.

Picard, H. W. J. 1972. *Masters of the castle: A portrait gallery of the Dutch commanders and governors of the Cape of Good Hope: 1652–1795, 1803–1806.* Cape Town.

Pogrund, B. 1990. *How can man die better . . . : Sobukwe and apartheid.* London.

Potgieter, S., and G. Abrahams. 1984. Gouda clay pipes from excavated historical sites in Cape Town. *Bulletin of the South African Cultural History Museum* 5:42–53.

Rae-Ellis, V. (see also Ellis) 1988. *Black Robinson: Protector of Aborigines.* Melbourne.

Ramenofsky, A. F. 1987. *Vectors of death: The archaeology of European contact.* Albuquerque.

Raper, P. E., and M. Boucher. 1988. Preface. In *Robert Jacob Gordon: Cape travels, 1777 to 1786,* by R. J. Gordon, ed. P. E. Raper and M. Boucher, 1: 11–37. Johannesburg.

Ras, A. C. 1959. *Die Kasteel en andere vroeë Kaapse vestingwerke 1652–1713.* Cape Town.

Rassool, C. and L. Witz. 1993. The 1952 Jan van Riebeeck Tercentenary festival: constructing and contesting public national history in South Africa. *Journal of African History* 34, 3: 447–68.

Raven-Hart, R. 1967. *Before Van Riebeeck: Callers at South Africa from 1488 to 1652.* Cape Town.

————.1971. *Cape Good Hope 1652–1702: The first fifty years of Dutch colonisation as seen by callers.* 2 vols. Cape Town.

Raymond, W. 1867. *Saldanha Bay harbour: Its special capabilities for colonization.* London.

Riou, E. 1990. *The last voyage of the "Guardian" Lieutenant Riou, Commander 1789–1791,* ed. M. D. Nash. Van Riebeeck Society II, 20. Cape Town.

Roberts, R. G., R. Jones, and M. A. Smith. 1990. Thermoluminescence dating of a 50,000-year-old human occupation site in northern Australia. *Nature* 345:153–56.

Robertshaw, P. T. 1977. Excavations at Paternoster, south-western Cape. *South African Archaeological Bulletin* 32:63–73.

————.1978. Archaeological investigations at Langebaan Lagoon, Cape Province. In *Palaeoecology of Africa,* ed. E. M. van Zinderen Bakker and J. A. Coetzee, 10:139–48. Rotterdam.

Robertson, H. M. 1945. The economic development of the Cape under Van Riebeek, Parts 1–4. *South African Journal of Economics* 13, 1:1–17, 2:75–90, 3:170–84, 4:245–62.

Robinson, G. A. 1966. *Friendly mission: The Tasmanian journals and papers of George Augustus Robinson 1829–1834,* ed. N. J. B. Plomley. Hobart.

Ross, R. 1983. *Cape of torments: Slavery and resistance in South Africa,* London.

————. 1991. The first imperial masters of colonial South Africa. *South African Historical Journal* 25:177–83.

Ryan, L. 1981. *The Aboriginal Tasmanians.* Vancouver.

————.1988. Review of *Black Robinson: Protector of Aborigines,* by V. Rae-Ellis. *Australian Historical Studies* 23, 91:211–13.

Sahlins, M. 1981. *Historical metaphors and mythical realities: Structure in the early history of the Sandwich Islands kingdom.* Ann Arbor, Mich.

————.1987. *Islands of history.* Pbk. ed. Chicago.

Saunders, S. 1990. Isolation: The development of leprosy prophylaxis in Australia. *Aboriginal History* 14, 2:168–81.

Schmitt, R. C. 1989. Comment. In *Before the horror: The population of Hawai'i on the eve of Western contact,* by D. E. Stannard, 114–21. Honolulu.

Schoonees, P. 1991. *Inscriptions on padrões, postal stones, tombstones and beacons.* Cape Town.

Schrire, C. 1980. An enquiry into the evolutionary status and apparent identity of San hunter-gatherers. *Human Ecology* 8:9–32.

————.1982. The Alligator Rivers: Prehistory and ecology in western Arnhem Land. *Terra Australis* 7. Australian National University, Research School of Pacific Studies, Department of Prehistory, Canberra.

————.1985. Aborigines and environmental politics. In *The future of former foragers in Australia and southern Africa,* ed. C. Schrire and R. (J.) Gordon, 83–92. *Cultural Survival Inc., Occasional Paper* 18. Cambridge, Mass.

————.1987. The historical archaeology of colonial-indigenous interactions in South Africa. In *Papers in the prehistory of the western Cape, South Africa,* ed. J. Parkington and M. Hall. *British Archaeological Reports. International Series* 332:424–61. Oxford.

————.1988. The historical archaeology of the impact of colonialism in 17th-century South Africa. *Antiquity* 62:214–25.

————.1990. Excavating archives at Oudepost I, Cape. *Social Dynamics* 16, 1:11–21.

————.1991. Is the Penn mightier than the shovel? A sally to a riposte. *Social Dynamics* 17, 1:106–9.

————.1992. The archaeological identity of hunters and herders at the Cape over the last 2000 years: A critique. *South African Archaeological Bulletin* 47:62–64.

————, ed. 1984a. *Past and present in hunter gatherer studies.* Orlando, Fla.

————.1984b. Wild surmises on savage thoughts. In *Past and present in hunter gatherer studies,* ed. C. Schrire, 1–25, Orlando, Fla.

————.1984c. Interactions of past and present in Arnhem Land, North Australia. In *Past and present in hunter gatherer studies,* ed. C. Schrire, 67–93. Orlando, Fla.

Schrire, C., J. Deacon, M. Hall, and (J.) D. Lewis-Williams. 1986. Burkitt's milestone. *Antiquity* 60:123–31.

Schrire, C., and J. Deacon. 1989. The indigenous artefacts from Oudepost I, a colonial outpost of the VOC at Saldanha Bay, Cape. *South African Archaeological Bulletin* 44:105–13.

————.1990. Reply to Wilson, van Rijssen, Jacobson and Noli. *South African Archaeological Bulletin* 54: 124–25.

Schrire, C., J. Deetz, D. Lubinsky, and C. Poggenpoel. 1990. The chronology of Oudepost I, Cape, as inferred from an analysis of clay pipes. *Journal of Archaeological Science* 17:269–300.

Schrire, C., and L. Meltzer. 1992. Coins, gaming counters and a bale seal from Oudepost, Cape. *South African Archaeological Bulletin* 47:104–7.

Schrire, C., K. Cruz-Uribe, and J. Klose. 1993. The site history of the historical site at Oudepost I, Cape. *South African Archaeological Society Goodwin Series* 7:21–32.

Schrire, I. 1956. *Stalag doctor.* London.

Schrire, T. 1966. *Hebrew amulets: Their decipherment and interpretation.* London.

————, ed. 1972. *Surgical emergencies: Diagnosis and management.* London.

Schrire, Y. L. 1879. *Shoshana novelet (The wilted rose).* Warsaw.

————. Ca. 1910. The history and happenings, reasons and adventures, from the day of my birth, to the day of my death, with a short critique in a clear language, in songs and prose, in remembrance for all time. Unpublished MS:1–152. Trans. O. Kacowitz and C. Schrire, 1993.

Sealy, J., and R. Yates. 1994. The chronology of the introduction of pastoralism to the Cape, South Africa. *Antiquity* 68, 58–67.

Searcy, A. 1907. *In Australian tropics.* London.

Serton, P. 1971. English summary of the introduction. In *Description of the Cape of Good Hope with matters concerning it (1726),* by F. Valentyn, ed. P. Serton, R. Raven-Hart, W. J. de Kock, with final ed. E. H. Raidt, trans. R. Raven-Hart, 3–13. Van Riebeeck Society II, 2. Cape Town.

Shain, M. 1981. Hoggenheimer—the making of a myth. *Jewish Affairs* 36:112–16.

————. 1983. *Jewry and Cape society: The origins and activities of the Jewish Board of Deputies for the Cape Colony.* Historical Publication Society 30. Cape Town.

————. 1992. Anti-Semitism and South African society: Reappraising the 1930s and 1940s. *South African Historical Journal* 27:186–97.

————. 1994. *The roots of antisemitism in South Africa.* Charlottesville, Va.

Shaw, T. 1991. Goodwin's graft, Burkitt's craft. *Antiquity* 65:579–80.

Shea, J. J. 1989. A functional study of the lithic industries associated with hominid fossils in the Kebara and Qafzeh Caves, Israel. In *The human revolution: Behavioural and biological perspectives on the origins of modern humans,* ed. P. M. Mellars and C. B. Stringer, 611–25. Edinburgh.

Shell, R. C.-H. 1994. *Children of bondage: A social history of the slave society at the Cape of Good Hope, 1652–1838.* Hanover, N.H.

Shimoni, G. 1980. *Jews and Zionism: The South African experience (1910–1967).* Cape Town.

Singer, R. 1978. The biology of the San. In *The Bushmen: San hunters and herders of Southern Africa,* ed. P. V. Tobias, 115–29. Cape Town.

Singer, R., and J. J. Wymer. 1968. Archaeological investigations at the Saldanha skull site in South Africa. *South African Archaeological Bulletin* 23:63–74.

————. 1982. *The Middle Stone Age at Klasies River Mouth in South Africa.* Chicago.

Sleigh, D. 1993. *Die buiteposte: VOC-buiteposte onder Kaapse bestuur 1652–1795.* Pretoria.

Small, A., and J. Wissema. 1986. *District Six.* Linden.

Smith, A. B. 1983. Prehistoric pastoralism in the Southwestern Cape, South Africa. *World Archaeology* 15, 1:79–89.

————. 1986. Competition, conflict and clientship: Khoi and San relationships in the western Cape. *South African Archaeological Society Goodwin Series* 5:36–41.

————. 1990. The origins and demise of the Khoikhoi: The debate. *South African Historical Journal* 23:3–14.

Smith, A. B., K. Sadr, J. Gribble, and R. Yates. 1991. Excavations in the southwestern Cape, South Africa, and the archaeological identity of prehistoric hunter-gatherers within the last 2000 years. *South African Archaeological Bulletin* 46: 71–91.

Smith, B. 1985. *European vision and the South Pacific,* 2d ed. New Haven.

Sollas, W. J. 1924. *Ancient hunters and their modern representatives.* 3d ed. London.

Solway, J. S., and R. B. Lee. 1990. Foragers: Genuine or spurious? Situating the Kalahari San in history. *Current Anthropology* 31, 2:109–46.

Soule, A., G. Dixon, and R. Richards. 1987. *The Wynand du Toit story.* Johannesburg.

Spencer, B. 1914. *Native tribes of the Northern Territory of Australia.* London.

————. 1928. *Wanderings in wild Australia.* Vol. 2. London.

————. 1931. Journal of the expedition to Tierra del Fuego. In *Spencer's last journey: Being the journal of an expedition to Tierra del Fuego by the late Sir Baldwin Spencer,* ed. R. R. Marrett and T. K. Penniman, 47–123. Oxford.

Spillett, P. G. 1979. *Forsaken settlement: An illustrated history of the settlement of Victoria, Port Essington, North Australia 1838–1849.* 2d ed. Dee Why West, N. S. W.

Spohr, O. H. 1963. The first Hottentot vocabulary, 1663. *Quarterly Bulletin of the South African Library* 18, 1:27–33.

Spriggs, M., and R. Jones. 1993. Professor. In *A community of culture: The people and prehistory of the Pacific,* ed. M. Spriggs, D. E. Yen, W. Ambrose, R. Jones, A. Thorne, and A. Andrews, 27–31. Occasional papers in prehistory, no. 21. Canberra.

Stack, E. M. 1983. Position paper on health in the Northern Territory. Darwin, Commonwealth Human Ecology Council Conference. MS 21 pages + 3.

Stanbury, M., ed. 1974. *"Batavia" catalogue.* Perth.

Stannard, D. E. 1989. *Before the horror: The population of Hawai'i on the eve of western contact.* Honolulu.

———. 1992. *American holocaust: Columbus and the conquest of the New World.* Oxford.

Stanner, W. E. H. 1965. Aboriginal territorial organization: Estate, range, domain and regime. *Oceania* 36, 1:1–26.

Sténuit, R. 1974. Early relics of the VOC trade from Shetland. The wreck of the flute *Lastdrager* lost off Yell, 1653. *International Journal of Nautical Archaeology and Underwater Exploration* 3, 2:213–56.

———. 1978. The sunken treasure of St. Helena. *National Geographic* 154:562–76.

Steyn, H. P. 1984. Southern Kalahari San subsistence ecology: A reconstruction. *South African Archaeological Bulletin* 39:117–24.

Stocking, G. W., Jr. 1987. *Victorian anthropology.* New York.

Supervising Scientist for the Alligator Rivers Region Annual Report. 1980. Canberra.

Swain, T. 1993. *A place for strangers: Towards a history of Australian Aboriginal being.* Cambridge.

Tatz, C. 1982. *Aborigines and uranium and other essays.* Richmond, Vic.

Templeton, A. R. 1993. The "Eve" hypotheses: A genetic critique and reanalysis. *American Anthropologist* 95, 1:51–72.

Ten Rhyne, W. 1933. *A Short Account of the Cape of Good Hope and of the Hottentots who Inhabit that Region. (1686),* trans. B. Farrington. In *The Early Cape Hottentots,* ed. and trans. I. Schapera and B. Farrington, 84–157. Van Riebeeck Society 14. Cape Town.

Theal, G. McC. 1911. Introduction. In *Specimens of Bushman folklore,* by W. H. I. Bleek and L. C. Lloyd, xxv–xl. London.

Thiele, S., ed. 1991. Reconsidering inequality. *The Australian Journal of Anthropology, Special Issue* 2, 2.

Thom, H. B. 1952. Introduction. In *Journal of Jan van Riebeeck.* Vol. 1, *1651–1655,* by J. Van Riebeeck, ed. and trans. H. B. Thom, xv–xliv. Cape Town.

Thorne, A., and R. Raymond. 1989. *Man on the rim: The peopling of the Pacific.* Ryde, N.S.W.

Thorne, A. G., and M. H. Wolpoff, 1992. The multiregional evolution of humans. *Scientific American* 266:76–83.

Tonkinson, R. 1980. The cultural roots of Aboriginal land rights. In *Northern Australia: Options and implications,* ed. R. Jones, 111–20. Canberra.

Toohey, J. L. 1981. *Alligator Rivers Stage II land claim. (Report by the Australian Land Commissioner Mr. Justice Toohey to the Minister for Aboriginal Affairs and to the Administrator of the Northern Territory).* Office of the Aboriginal Land Commissioner. Interim ed., Darwin, N.T.

Tooley, R. V. 1963. *Early maps and views of the Cape of Good Hope.* London.

Treaty 88 Campaign. 1988. Aboriginal sovereignty—never ceded. *Australian Historical Studies* 23, 91:1–2.

UNESCO 1972. *Apartheid: Its effects on education, science, culture and information.* 2d ed. Rev. and enl. Paris.

Urry, J., and M. Walsh. 1981. The lost "Macassar language" of northern Australia. *Aboriginal History* 5, 2:91–108.

Valentyn, F. 1726. *Oud en Nieuw Oost-Indien. Vol. 5 (2). Beschryving van . . . Mala-bar. . . . Japan . . . KaapMDDŇ der Goede Hoop.* . . . Dordrecht and Amsterdam.

————. 1971. *Description of the Cape of Good Hope with matters concerning it. (1726),* ed. P. Serton, R. Raven-Hart, W. J. de Kock, with final ed. E. H. Raidt, trans. R. Raven-Hart. Van Riebeeck Society II, 2. Cape Town.

————. 1973. *Description of the Cape of Good Hope with matters concerning it. (1726),* ed. E. H. Raidt, trans. R. Raven-Hart. Van Riebeeck Society II, 4. Cape Town.

Van den Boogaart, E. 1979. Infernal allies. The Dutch West India Company and the Tarairiu 1631–1654. In *Johan Maurits van Nassau-Siegen 1604–1679: A humanist prince in Europe and Brazil,* ed. E. van den Boogaart, in collaboration with H. R. Hoetink and P. J. P. Whitehead, 519–38. The Hague.

Van der Stel, S. 1932. *Simon van der Stel's journal of his expedition to Namaqualand 1685–6,* ed. G. Waterhouse. London.

————.1979. *Simon van der Stel's journey to Namaqualand in 1685,* rev. G. Waterhouse, transcr. C. G. de Wet, trans. R. H. Pfeiffer. Cape Town and Pretoria.

Van Riebeeck, J. 1952. *Journal of Jan van Riebeeck. Vol. 1, 1651–1655,* ed. and trans. H. B. Thom. Cape Town.

————. 1954. *Journal of Jan van Riebeeck. Vol. 2, 1656–1658,* ed. and trans. H. B. Thom. Cape Town.

————. 1958. *Journal of Jan van Riebeeck. Vol. 3, 1659–1662,* ed. and trans. H. B. Thom. Cape Town.

Van Ryneveld, W. 1942. *Aanmerking over de Verbetering van het Vee aan de Kaap de Goede Hoop, 1804,* ed. H. B. Thom. Van Riebeeck Society 23. Cape Town.

Vigilant, L., M. Stoneking, H. Harpending, K. Hawkes, and A. C. Wilson. 1991. African populations and the evolution of human mitochondrial DNA. *Science* 253:1503–7.

Walker, A., and R. D. Zorc. 1981. Austranesian loanwords in Yolngu-Matha of northeast Arnhem Land. *Aboriginal History* 5, 2:109–134.

Wallerstein, I. 1980. *The modern world-system II: Mercantilism and the consolidation of the European world-economy, 1600–1750.* Pbk. ed. New York.

Ward, R. G., J. W. Webb, and M. Levinson. 1976. The settlement of the Polynesian outliers: A computer simulation. *Polynesian Society Memoir* no. 39:57–68.

Watson, S. 1991. *Return of the moon: Versions from the /Xam.* Cape Town.

Webster, E. M. 1980. *Whirlwinds in the plain: Ludwig Leichhardt—friends, foes and his-tory.* Melbourne.

Weibe, R. 1989. *Playing dead: A contemplation concerning the Arctic.* Edmonton.

Werz, B. 1993. Maritime archaeology project Table Bay: Aspects of the first field season. *South African Archaeological Society Goodwin Series* 7:33–39.

Westbury, W., and C. G. Sampson. 1993. To strike the necessary fire: Acquisition of guns by the Seacow Valley Bushmen. *South African Archaeological Bulletin* 48:26–31.

White, J. P. 1972. Ol tumbuna: Archaeological excavations in the eastern central highlands, Papua New Guinea. *Terra Australis* 2. Canberra, Australian National University, Research School of Pacific Studies, Department of Prehistory.

White, J. P., and J. F. O'Connell. 1982. *A prehistory of Australia, New Guinea, and Sahul.* Sydney.

White, J. P., and R. (J.) Lampert. 1987. Creation and discovery. In *Australia to 1788,* ed. D. J. Mulvaney and J. P. White, 3–23. Broadway, N.S.W.

Wilson, M., and A. Mafeje. 1963. *Langa: A study of social groups in an African township.* Cape Town.

Wilmsen, E. N., and J. R. Denbow. 1990. Paradigmatic history of San-speaking peoples and current attempts at revision. *Current Anthropology* 31, 5:489–524.

Wilson, M. L., W. J. J. van Rijssen, L. Jacobson and H. D. Noli. 1990. Comments on the indigenous artefacts from Oudepost I. *South African Archaeological Bulletin* 45:122–24.

Wolf, E. R. 1982. *Europe and the people without history.* Pbk. ed. Berkeley.

Wolpoff, M. H. 1989. Multiregional evolution: The fossil alternative to Eden. In *The human revolution: Behavioural and biological perspectives on the origins of modern humans,* ed. P. M. Mellars and C. B. Stringer, 62–108. Edinburgh.

Woodward, C. S. 1974. *Oriental ceramics at the Cape of Good Hope 1652–1795.* Cape Town.

Wright, R. V. S. 1971. Prehistory in the Cape York Peninsula. In *Aboriginal man and environment in Australia,* ed. D. J. Mulvaney and J. Golson, 133–40. Canberra.

Yates, R., and A. B. Smith. 1993. A reevaluation of the chronology of Oudepost: A reply in part to Schrire. *South African Archaeological Bulletin* 48:52–53.

Zouros, E., K. R. Freeman, A. O. Ball, and G. H. Pogson. 1992. Direct evidence for extensive paternal mitochondrial DNA inheritance in the marine mussel *Mytilus.* *Nature* 359:412–14.

Unpublished Documents
Algemeen Rijksarchief, The Hague

VOC 4004. Overgekomen brieven en papieren van Kaap de Goede Hoop 1669. Folio 558–652. Journael en grootboeck van de winckel.

VOC 4098. Register der brieven en papieren van de Caap overgekomen, 1726. Eerste deel. Folio 309. Lijste van t' verstrekte vers vleesch aan Comps. passeerende schepen, Hospitalen etc. zedert Po. February 1725 tot Ulto. January 1726.

VOC 4101. Register der brieven en papieren van de Caap overgekomen, 1727. Eerste deel. Folio 101. Lijste van't verstrekte vers vleesch aan Comps. passeerende schepen, Hospitalen etc. zedert primo January tot ult. decemb. 1726.

VOC 4104. Register der brieven en papieren van de Caap overgekomen, 1728. Eerste deel. Folio 106–113. Lijste van t' verstrekte vleesch ten behoeve als voren gedurende den Jare 1727.

VOC 4107. Register der brieven en papieren van de Caap overgekomen, 1729. Eerste deel. Folio 175. Origineele lijst van 't verstrekte vleesch aan 's Comps. passeerende schepen, Hospitaal etc. zedert primo January tot Ulto. December 1728.

VOC 4111. Register der brieven en papieren van de Caap overgekomen, 1730. Eerste deel. Folio 107–17. Rapport van Gecommitteerdens wegens hunne bevinding van de Bay Fals, Tafel en Saldanhabay gedateerd 18 December 1729. N.B. Opgenomen in de kaartencollectie.

VOC 4111. Register der brieven en papieren van de Caap overgekomen, 1730. Eerste deel. Folio 134. Lijste van het verstrekte vleesch aan Comps. passeerende schepen, Hospitaal etc. sederd po. January tot ulto Decemb. 1729.

VOC 4115. Register der brieven en papieren van de Caap overgekomen, 1731. Eerste deel. Folio 849. Origineele leyst van 't verstrekte vleesch aen 's Comps. passeerende schepen, Hospitael etc. gedurende den jare 1730.

VOC 4117. Register der brieven en papieren van de Caap overgekomen, 1732. Eerste deel. Folio 913. Lijste van het aan de Caap verstrekte vlees aan Compagnie passeerende schepen, hospitaal etc. gedurende het voorm. jaar.

VOC 4120. Register der brieven en papieren van de Caap overgekomen, 1733. Eerste deel. Folio 1183. Lijste van het aan de Caap verstrekte vlees aan Comps. passeerende schepen, hospitaal etc. gedurende het voorm. jaar.

Archives of the Jagger Library, University of Cape Town

MS. 04.03.03. B. M. Fagan to R. R. Inskeep, "Handing over Notes." 1960.

Australian Institute of Aboriginal Studies, Canberra.

MS 9568. Cahill, P. Letters to Sir Walter Baldwin Spencer. April 27 1913 to November 24 1921.

Cape Archives Depot, Cape Town

C1876. Dagregister, 1663.

C1879. Dagregister, 1673.

CJ1. Deel (II) Oorspronklike Regsrolle en Notule (Krimineel en Siviel) Original Rolls and Minutes (Criminal and Civil) 1652–1673.

C336. Criminele Processtukken. Verklaring van P. Steenmetz.

C432. Inkomende Briewe. P. Steenmetz to Governor J. de la Fontaine.

LM 9. Precis and translation of the Journal, 1677–1683. H.C.V Leibbrandt c. 1900.

LM 10. Precis and translation of the Journal, 1684–1687. H.C.V Leibbrandt c. 1900.

LM 11. Precis and translation of the Journal, 1689–1692. H.C.V Leibbrandt c. 1900.

LM 12. Precis and translation of the Journal, 1693–1695. H.C.V Leibbrandt c. 1900.

LM 20. Precis and translation of Letters Received 1726–1732. H. C. V. Leibbrandt, c. 1900.

LM 23. Precis and translation of Letters Despatched, 5th January 1723 to 29th December 1725. H.C.V Leibbrandt c. 1900.

LM 24. Precis and translation of Letters Despatched, 5th January 1726 to 27th July, 1728. H.C.V Leibbrandt c. 1900.

VC7 Dagregister, 1676.

Cape Archives Catalog of Maps

M1/84 Map of Saldanha Bay showing islands, etc. 1660. Photocopy. Leupe Collection.

M1/874 Map of the Cape of Good Hope from False Bay to the Swartland showing farms with the owners' names, etc. Sheet 1. 1786. Photocopy.

M1/888. Map of the coast and adjacent area from False Bay to St. Helena Bay. Sheet 1. 1788. JC Friderici. Compiled by order of Governor Van de Graaff. Photocopy.

M1/951. Map of Saldanha Bay with soundings showing the inland expedition of Admiral Johnstone in 1781. 1786. Van Gennip. Photocopy.

M1/954. Map of Saldanha Bay. c. 1790. Photocopy.

M1/1172. Hydrographical map of Saldanha Bay and islands with note showing various landmarks. c. 1755. N. Bellin. Photocopy. Leupe Collection.

M1/1176. Hydrographical map of the south western part of the Cape from False Bay to Saldanha Bay and adjacent interior. 17th Century. J. van Keulen. Photocopy.

M1/1177 (a). Hydrographical map of the south western part of the Cape from False Bay to Saldanha Bay and adjacent interior. Sheet 1. 17th Century. J. van Keulen. Photocopy.

M1/1177 (b). Hydrographical map of the south western part of the Cape from False Bay to Saldanha Bay and adjacent interior. Sheet 2. 17th Century. J. van Keulen. Photocopy.

M1/1183. Map of the Cape of Good Hope showing location of Hottentot tribes, etc. c. 1710. F. Valentyn. Photocopy.

M1/1331. Map of Saldanha Bay showing the position of the British fleet under Admiral Elphinstone and those of the Batavian forces under General Lucas. 1795. JS Henry. Photocopy.

M1/1396. Hydrographical map of Saldanha Bay showing the Company's Post, farms, etc. 1796. J Elphinstone. Photocopy. Leupe Collection.

M4/31. Survey map of part of Saldanha Bay showing islands, coastline, surrounding country etc, 1820. Drawing. Royal Engineers.

Cape Archives Depot
1. Morrison Collection

M108. The landing of Jan van Riebeeck at the Cape of Good Hope, 1652.

M121 Camp of Simon van der Stel, Copper Mountains, 1685.

M143 Exchanges of fish for beads at the Cape of Good Hope.

M748. Plan of Saldanha Bay showing the operations of the squadron of Commodore Johnstone in his attack on the five Dutch East India Company's ships on 21/7/1781.

2. Schrire Collection

SH1–27. List of the Schrire Photographic Collection. Cape Archives Depot, State Archives Service, June 1989.

Government Documents, Canberra

Official Hansard Report of the House of Representatives Standing Committee on Aboriginal Affairs (Reference: Aboriginal Health). Alice Springs, Monday 26 June 1978.

Mitchell Library, Sydney, State Library of New South Wales

MS. C. 155. Leichhardt, L. 1845. Continuation of my Log from the Abel Tasman to Port Essington: September 8, 1845.

South African Library

SAL, PHA, Table Bay: 1626. Natives of "Souldanja" (later "Table") Bay, as seen around 1626.
SAL, PHB, Baartman. Saartjie Baartman, The Hottentot Venus. Detail ex Encyclopedia Français (1936).
SAL, INIL 2984. Bushmen at the Empire Exhibition, Johannesburg, 1936–7.
SAL, MSC 57; 27. Portraits in the Bleek collection, namely, Tuman, Trucanini, *Pithecanthropus alalus,* A Breakwater group, svinxa=Klaas, and King Billy.

South Australian Archives, Adelaide

Edmunds, R.H. Diary of McKinlay's Expedition 1865–1866. South Australian Archives, unpublished MS.

Index

Illustrations are italicized.